Values and Ethics in Counselling and Psychotherapy

Values and Ethics in Counselling and Psychotherapy

Gillian Proctor

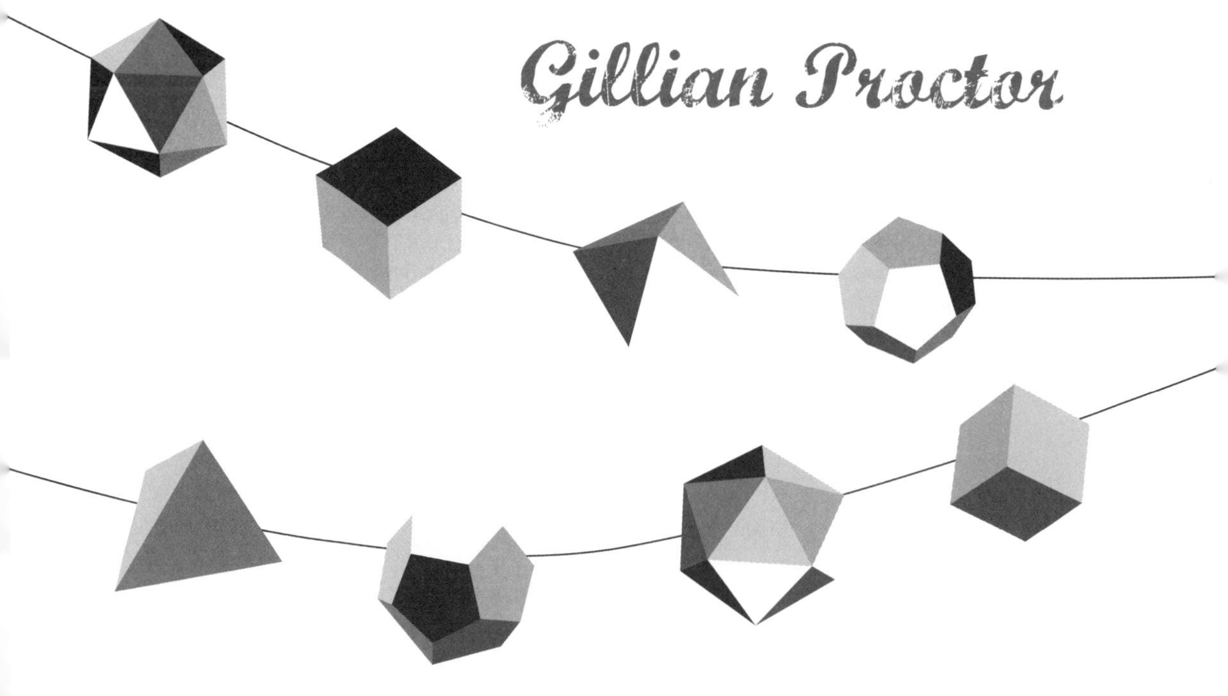

SAGE

Los Angeles | London | New Delhi
Singapore | Washington DC

SAGE

Los Angeles | London | New Delhi
Singapore | Washington DC

SAGE Publications Ltd
1 Oliver's Yard
55 City Road
London EC1Y 1SP

SAGE Publications Inc.
2455 Teller Road
Thousand Oaks, California 91320

SAGE Publications India Pvt Ltd
B 1/I 1 Mohan Cooperative Industrial Area
Mathura Road
New Delhi 110 044

SAGE Publications Asia-Pacific Pte Ltd
3 Church Street
#10-04 Samsung Hub
Singapore 049483

Editor: Susannah Trefgarne
Editorial assistant: Laura Walmsley
Production editor: Rachel Burrows
Marketing manager: Tamara Navaratnam
Cover design: Shaun Mercier
Typeset by: C&M Digitals (P) Ltd, Chennai, India
Printed in Great Britain by Henry Ling Limited at
The Dorset Press, Dorchester DT1 1HD

MIX
Paper from responsible sources
FSC™ C013985

First published 2014

Library of Congress Control Number: 2013947177

British Library Cataloguing in Publication data

A catalogue record for this book is available from the British Library

ISBN 978-1-84920-613-6
ISBN 978-1-84920-614-3 (pbk)

To my son Zeb, who has fulfilled a lifelong dream.

Contents

About the author

I am a clinical psychologist, person-centred therapist and research supervisor. I worked in the NHS for 22 years and recently left to become self-employed. I am passionate about the ethics and politics of life, relationships and therapy. I love writing and my aim is to bring academic thinking from various disciplines (predominantly counselling and psychotherapy, psychology, sociology and philosophy) together with clinical practice in an accessible way. My initial interest in power in therapy led me to the relevance of politics and the sociopolitical context in therapy. In addition to reminding us that therapy occurs within a much wider context than the therapy dyad, issues of power also pointed within the person of the therapist to our own personal history, our values and beliefs, and how these influence our ethical decisions. I also love exploring these issues of relational dynamics by facilitating encounter groups.

I have previously authored *The dynamics of power in counselling and psychotherapy: ethics, politics and practice* (PCCS Books, 2002), and co-edited *Encountering feminism: intersections of feminism and the person-centred approach* (with Mary Beth Napier; PCCS Books, 2004) and *Politicising the person-centred approach: an agenda for social change* (with Mick Cooper, Pete Sanders and Beryl Malcolm; PCCS Books, 2006). I have also authored numerous book chapters and articles on these topics and other related issues such as the diagnosis of borderline personality disorder and working in forensic services.

Acknowledgements

This book has been a long time in labour, having been commissioned before I became pregnant with my son Zeb. During this process, many people have offered invaluable support. Linda Smith has provided a lending library of her extensive philosophy and therapy collection and through dialogue has been an integral part of the development of the ideas I present. My parents, Joyce and Eric Proctor, have looked after their grandson Zeb on numerous occasions whilst I worked on draft after draft. Zeb (now age three) has been very patient with my spending bursts of time at my computer. Thanks also to the Mallott-Mannings for celebratory curries at the end of each draft!

Several people have helped shape this final polished manuscript by commenting on previous drafts, which provided essential help for me to improve the relevance and accessibility. Thanks go to: Christine Bousfield, Leah Davidson, James Gerrard, Patrick Harper, Linda Smith and Sheila Youngson. All the staff at Lynfield Mount Hospital library were endlessly helpful with my requests for books and articles. I am very grateful for the detailed guidance from several reviewers and for the editorial skills of Susannah Trefgarne at Sage, whose suggestions have improved this final version no end. Finally, I really appreciate those who have taken the time to read and endorse this book.

Introduction

This is a book about you. It's also about me. I am writing about each of us and all people, both individually and in our shared humanity. It is about the nature of being human. Considering values and ethics is a very personal affair; I shall argue that our values are intricately related to our identities or who we are as unique people. Ethics are also a matter for judgements, of right and wrong, good and bad. Ethics and morals are about how we treat other people and interact with the world around us; they are the stuff of life. I agree with Gordon (2009: iii) that 'Therapy is inherently an ethical endeavour ...'. I suggest values and ethics are involved in every part of how we are in therapy; this book is not just about common 'ethical dilemmas' but also about our decisions concerning how we respond to our clients at every moment.

How do we deal with our responsibility as counsellors and psychotherapists? Given the power in our role and the potential vulnerability of the people we work with, how do we take this responsibility seriously? Self-awareness and personal development are emphasised in counselling training and are frequently mentioned imperatives for counselling practice, which involve trying to be aware of our motives for our decisions about how to be with clients. This concerns values and ethics. It also involves us in the debate about how much any of us can know ourselves, and even less, know what our impact might be on someone else in a relationship. Moreover, logical explanations about why we do what we do often fail to capture the way these decisions are actually made, with evidence that intuition and emotions are much more important (and much more unpredictable). Given these minefields in our investigation into our own consciousnesses, how do we still try and fulfil our role with responsibility?

Purpose of the book

The purpose of this book is to give therapists and healthcare workers tools to think about values and ethics in practice. As such, I want to use examples from counselling practice throughout, not to demonstrate or indicate the 'right' ethical answers, but to suggest various ways of approaching the problems. I have chosen to do this by creating four characters, or students, who are embarking on a module on values and ethics as part of a diploma in counselling. They have already been introduced to basic counselling theories in various models and have all been on placements working as counsellors. I shall present a brief synopsis of these characters in this introduction, and you shall then meet them throughout the book. The book is full of exercises or questions to provoke consideration of the opinions I present, and one or more of these characters completes each exercise. I shall use them – much in the same way that the Ancient Greeks used characters in their dialogues about ethics and philosophy – to present various viewpoints, and sometimes to debate with each other. This literary device will hopefully serve to both ground theory in practice and present various sides of debates without making any claims to which side is better or more 'right'. All of the characters and the course tutor (who also appears) sometimes represent my own opinion, and many other opinions in addition. At the same time, the exercises invite you, the reader, to think about your own responses to the questions.

I also present some of the key ideas in western moral philosophy. My aim in presenting these ideas is to introduce you to concepts which are the result of previous contemplation on the nature of being human and the nature of morality (from the genre of western moral philosophy), to engage you in a dialogue and provoke your contemplation on these ideas, informing your process of thinking rather than providing answers. Western moral philosophy provides the foundations for the ethical frameworks and codes used in the profession of counselling and psychotherapy. I have presented the ideas of the philosophers and key philosophical concepts that I refer to throughout the text in the three appendices at the end of the book. Each time a concept is mentioned which is further explained in the appendix, the concept appears in **bold** and this icon apperas in the margin.

For some, religion or spirituality is an important part of values and ethical beliefs. This book refers sparingly to these as this is not the framework from which I understand values and ethics. However, the framework of this book does allow room for you if you see religion or spirituality to be a fundamental part of your values and ethics.

Structure of the book

In Part I of the book (Values), two chapters discuss our values in detail and how they inform who we are as people and as counsellors. They are full of exercises to provoke personal consideration of values and beliefs. Each section in these chapters can be used as a stimulus for discussions about values and beliefs, each probably needing time to be considered and debated. This part may work best as a resource to stimulate thought and debate rather than be read and considered in one sitting.

The next five chapters (Part II: Therapy ethics) review the literature on ethics in healthcare (one chapter) and then in counselling and psychotherapy (two chapters). Counselling and psychotherapy are placed within a healthcare context here, as it is from this context that ethical codes and frameworks in counselling originate. However, practice examples throughout are not restricted to counselling and psychotherapy in healthcare settings. The fourth chapter in this section considers the context of ethics in counselling and therapy and the importance of life outside the therapy room. The final chapter in this section focuses on the concept of 'ethical mindfulness' and particularly considers self-awareness, self-care and the importance of supervision.

Part III (Practice issues) considers specific issues within ethics in practice. The first chapter discusses putting specific models of therapy into practice, considering the values implied in specific models and particular ethical questions in each model. The second chapter presents ethical dilemmas when the principles of autonomy and beneficence are in competition, and the third specifically considers confidentiality. The fourth and fifth chapters both look at issues of 'boundaries'. These practice issues were chosen owing to their popularity as issues for discussion in the literature and in practice. There are clear omissions, such as issues like assessment and record-keeping. I hope readers can apply the ideas of this book to other practice issues.

The final chapter concludes the book with a summary of the approach of this book and a summary of what our four students have learned from the module on values and ethics. This is followed by the three appendices, which are to be used as a reference section and summarise the ideas of the philosophers and philosophical concepts referred to throughout the book (and indicated by the icon in the margin).

Terminology

I use counselling and psychotherapy interchangeably. I use the terms 'counsellor' and 'therapist' interchangeably throughout to refer to counsellors and psychotherapists, working short-term and long-term with clients from any model of therapy. I sometimes refer to literature about the practice of psychology or other healthcare practices where there is obvious relevance to the practice of psychotherapy.

I always refer to the 'therapy relationship', following my previous work (e.g. see Proctor, 2002), rather than the more customary 'therapeutic relationship', as I do not believe we can automatically assume each relationship is 'therapeutic'. I think using the term 'therapeutic' to describe a relationship also obscures the values intrinsic to a therapist's decision of what they believe to be helpful.

I use 'ethics' and 'morals' fairly interchangeably throughout this book, following Kitchener and Anderson (2011) who argue that distinctions are not consistent. However, I mainly refer to 'ethics', reflecting my focus on a personal process of making decisions rather than agreed customs or rules, which is a fairly common distinction. Adshead (2005) discusses the roots of these words – morals coming from the Latin *mores*, meaning customs or practices; and ethics from the Greek *ethos*, meaning character. She consequently suggests that morals in psychotherapy refer to its codes and contracts, and ethics to the values and attitudes that underpin identity. For **Habermas** (1993), ethics are personal decisions, and moral matters are about how we live together in society. I remain unconvinced by the possibility of this separation.

Definitions

Values: 'beliefs of a person or social group in which they have an emotional investment.' (www.thefreedictionary.com)
Ethics: 'The rules or standards governing the conduct of a person or the conduct of the members of a profession.' (http://medical-dictionary.thefreedictionary.com)
Morality: 'accordance with widely shared conventions of right or good conduct that form a stable, but usually incomplete, social consensus; it includes the concept of moral ideals.' (http://medical-dictionary.thefreedictionary.com)

Presenting the characters

When you read the following synopses, notice if you have any reactions to the characters – do you make any assumptions or predictions about what kind of people they are? Do you think you would like to meet them and, if so, do you think you would like them or relate to them? Can you imagine their potential responses to counselling training? Can you predict the course of their personal development? Do you think they will like each other, or can you foresee conflicts between our counselling students? Which of them would you like to see as a counsellor? Try and think on what basis you answer each of these questions and what your deliberations tell you about your values.

Anne

Anne is 45 and her three children are all in their late teens. She had always planned to go back to her teaching career when her children were at secondary school, but now the job seems to have changed so much since she was last a teacher, she has decided to retrain. She is also Brown Owl at the local Brownie pack and currently is worried about one of her Brownies in particular who has confided in her about troubles at home. She has tried giving the girl advice but is worried that she could be more helpful if she knew more about what to do in these situations. She has been told by many friends that she is a good listener. All of these factors combined to lead Anne to make enquiries about training as a counsellor. When she spoke to a friend who has already trained and talked about the benefits of working for yourself and working flexibly from home, she was convinced this was the career for her. Her husband agreed this was a good way for her to get involved in bringing some money in without compromising being there for her children too much.

Maxine

Maxine is 35 and is out of work. She has been in therapy with a counsellor for six months through a voluntary sector agency. She sought therapy after leaving a violent relationship, and feels that she has benefitted greatly from the experience. She is intrigued as to how therapy works, as she feels so much better about herself and decides that she would like to undertake some counselling training to further understand herself and the process she has been through. The local course, which she is able to access at no cost as she is on benefits, is run by her counsellor. They have discussed over some time during therapy the implications of this and the counsellor has brought up the potential difficulties that entering this dual relationship could entail. However, after discussion, they agree to end counselling and that Maxine will begin the course that her ex-counsellor is running a month later. The counsellor reassures Maxine that any information she knows about her through counselling will not be disclosed to anyone during the training and they agree to meet regularly during the training to discuss their feelings and experiences of this dual relationship.

Rubina

Rubina is 24 and since finishing a degree in psychology has worked for several years for a voluntary sector agency which supports South Asian women who have experienced domestic violence. Rubina is particularly interested in issues of domestic violence as her sister left a violent marriage. She is recently married, an arrangement that she happily agreed to, and she lives with the parents of her husband, her new in-laws. She has settled well in her new family and is enjoying working out how to be with her new husband with whom she shares many values. She is close to her parents and sister who live nearby, and is involved in her local cultural and religious community. She has been encouraged and supported financially by her employers to go on a counselling course. She is interested to see if it can help her think about issues of confidentiality and self-disclosure. One of the difficulties she has found in trying to support women in her organisation is that a lot of the women know her family and are more interested in discussing her parents than in talking about their own experiences. She is also interested to see how much the values of counselling are compatible with her Islamic ethics.

Tom

Tom is 28 and works in a bank. He has been seeing a psychiatrist since he was 18 and experienced mood swings, and was prescribed lithium and diagnosed with bipolar disorder. However, a few years ago he began to wonder if there was another way of dealing with his mood to be able to come off his medication, as he felt it was taking the edge off his feelings and he was worried about the risks of continuing this medication in the long-term. He read about alternative approaches and got some help from a psychologist to come off his medication and to manage his moods himself. Over the last few years, he has begun to be much more aware of his own moods and what he needs, depending on how he feels. He has taken some time off work when feeling down but has learnt how to look after himself and accept feeling down, so consequently he is usually able to work again within a week or so. However, he has started to become disillusioned with work and has wondered about trying to understand and help other people. He began some voluntary work with a youth offending scheme and they suggested that he could benefit from doing some training in counselling.

Exercise

If you were a character in this book, how would you be described? Can you write a thumbnail sketch of yourself, similar to the character descriptions, to say something about who you are and what has led you to become a counsellor or therapist?

Summary

This introduction has proposed the idea that our values shape all of our ongoing decisions as therapists. Values are a personal affair and we each have the freedom and responsibility to develop our own. In the way this book is constructed, through dialogue between students and the tutor, and in dialogue between my ideas and those of philosophers and theoretical ideas about therapy, I hope it is clear that I am not advocating any 'right' answers, but am trying to encourage personal and critical thinking. I declare my hope that this book will promote the ethical responsibility that I believe comes with the power of being a therapist, with respect to both increasing our awareness of values and motives for behaviour, and increasing our understanding of the philosophical beliefs that help us make sense of our values, beliefs and how we make ethical decisions.

PART ONE

Values

ONE What are your personal values?

Introduction

This chapter will encourage and suggest exercises for us to assess our own values and beliefs. It will touch on the notion of identity and the relationship between identity and values. It will consider how we perceive the values of others and whether sharing values is an important foundation of relationships. We will think about origins of values and the concept of 'conscience'. Each of the exercises will be illustrated by at least one of the four students completing them, so we learn more about each of their identities and values.

What are values?

I argue that every decision we make is underpinned by what we value in life: every action and inaction. Our values shape everything we do; they underpin human agency, choice and autonomy. Values express what it means to be human and make choices about our behaviour. Values are inescapable and inherent in our behaviour and everyday decisions. For **Sartre**, we are always engaged in a world of values, saying, 'my acts cause values to spring up like partridges' (1943/2003: 62). Behaviour acquires value through the culturally agreed social significances of acts. Sartre explains: 'Values are sown on my path as thousands of little real demands, like the signs which order us to keep off the grass' (1943/2003: 62). How much do you think values influence or even determine your behaviour?

Exercise

1. Think of the first decision or choice you made today.
2. Explore what your options were at that time.
3. Work out what value was behind you picking the option you picked.
4. Repeat for the next three decisions you made and see if there are any commonalities in the list of values you acquire.

Maxine

The first decision Maxine thought about was the decision on whether or not to turn up to the counselling course that morning. She had been very nervous and apprehensive and had identified that she was worried what her ex-counsellor and new tutor would think of her in this new context. She had felt fairly confident in their therapy relationship that her counsellor had liked her and she did not want this to change. However, Maxine did not want to discuss this situation with her peers or with her tutor so thought again what decision to discuss. She instead chose to talk about her decision about what to wear that morning. She noted that she hadn't wanted to look as though she had made an effort to dress up but wanted to appear informal and casual. She also noted that in one of her favourite tops, she was particularly aware of the shape of her breasts and she did not want to draw attention to this or for other students to perceive her as overtly sexual or sexually available so she rejected this option. She was also aware she would be sitting still all day and wanted to wear something she felt comfortable in so did not choose a pair of trousers that were a little too tight around her waist. She identified that the values she had prioritised in her decision of what to wear were comfort, wanting to belong and not intimidate or distance people, and wanting to feel good about herself (feeling attractive but not overtly sexual which to her would feel desperate or needy as opposed to self-contained and content).

Rubina

Rubina could not decide what decision to discuss and finally decided to discuss the decision of what to discuss! She found it difficult to assess how much information she wanted to disclose about herself and her life, as she did in her work. She considered that the values important to her about this decision were privacy, openness and humility. She was interested to think more about the value of humility and consider how much she felt vain and selfish to talk about herself, and concluded that this value was possibly much more deeply held and influential than she had previously realised. She decided that this course was an opportunity to challenge her usual mode of saying very little about herself.

We can see from these examples that our personal values are many and various and different ones may be prioritised at different times, depending on our physical and emotional needs at the time and the context of each decision.

Identity

To the extent that our values are personal to us (although developed intersubjectively), they are connected to how we describe or think about our identity. I see identity not as fixed but as developing and being actively shaped by us according to our values and in response to our context. The features or characteristics we think are important to describe ourselves reflect our values. Values are the root of ethical decisions and **Sartre** is adamant that there is no justification for our values; we are free to choose them. Our values, developed from our social intersubjective context, shape who we become and this in turn further shapes our values.

Exercise

This and the following two exercises came from Sue Wood[*], who worked with me on the School of Health's Postgraduate Certificate in Citizenship and Community Mental Health, University of Bradford. She works as a freelance creative writing facilitator with at-risk groups and in professional health training.

1. Choose three adjectives to describe yourself.
2. Which three adjectives do you think you would have chosen 10 years ago?
3. Which three adjectives do you think you would have chosen 15 or 20 years ago?

Anne

Anne completed the exercise above very quickly. Without hesitation she described herself currently as caring, responsible and fun. She thought more carefully about how she was 10 years ago and situated herself in

[*] suewood45@hotmail.com

recollecting that at that time her children would all have been in primary school and she was very involved in their everyday lives. She chose for that time: caring, exhausted and proud. Thinking back further, she reminded herself of her life 20 years ago, before she had become a mother, excited to have just met her husband and just begun her career in teaching. She chose for then: excited, loving and hopeful.

Tom

Tom spent a lot of time trying to work out which three adjectives to pick, finding great difficulty as he experienced himself as changing so much in his moods. After much deliberation he chose: self-confident, emotional and concerned. Thinking back to being 18 was a distressing thought for Tom as being diagnosed with a major psychiatric illness was not a positive experience for him, although the resulting medication did make his life temporarily easier. The adjectives he decided on were: unhappy, unconfident and worried. Finally thinking back to being eight years old was easier for Tom. He described himself aged eight as: carefree, emotional and interested.

The students spent much time discussing how they saw themselves and how this had changed over time, noting what characteristics had remained constant and which had changed or developed and why. They noted how their identities can be vulnerable to how others see or treat them, and also discussed with some sadness what parts of their identities they felt they had lost and would like to reclaim. They also noted how their descriptions of themselves were so dependent on their self-esteem and how positively or negatively they saw themselves at any one time. As a result, their tutor suggested a further exercise.

Exercise

1 Choose three adjectives to describe how you'd like to be.
2 Compare these to the adjectives you have chosen to describe how you think you are. If these are very different, this can be an indication of low self-esteem, whereas if they are similar, this suggests high self-regard or esteem.

The students

The group discussed this exercise and its usefulness as a measure of self-esteem, and generally agreed they felt it was more useful to help them identify areas for self-development than to use as a measure. They discussed how it highlighted that their identities are connected to their values, with the characteristics they chose showing what they value, whether they are characteristics they would like or that they think they already have.

Identity and roles

Our identity is also tied up in how we see ourselves in terms of the roles we fulfil. The roles that are central to our identity may say something about our values too.

Exercise

1. List all the roles that you have in life and list them in order of how central each is to your identity.
2. Write a poem, beginning each line with 'I am a ...'. Include all your roles; more than one can complete each line.
3. Think about how much this poem reflects your identity.
4. What aspects of your identity does it miss?

Anne

Anne listed in order of centrality to her identity: mother, wife, daughter, sister, friend, listener, Brownie leader, singer, swimmer, reader, cleaner, cook, ironer, tidier of clutter, appreciator of flowers, gardener, accountant, first-aider. She wrote the following poem:

I am a mother, a wife, a daughter and sister,
I am a woman in relationships.
I am a helper, a listener, a Brownie leader;
I am a singer, a swimmer, a reader and gardener;
I clean, I tidy, I iron, I count money and
I apply plasters to sores.

She reflected how much time she spends in her life fulfilling roles that are important to her sense of identity as a caring and nurturing woman. She also reflected that singing, swimming and reading are important parts of her identity that she rarely fulfils now, and decided she must prioritise these activities more highly. She was glad that the counselling course will involve a lot of reading and is determined to make time for this and be clear with her children that she is unavailable for their needs when she is focusing on this.

Values and ethics

Exercise

How do you define what is ethical for you? What are the most important values in your life? Try and complete the sentence: 'An ethical life for me is ...' Compare your answer to the examples in the box below of my interpretations of how various philosophers have defined an ethical life.

An ethical life is ...

- Rational to pursue by developing virtues, particularly wisdom, courage, temperance and justice (Plato: virtue theory)
- Good habits and virtues, by developing the reasonable and appropriate balance between extremes (e.g. between selfishness and altruism) (Aristotle: virtue theory)
- Pursuing your own pleasure (Epicureans)
- Seeking to be in tune with the universe (Stoics)
- Following human reason and the scriptures to divine God's purpose (Aquinas)
- A duty to treat others equally and as you would be treated and without using people for your own means (Kant: rationalism/deontology)
- Conscious awareness of ourselves and nature to become active rather than passive with our reactions and emotions (Spinoza)
- Critical rational thought and awareness of oneself (Hegel)
- Following your immediately compelling rational intuitions about what is self-evident (Moore: intuitionism)
- Following our emotions and passions which are informed by observation and experience (Hume: empiricism)
- Judging an action by its consequences and choosing that which is most favourable to most people (Bentham: consequentialism/teleology)
- Following rules laid down by various societal institutions (Hobbes: contractarianism)
- Becoming habitually sensitive to the needs and interests of others, and evaluating our habits to check their appropriateness in changing circumstances (Dewey: pragmatism)
- Caring for others according to our relationships with them, including compassion for unknown others and self-care (Gilligan: care ethics)
- The duty of love for all (Kierkegaard)
- Searching for meaning and developing ourselves as unique people (Nietzsche)
- Authenticity (being true to oneself), and resoluteness (taking on personal responsibility for the choices we make) (Heidegger)

- To respond to the Other who is different from me – heteronomy – starting with the Other (Levinas)
- Encounter in I–Thou relations (Buber)
- Grasping our freedom to develop our authentic selves and make our ethical decisions without justification and without excuse (Sartre)
- Awareness that most philosophical thinking in answer to this question has been done by men who often see women as 'other' and not a subject in their own right (De Beauvoir)

(More on these philosophical concepts can be found in the **Appendices**)

Religion and philosophy

God

God and Christianity are invoked regularly throughout western moral philosophy, sometimes assumed and sometimes argued against. The **Stoics** believe that each individual fits within a divine plan for the whole universe, and morals should consist in seeking to be in tune with the universe, and to act with integrity to be part of the wider world soul. The later 'natural law' theory of Aquinas added Christianity to the idea of the Stoics' divine plan for the universe, suggesting that God gives human reason to be supplemented by the Scriptures, although human reason has been flawed since the 'fall of Man' such that we must look to God's purpose primarily. **Kierkegaard** argues that individual choice is sovereign and advocates that the ethical choice is to obey God and to love others. At the same time he argues that there are no outside criteria to make any choice more right than any other. He critiques **Hegel**, who tried to present religion as rational and thus reduces it to something other than itself. **Nietzsche** accuses Christianity of a systematic devaluation of this world in favour of the next, thus destroying all moral values. He claims that God is dead and defines power as the human goal.

Anne and Tom

Anne decided that for her 'an ethical life is to love and care for others'. She thought her philosophy was close to Gilligan's ethics of care and Kierkegaard. She was aware that Kierkegaard's injunction of love was for all without preference, whereas the ethics of care focuses on preferential relationships, and thought that her approach was probably closer to the ethics of care. Tom thought that for him 'an ethical life is to be true to myself whilst treating others and the world with respect and care'. He considered the list of philosophers and decided that his approach had aspects of the Stoics, Kant and Heidegger. He liked Heidegger's idea of resoluteness to add to his philosophy of life. He also really liked Spinoza's ideas of being active rather than passive whilst experiencing himself.

Values and friendship

Often our values are important to us in who we choose as friends. Most of us choose friends who are like ourselves in some way, often people who share our values or what is important to us. Perhaps values are equally involved when relationships break down where conflicting values come into play, or perhaps when our values move us in different directions away from each other.

Exercise

1 What characteristics do you value in other people?
2 Think of your friends – how much do they share these characteristics?
3 In relationships or friendships that have broken down, did this reflect a conflict or divergence of values?

Tom

Tom thought about whom he likes spending time with, both in terms of his friends and colleagues or people he has turned to for help, such as his psychologist and psychiatrist. He reflected that he really values an ability to question what can be taken for granted, and noted this quality in his psychologist and several of his friends. He also reflected that he likes people to be confident but not arrogant; to have opinions but also be interested in the opinions of others. Finally he decided that he really valued a dry sense of humour and that humour was an important antidote to his serious questioning of life.

Origin of values

How much do you think nature or nurture influences your values? What aspects of your context and culture most influence your values? For some, religion or spirituality is an important part of values and ethical beliefs. Values and beliefs influence each other such that behind each of your values you can find some beliefs about yourself, others and the world. In turn your values influence how you perceive yourself, others and the world.

Exercise

1 Consider yourself at the ages of 5, 10, 15 and 20 years old and list for each age all the influences on you (include significant people, institutions and broader cultural influences such as the media).
2 For each influence, list the values that you were taught.
3 Decide how important each of these values is to you still now.

Maxine

Maxine thought back to when she was five years old. At that time she spent most of her time with her parents, her aunt, uncle and cousins, and at school. The values taught all seemed similar from her family and were values of enjoyment and freedom. She remembered being allowed to watch a bit of television but limited to cartoons or children's programmes which she could not recall influencing her. By the time she was 10 years old, the influences on her had broadened. She was a keen gymnast and competed for her county, spending a lot of time with her gym teacher, who supported and encouraged her enormously, giving her the values of care, effort and achievement, and valuing her body. She also had friends from different schools through gymnastics. She played with a couple of other similar-age girls on her street who attended different schools, one of whom was of African-Caribbean descent, so she was also aware of different cultures. From these friends and their families, she came across the values of politeness, curiosity and respect for different opinions. At age 15, Maxine spent a lot of time with a few girlfriends who were interested in shopping and boys, from whom she learnt the values of appearance and covering up feelings. However, she also had other local friends who she relaxed with much more and learnt the values of having fun and being herself. She realised that nearly all the values she had learnt were still important to her now, depending on context and how she was feeling about herself. It made her wonder if any of her values were *hers* alone, as opposed to influences from other people. She considered whether her interest in other people is just *her* but realised that she has been influenced by others who have shared this value, such as her gym teacher.

Impact of life experiences on values

Major events or changes can have big impacts on our values or be critical events in leading us to re-evaluate our values. For example, the experience of someone dying who was important to us can lead us to evaluate the impact of their values on us and can help us prioritise our values in considering whether we are leading the life we want to live, having been reminded of the finiteness of life. Of course, the values we already hold also influence how we react and respond to such events.

Conscience

The conscience is often referred to as though it were a separate entity: we might say 'She has no conscience' or 'how does your conscience let you do that?' It seems to refer to the most strongly held values we have that influence our behaviour. Could the idea of a 'conscience' represent the way our most deeply held values influence us?

For **Heidegger**, we are called upon by the nature of our being to make our own choices, to choose to choose, and then we can have an individual conscience.

Exercise

1 List any behaviours that you think would be against your conscience.
2 How would you feel if you carried out each of these behaviours?
3 Can you remember a time when you acted against your conscience?

i Why did you do this?
ii How did you feel as a result?
iii How did you deal with this feeling?

Anne

Anne listed various behaviours as being against her conscience: killing, stealing, hurting someone else, lying and breaking a promise. She remembered a time when she stole a sweet from a shop when she was seven, but decided she was too young then to think fruitfully about this now. She then considered a time when she felt she had broken a promise to her mother to always look after her father when she had gone. She thought about how guilty she had always felt about putting her father in a care home when he had dementia and was unsafe on his own, and she felt it would be too much and possibly dangerous for her children (who were young at the time) for her to bring him to live with her. As she reflected on how guilty she has always felt as a result, she decided she had probably never really dealt with this feeling; it just returned intermittently with all the same intensity. She was tearful when relating this experience and no reassurance from the other students that she had done what she could seemed to reassure her. She realised how deeply she felt the guilt as she had acted against such a deeply held value to her, of caring for those close to her and keeping promises.

Rights

We live in a legal framework of rights and responsibilities, with legislation such as the human rights framework. Legislation uses the discourse of rights and responsibilities to enshrine moral duties in law.

Exercise

1 What do you think should be the human rights of every individual?
2 List these in order of priority so if there is a conflict between rights you know which you would prioritise.
3 What do you think should be our responsibilities?
4 Are there any circumstances in which, or for any individuals, you believe these rights or responsibilities should be waived?

Tom

Tom considered the rights he would defend and begins with the right to life and the freedom to make our own choices about how to live that life. He continued with the rights to follow a religion of our own choosing, the right to choose our own sexual orientation and sexual expression without discrimination, and after a little thought about how he would exclude the rights of people to have sexual relationships with children, he adds the condition of not impeding the freedom of others. He started to think of the kind of life he believes everyone in the world should be able to live whilst knowing that many currently do not. He added the right to have enough money to live on, and the right to have enough food, water, comfort and warmth. He then began to think more psychologically about welfare and added the right to be free from fear of violence. Finally, he thought about a life of flourishing rather than just existing and added the right to be occupied in productive and valued activity, the right to friendships and valued relationships, and the right to choose whether or not to reproduce.

Tom wondered about how to prioritise among all these rights and considered Maslow's (1943) hierarchy of needs, where our needs move up the hierarchy when the lower needs are fulfilled. According to Maslow's hierarchy, basic survival rights would have to be prioritised above rights to flourish. Tom was clear that we all have responsibilities not to impede the rights of others and more actively to help others to access their rights and be able to flourish.

Maslow's hierarchy of needs (1943)

- Self-actualisation
- Esteem
- Belongingness and love
- Safety
- Physiological

Tom was unsure when these rights or responsibilities should be waived, and worried about what this would mean to designate a group of people to not have these rights. However, he did think there is a limit to how much children can be expected to be autonomous individuals with rights and responsibilities, suggesting instead that adults have a particular responsibility to protect the future rights of children for them. He considered people with dementia and people with mental health problems and thought that there are perhaps some circumstances in which people may not have the capacity to make autonomous decisions and therefore need to be protected.

Values, beliefs and judgement

Judgement can occur when we believe others to hold different values from ourselves. It can be difficult to hold values for ourselves without judging those who hold different values. It is important for us to be aware of our own basis for judging others, so we can question these judgements, try and understand why another's values are different from ours, and work to prevent acting unfairly. If we can deduce the beliefs behind our values, this can sometimes be an easier basis from which to understand different beliefs of others and thus be able to accept different values.

Exercise

1 What values do some other people hold that you strongly disagree with?
2 When you meet someone who seems to hold a value that you strongly disagree with, how do you feel about them?
3 Think of an example of this situation:

   i Do you have any understanding of why this person held such a value?
   ii Does your understanding change your feelings towards them?
   iii How did your feelings towards them influence how you acted towards them?

Maxine

Maxine considered the value of having fun, which is important to her. She remembered a conversation with another woman who goes to a yoga class with her who questioned why Maxine had a hangover during yoga and why she would drink to the extent of her feeling poorly the following day. Maxine interpreted this question as this woman not valuing having fun as she generally found her very serious and completely focused on healthy living to the exclusion of all else. After this challenge, Maxine had avoided her. She realised how much she has kept away from her after assuming that this woman did not share her value about having fun and also realised she had made a lot of assumptions about this woman's values and why she challenged Maxine's hangover. Other students suggested that this woman may have had her own historical reasons for questioning Maxine's drinking, perhaps having a history of drinking too much herself and seeing it as progress to move to a point of prioritising looking after herself by not drinking. Maxine realised that, for her, having fun is a key value connected to looking after herself, as it is about valuing her freedom from being controlled by or having to answer to anyone else. She wondered whether on this level she actually shared a value with the woman at yoga and decided she would like to speak to her more to understand better her questioning of Maxine's drinking.

Summary

This chapter has been designed with the hope of stimulating you to think about your own values and underlying beliefs about yourself, others and the world. The exercises demonstrate how our values shape our interactions with the world and others and are foundational in our decisions about how we live our lives. Our relationships provide sources for the origins and development of our values, and then our values inform our choices in relationships.

Values are intrinsic to notions of identity and the various roles that we fulfil. This is one area where values are relevant to therapy, with respect to therapist identities and how we define ourselves. For example, do you call yourself a counsellor or a therapist, and why? It is likely that behind your answer to this question lie values that are important to your identity. What kind of therapist, or counsellor do you define yourself as? If you identify with a particular approach to counselling or therapy, what led you to this particular approach? Again, it is likely that your values lie behind your answers to these questions.

This leads us to the following chapter, which looks specifically at our values in the context of being a counsellor or psychotherapist and how these relate to ethical practice.

TWO How are values relevant to therapy?

Introduction

This chapter is full of questions to provoke thought about what beliefs and values and principles we have that lie behind our practice as counsellors and therapists.

This chapter will consider the BACP Ethical Framework specifically, as the UKCP (2009) Ethical Code focuses on principles as opposed to values. The BACP Ethical Framework (2013: 1) explains the connection between values and principles, saying 'Values inform principles. They represent an important way of expressing a general ethical commitment that becomes more precisely defined and action-orientated when expressed as a principle.'

Our values express our ideas about how we want to live our lives. As we have seen in Chapter 1, our values are related to our identity and can change and develop over time. Values and ethics are related to both reason and emotion, and various philosophers have stressed each of these aspects.

Relevance of values and beliefs to therapy

Surely the values and beliefs of a therapist should not matter? Bion suggests we should be 'without memory ... or desire' (1967/1984: 18), perhaps suggesting our value base should be suspended during therapy. The traditional psychoanalytic idea of the therapist as a blank screen implies that the subjectivity of the therapist should be left outside the therapy room. But is it possible to have a relationship, therapy or otherwise, that leaves behind the subjectivity of one person?

Lomas (1999) discusses the myth of neutrality and the inevitability of moral influence. Clarkson (2000) states that we cannot be value-free or objective as counsellors in relationships. Furthermore, she calls the idea of neutrality 'impossible, delusional and dangerous' (2000: 67).

Exercise

Do you think it is possible or desirable to be neutral as a therapist?

Anne

Anne thought that the idea of the blank screen made some sense to her, in terms of creating the maximum space for the client to bring all their own self, free from influence or constraint by their perception of the therapist. However, she also reflected that even if this was ideal, it was impossible to achieve in reality with even factors such as the therapist's gender influencing how the client perceives them. She also understood the importance of self-awareness, for therapists to be aware of their own values and therefore limit their influence on clients. She wondered whether trying to be neutral was such a good idea given her thinking about the importance of reclaiming her subjectivity as a woman (following **Hegel** and **De Beauvoir**), and considered that it may be more worthwhile for a client to feel accepted by another subject than by an object with no personhood.

BACP Ethical Framework

The BACP Ethical Framework lists the fundamental values of therapy and counselling as including a commitment to:

- Respecting human rights and dignity
- Protecting the safety of clients
- Ensuring the integrity of practitioner–client relationships
- Enhancing the quality of professional knowledge and its application
- Alleviating personal distress and suffering
- Fostering a sense of self that is meaningful to the person(s) concerned
- Increasing personal effectiveness
- Enhancing the quality of relationships between people

- Appreciating the variety of human experience and culture
- Striving for the fair and adequate provision of counselling and psychotherapy services. (2013: 1)

The students

The four students discussed the values specified in the BACP Ethical Framework and decided that all the values listed were compatible with their own personal values although each of them would prioritise different values. Anne decided 'alleviating suffering' was the value that resonated most strongly with her, whereas Rubina prioritised 'protecting safety' and 'increasing personal effectiveness'. Maxine was drawn towards 'fostering a meaningful sense of self and 'increasing personal effectiveness', whereas Tom felt that 'respecting human rights and dignity' and 'appreciating variety' were most important to him. They thought the differences in their respective choices reflected their different personal and professional experiences and the various reasons which they each had for wanting to be counsellors. Whereas they all felt they could agree with all the values listed, they also wondered if there would be times when the values could be in conflict and they would have to prioritise, which is when their differences would come into play.

Values and counselling theory

How do you see theory in psychotherapy and counselling? Is theory scientific knowledge that as we learn more gets closer and closer to the truth? Are different theories different stories that could all equally be valid or true, depending on the context or individuals? Or is there no such thing as truth in relation to theories of therapy, the theory ascribed to by any individual therapist being the one that fits them in particular? Or do you see scientific theories as reductive and assaults on the complexities of people and life? How do you interpret the various findings and conclusions drawn from research in psychotherapy, from the various conclusions that the therapeutic relationship or alliance is far more important than techniques or models (e.g. Wampold, 2001) or that some models of therapy have much more proven effectiveness than others, particularly for certain conditions (see Cooper, 2008)? Is one of these conclusions 'wrong' – a result of incorrect application of scientific principles or procedures? Or do they represent different stories reflecting the vantage point of the authors or the power structures involved?

It is impossible to use scientific principles or rationality to determine the truth of rationality, or to use our concepts of what determines right and wrong to argue about whether the concepts of right and wrong are valid concepts, just as it is impossible to use God to argue for the existence of God. Of necessity, we have to move beyond any rational arguments to our values to argue for or against the use of rational arguments. We cannot use scientific proof to argue for the value of science; we can only explain how science works and argue for or against its validity.

Do you decide which theory (or theories) of therapy you ascribe to by using reason to examine evidence and proclaim which one is rationally superior (which would make you a **rationalist**)? Or is your theory the one that feels right? Is your theory the one that appeals to your intuition, which comes from accumulated experiences in life (making you an **intuitionist**)? Or is your theory the one that you use to make most sense of *yourself*? Or are your theories the ones that you know from experience of trying different things with various clients at various points, the ones that you have experienced being most helpful at the times you use them (this is an **empiricist** or pragmatist (see **Dewey**) approach)?

Beliefs about 'mental health'

How do you see 'mental health'? Do you believe in disorders of the brain that science is getting closer to understanding all the time? Or do you believe 'mental health problems' are a result of people's thoughtless or misinformed choices about how to live their lives? Or are mental health problems a result of traumatic experiences that some people are more resilient to than others? Or are people with mental health problems the unlucky ones that have had more traumatic experiences? Or do you believe the whole notion of mental health problems is misguided – we all live our lives in different ways as unique people and nothing should be labelled a problem? Is it a matter of problems in living being medicalised – last century we had everyday misery, now we have depression? Or does mental health not concern you as a counsellor or psychotherapist – instead you are interested in personal development? In which case, do you believe that counselling is not for people experiencing a lot of emotional distress, but only for clients who are relatively 'stable'? This list of possibilities is not at all exhaustive, but designed to prompt you to think about your personal beliefs and attitudes.

Exercise

1 What do you think causes what are commonly called 'mental health problems'?
2 What has informed your belief in these causes? Try and identify the assumptions you make underlying these beliefs.
3 What values do these beliefs imply?

The students

Rubina and Anne agreed that they believed mental health problems to be caused by trauma or unfortunate experiences. They felt strongly that these experiences should not be labelled and that sufferers deserve compassion. Anne pointed out that mental health problems should have no more stigma than physical health problems. Maxine added that there is constantly new research about brain differences and that we do not know enough to know whether experiences cause chemical differences or whether our chemicals determine how we react to experiences. She also wondered about the impact of our different personalities, psychologically and spiritually, and wondered whether some people are better able to deal with trauma than others. Tom felt angry about this discussion and felt patronised by people seeing him as 'unfortunate' as he had clearly experienced mental health problems and had discussed this in the group. He questioned whether the other students believed that 'mental health problems' were a qualitatively different experience from the emotions that they had experienced and suggested that it is more the rise in power of medicalisation that defines what people see as 'mental health problems'. He further suggested that the way they were talking about 'mental health problems' implied a 'them and us' value which would come through if they were counselling people with this attitude.

Beliefs about truth and memory

What do you think the truth status is of what clients say about themselves? Are their stories constructed and told and can always change depending on context and time? Are they the best recollection possible of memories of facts and events? How much can we trust memory? Is it important to try and check out the veracity of what clients say, perhaps through encouraging them to check out memories with other people or discussing clients with other people who know them (obviously with consent)? Or is the truth status of clients' accounts irrelevant, and what their stories mean to the clients is what matters? What about in circumstances where a client is telling you about someone being in danger? Does truth matter here and if so how do you assess it? Are two people's different accounts of the same event equally valid? Or can one be truer than the other? If truth doesn't matter and you want clients to be able to tell the most useful stories for them, what about the impact on other people in their lives if, for example, they decide they were abused by a family member?

Exercise

1. How do you assess the 'truth' value of what clients tell you and when does it matter?
2. When if ever do you share your beliefs about truth with clients? Is this relevant if clients ask you if you believe them?

Anne

Anne remembered a time when a Brownie had arrived with a broken arm and said she had broken it in a play fight with her father. Anne had been concerned about this and questioned her further. The Brownie had said that she was sure her father had not meant to hurt her and that he had not realised his own strength as he had been drinking. Anne's concern increased and she spoke to the girl's mother about her concerns when she came to collect her. The girl's mother was furious with the girl, saying she was 'lying again' and that she had broken her arm at school playing hockey. Anne decided she was unsure who to believe and decided to contact the school, who confirmed that the girl had broken her arm at school. Anne was left confused as to why the girl would say it was her father, and she decided she would not encourage the girl to speak to her anymore as she could not trust what she was saying.

The tutor suggested that Anne could have discussed this situation further with the girl as she thought that she was clearly having some difficulties in her relationships with her parents. She wondered if Anne could have suggested the girl access formal counselling through school.

Values about the purpose of therapy

What are you hoping for or aiming for as a therapist for your clients? To be of use to them in a way they experience? For the therapy relationship to be of use to them? Do you hope to be helpful to clients? To help them understand themselves better? To help them understand other people better? To feel happier or better about their lives? To lead more fulfilled or self-aware lives? To develop more autonomy or make freer choices about their lives (**Heidegger**)? To discover or rediscover their own resourcefulness or ability to make decisions? To love more (**Kierkegaard**)? To fulfil their duty as good citizens better and be more content with this obligation (**Kant**)? To become more fully themselves or more authentic (**Sartre**)? To be able to think more helpfully? To be able to think more rationally? To be able to function more effectively in the world (societally: fulfilling socially acceptable roles; or subjectively: being able to do what they want to be able to do)? To use what's been learnt during therapy to find this learning useful in everyday life? To accept themselves as unique individuals and to value themselves? To draw new conclusions from old beliefs? To increase their ability to be compassionate towards themselves? To develop capacity for trust and reduce anxiety in relationships? To be able to more objectively observe themselves (their thoughts and feelings), to evaluate more effectively? To be more in tune with the universe (**Stoics**)? To suffer less? To live more fruitfully? To become more integrated and individuated? Again this list is not exhaustive but a prompt for your personal exploration.

Exercise

1 What is your aim as a therapist with clients (for clients)?
2 What values are implied by this/these aim(s)?

Anne

Anne thought that her aim was for clients to feel happier and more positive about themselves and to understand themselves better. She thought that these aims implied her values of contentment and understanding. She wondered whether she also aimed for her clients to love more or have better relationships, and thought that she hoped this would be an outcome which followed from them feeling happier about themselves.

Values about being a therapist

What do you aim to do as a therapist? To convey your understanding of your client in such a way that the client can find this helpful (Aveline,

2001: 132)? To be authentic and responsive to your client? To try and understand your client as if you were them? To interpret their unconscious and help them better understand their unconscious processes? To build a trusting relationship with your client so they can then get the most out of therapy? To build the client's capacity for self-awareness and autonomy to the extent that they no longer need therapy? To encourage and allow the client's healthy dependence on you to provide a reparative, emotionally corrective relationship, from which the client can develop towards secure and healthy independence? To develop a relationship modelling healthy interdependence? To be accepting and valuing of the unique individual client? To educate the client about how their inner world is constructed, to enable them to have more insight and control over their own thoughts, feelings and behaviour?

What rewards do you get from being a therapist? Martin suggests: 'Being trusted to enter intimately into the lives of people. ... To observe the gradual blossoming of a person' (2001: 171). How does being a therapist fit with what you think is important in your life? How do you judge success or failure in therapy? Murdin (2001) suggests that this depends on the theoretical training and individual personal value system of the therapist.

Exercise

1 What are your aims for yourself as a therapist?
2 Complete the sentence: 'For me, being an ethical therapist is ...'. Compare this to your previous sentence in Chapter 1 about living an ethical life.
3 What rewards do you get from being a therapist?

Rubina

Rubina thinks that her aims are to try and understand her client, care for them and build their capacity for autonomy to no longer need therapy. She completes the sentence saying: 'For me, being an ethical therapist is responding as much as possible to the needs of my client whilst taking care of my own needs.' She related this to her previous sentence about an ethical life and was pleased to see how consistent they were. This reflected her belief that being a therapist fitted with how she wanted to live the whole of her life. She noted that she found it very rewarding to feel useful and important to her clients and noted that being a therapist gave her a positive sense of identity. She also enjoyed being able to hear about and learn from the lives of others.

Judging other therapists

Do you believe that there are certain ways that therapists should behave in therapy? When you make a moral judgement about another therapist's behaviour that goes against how you think they should behave, what are you saying? Are you saying they are morally 'wrong'? Are you saying they are doing something you disapprove of? Or are they going against a social convention, thus courting disapproval? If you believe there are certain things that are morally right or wrong, how do you know what these things are or on what basis do you argue the evidence for them? Do you judge a therapist's behaviour to be wrong when it leads to harm for the client (**consequentialist**)? Or is it wrong when the therapist's motivation is self-interest (**Kant**)? Or is it wrong when the evidence of previous similar behaviour has often led to harm for clients (**empiricism**)? Or is it wrong when the therapist has acted quickly, and without reflection or responsibility (**Heidegger**)? Or can behaviour not be judged right or wrong, but only understood according to the values and principles which people hold at a particular time in a particular culture (**relativism**)? Often when moral judgements are made, these distinctions are not clear.

Concerns about a colleague's conduct are often reported as examples of ethical dilemmas. Clarkson (2000) asked psychotherapists about their ethical dilemmas and found that concerns about a colleague's conduct ranked as the second most important theme, following confidentiality. The two most cited subthemes were concerns about a colleague's competence and sexual misconduct with clients or students. Nearly half of the therapists who discussed their response to a dilemma involving concerns about a colleague's conduct took no action, whereas a little over half took some action.

The BACP Ethical Framework, under 'Responsibilities to all clients', suggests that:

- Practitioners have a responsibility to protect clients when they have good reason for believing that other practitioners are placing them at risk of harm.
- They should raise their concerns with the practitioner concerned in the first instance, unless it is inappropriate to do so. If the matter cannot be resolved, they should review the grounds for their concern and the evidence available to them and, when appropriate, raise their concerns with the practitioner's manager, agency or professional body. (2013: 8)

The UKCP Ethical Principles and Code of Professional Conduct similarly addresses this situation under the 10th principle of professional integrity and states:

> The psychotherapist commits to report potential breaches of this Ethical Principles and Code of Professional Conduct by themselves or by other psychotherapists to the relevant organisational member or UKCP. (2009: 7)

Exercise

1. How do you decide that another therapist is behaving unethically?
2. How do you distinguish between another therapist doing something different from you or being unethical?
3. What reasons do you have for not acting if you believe another therapist has behaved unethically?

Importance of shared values between therapist and client

What happens when you and your client have different values or ethical beliefs? Do you interpret and pathologise your client's belief using your preferred theory of therapy (for example, 'She has catastrophic and rigid thinking in not believing her anxiety will reduce if she faces the situation'; 'He wants me to be warmer because he experienced his mother as cold and distant'; or 'She doesn't value herself due to her internalised conditions of worth')? How much do you believe therapy is a conversation and mutual dialogue about values by which we live our lives? Or should therapy be an educative enterprise whereby the therapist can teach or convey better values to the client to thus lead a better or more fulfilling life? Does therapy result in you questioning your values as a therapist?

Can you work with a client who holds different fundamental values from you? Would you struggle to work with either of the following two clients? Consider how you would work with a client who was unhappy being gay and wanted therapy to help them become heterosexual? Or a client who wanted to learn how to accept their son's gay sexuality? Brodley (2011a) argues that the therapist must agree with the client's ethical aims for therapy. She states that if the therapist cannot agree with the client's aim, this will mean they cannot help but be judgemental of the client, and the therapist needs to refer on, or be clear with the client what they cannot help with (assuming they can accept the client apart from a particular aim).

Exercise

1. When do you discuss values or ethical beliefs with clients?
2. Do you explain your model of therapy with reference to the implicit values to assess if clients agree with these values and share the aims?
3. What do you do when a client has an aim for therapy that goes against your values as a counsellor?
4. When is it important for you as a client to know something about your therapist's values?

Tom

Tom considered the difficulties of explaining his aims and values to clients when he draws from a range of approaches. He remembered working with a client who had been diagnosed with depression and prescribed anti-depressants. Tom had questioned how the medication was affecting her and she had explained that she needed her medication to fix the chemical imbalance in the brain. Tom had decided to explain to her his understanding of depression to be clear why he had asked the question and to ask if she was interested in seeing depression in a different way. His client had been angry that Tom was questioning what her doctor had told her and thought that he might be suggesting she was responsible for feeling so low. Tom tried to explain further but also to acknowledge that if that was her belief that was fine and they could work with that. However, the client did not return after that appointment. Tom still felt uncertain about how he had handled this situation. He felt it had been important to say something about his values but wondered if there was a better way to do this without it being so threatening to his client. He also wondered how well he could have worked with someone with such different beliefs to his own.

Professional identity

Values and identity are intricately connected and so both our personal and professional values are relevant to therapy and our personal and professional identities. Kitchener and Anderson (2011) consider the importance of the intersection between our personal and professional identities. They use the idea of acculturation to think about the development of a professional ethical identity, considering the meeting of our professional and personal identities as analogous to the meeting of two different cultures.

Definition

Acculturation:

1. The modification of the culture of a group or individual as a result of contact with a different culture.
2. The process by which the culture of a particular society is instilled in a human from infancy onward. (From www.thefreedictionary.com/acculturation)

They consider four possible acculturation strategies: integration, assimilation, separation and marginalisation. They advocate the ideal of integration, which represents the greatest congruence between the ethics and values of the person and the profession. They stress the dangers of assimilation, where the professional ethics are adopted to the exclusion of the personal ethics, which can mean that under personal stress, professional ethics are abandoned. In contrast, with the strategy of separation, personal ethics are adopted and professional ethics ignored, which may arise from ignorance of professional ethics or disagreement. They also mention the strategy of marginalisation, where there is neither a strong base of personal nor professional ethics and consequently no ethical compass. They stress the importance of ongoing reflection for the process of acculturation into a profession and cultural maintenance.

Exercise

1. What personal values did you have challenged in the process of training as a counsellor? What acculturation strategies have you used? Have you been more likely to prioritise your personal values (separation), your professional values (assimilation) or to try and integrate the two?
2. Are there personal values which lead you to behave differently in your personal relationships in contrast to professional relationships?
3. Have your personal values and the values of the therapy profession ever seemed so incompatible that you have wondered if you should stop being a therapist? If so, how have you resolved this dilemma?

Rubina

Rubina considered how much her value of being part of an extended family (as opposed to being an individual) had been challenged in her counselling training. She thought that she had also been brought up to be autonomous and be her own unique self, so in trying to integrate her personal family values with her professional valuing of autonomy she focused more on her family's promotion of her autonomy than on the importance of a shared family identity. She wondered if she had perhaps lost some sense of her being part of a family as a result of the focus on individual autonomy in therapy, and she felt sad about this. She resolved to hold onto this aspect of her identity in discussions of autonomy and look more into whether there was counselling literature on this issue (see e.g. Lago & Thompson, 1996; Moodley, Lago & Talahite, 2004; Sembi, 2006).

Summary

This chapter has asked questions about how and who we are as therapists. At the root or core of the answers to all these questions are our values, which influence our beliefs and from which are constructed our ethical or moral principles, in turn both shaping and justifying our behaviour. The range of these questions demonstrates the extent to which values and beliefs shape who we are as people and in particular who and how we are as therapists. Our personal values influence us to become counsellors and psychotherapists and affect our choices of the particular model or models of counselling that we use and how we work. In turn the values of the profession and the values of our counselling theories affect our personal values and how we see the world. Awareness of our values is imperative for us to take responsibility for the decisions we make in our work.

The next section of this book continues to discuss in more detail the articulation of our professional values, from the foundation of healthcare ethics and counselling ethics in particular.

PART TWO

Therapy ethics

THREE Ethics in healthcare

Introduction

Ethics in counselling and psychotherapy have developed from the framework of healthcare ethics. This history has implications for the profession, and how we understand and use ethical codes is important for our ethical practice. Tjelveit (1999) discusses the history of psychotherapy in terms of its roots in medical practice and the implications of the biomedical roots of its ethical codes and frameworks. He points out the importance of the social idea of the professional who strives to benefit clients and public welfare, and how this is threatened by the notion of the therapist as a mere provider of services. He also stresses the individualistic roots of the notion of the patient, which can lead ethics in psychotherapy to be too individualistic without consideration of society, relationships and the natural world on which we are all dependent.

This chapter summarises traditional biomedical (**deontological**) and alternative approaches to ethics in healthcare and some critiques of each. I present 'doing ethics', which can also be termed the 'ethics of justice', and critiques of this approach. Until the 1990s, ethics in healthcare focused almost solely on a single moral framework, that of the four principles or 'ethics of justice' approach of Beauchamp and Childress (2001). This approach is based in **deontological** and **consequentialist** approaches to ethics. However, since then healthcare ethics has become far more methodologically diverse, focusing more on the actor and the process of deciding than the action, and these other approaches, which fall into 'being ethics', are also presented in this chapter. 'Being ethics' include 'values-based practice', the 'ethics of care' and other philosophical approaches informed by **phenomenology** and **relativism/post-modernism**/deconstruction.

Duty and consequentialist theories: the ethics of justice

Duty (**deontological**) theories founded in the philosophy of **Kant** emphasise our ethical or moral duty to behave a certain way towards others; motive is crucial. In contrast, consequentialist or utilitarian (**teleological**) theories decide what is ethical by considering purely the consequences of any particular action, the ethical choice being the one that leads overall to the greatest good and the least harm. Various philosophers (such as **Ross**, **Hare** and **Rawls**) followed the rationalist deontological tradition of **Kant**, and combined this with utilitarianism, forming the base of what has become known as the 'ethics of justice' (Banks, 1995: 34). Beauchamp and Childress (2001) put together developments of deontological and teleological approaches to devise the principle ethics which are most commonly applied in healthcare. These 'ethics of justice' have usually been split into four principles which are: doing good, avoiding harm, justice (all from teleology) and respecting autonomy (from deontology). These principles have traditionally formed the foundation of most ethical codes or rules in caring professions. Beauchamp (2007) explains their goals when they derived these principles. They wanted to shift the traditional focus in healthcare ethics from beneficence or paternalism in the direction of autonomy and social justice. He further states that the four principles 'are the most general and basic norms of the common morality' (2007: 7). By common morality, he means norms applying to all persons everywhere that have arisen to promote human flourishing and to limit difficulties in social relationships among us.

The ethics of justice: principles

Beneficence: 'the doing of active goodness, kindness, or charity, including all actions intended to benefit others.'
Non-maleficence: 'a principle of bioethics that asserts an obligation not to inflict harm intentionally.'
Autonomy: 'in bioethics, self-determination that is free from both controlling interferences by others and personal limitations preventing meaningful

choice (such as inadequate understanding or faulty reasoning). Having the capacity to act with autonomy does not guarantee that a person will actually do so with full understanding and without external controlling influences.'
Justice: 'a principle of bioethics that means giving others what is due to them; it is comprised of a group of norms for the fair distribution of benefits, risks, and costs.'
Source: http://medical-dictionary.thefreedictionary.com

Exercise

1 Consider Beauchamp and Childress's principles for healthcare ethics. Can you think about a time when you or a close friend or relative was a healthcare patient? Were these principles followed by the healthcare workers? Describe how they were or were not. Is it clear how they are applied in practice? Are there times when they are in conflict?
2 How clear do you think these principles are to follow in practice?

Anne

Anne remembers when she was in hospital giving birth to her first child. She discussed the different approaches among the healthcare workers involved. She decided that the obstetrician clearly prioritised the principles of beneficence and non-maleficence and strongly advised her of decisions that she thought would be the best for her. In contrast, one of the midwives clearly respected her autonomy above all other principles and worked hard to give her many possible options and encouraged her to trust herself to decide what felt right for her. Anne was also aware that both were aware of justice in dividing their time between her and the other patients also in labour at the time.

The students

Each student considered one of these principles to discuss how clear they are to follow. They noted after discussion that each involves value judgements to decide meaning and application.

Tom – Justice

Tom considered the principle of justice, which he regarded the most important. He wondered if justice is the same as treating people fairly, which could mean everyone being offered the same number of counselling sessions.

Rowson suggests that treating people fairly involves treating people alike 'unless some relevant difference between them requires us to treat them differently' (2001: 16). In contrast, treating people justly is treating each 'according to his/her due'. The key for Rowson is identifying the attributes that should be taken into account when deciding it is fair to treat people differently.

Toulmin argues for equity to balance law, and emphasises that equity is not synonymous with equality; instead equity is about 'reasonableness or responsiveness in applying general rules to individual cases. Equity means doing justice with discretion' (1981: 34). He notes that in a world of strangers, only equality is left and asks how we can strike the balance between the ethics of intimates and the ethics of strangers, between equity and equality.

Anne and Rubina – Beneficence and Non-maleficence

Anne considered the principle of beneficence and Rubina the principle of non-maleficence. They noted the difficulty of defining 'happiness' or even 'harm' for others. How do we know what will be good or harmful for another? They thought that making this decision for someone else was paternalistic and should only be used if the person was not in a position to decide for themselves. They thought that the principle of autonomy should be prioritised above these paternalistic principles in counselling. However, they noted that perhaps the paternalistic approach was more prevalent in healthcare where experts have a lot of information which they need to put together to decide what is best for the patient. Given the importance of not being an expert as a counsellor, they considered that the principles of healthcare ethics may not be the most suitable model to apply to counselling.

Maxine – Autonomy

Maxine thought about the principle of respect for autonomy, and decided that she thought this should be the most important principle in counselling and, for her, in life.

Stoljar (2007) suggests that current theories of autonomy treat people not as isolated individuals, but consider autonomy in the social context. She stresses that respecting autonomy as a healthcare professional involves not only provision of information, but also a consideration of how to enhance environmental conditions and the healthcare relationship to minimise oppression and to increase autonomy.

Conflict between principles

Putting together the principles of beneficence, non-maleficence and justice follows the addition of the principle of justice to **consequentialism** by Mill (1871/1998). However, as with this move in moral philosophy, the issue here is how to prioritise one of these principles over another when they are in conflict. Beauchamp and Childress (2001) do acknowledge that sometimes principles will be in conflict and one will be prioritised over another. Although they do not suggest how this should be done, they do suggest that when one principle is overridden in favour of another, 'the infringement selected must be the least possible infringement, commensurate with achieving the primary goal of the action' and 'the agent must seek to minimize the negative effects of the infringement' (2001: 20). Beauchamp (2007) is clear that the principles approach does not specify how to apply them in practice and also notes that they are not absolute, but, following **Ross**, act as prima facie duties, meaning they are acted upon unless they conflict with another duty on a particular occasion. He states that there is no supreme principle to decide how to act when principles compete; thus 'discretionary judgment becomes an inescapable part of moral thinking that relies on principles' (2007: 8).

Having considered all the principles, the students decided that principlism is not an easily applicable method for making decisions, but involves much reflection and consideration of one's own individual values in how to apply the principles. McNaughton (2000: 284) lists what is involved in applying moral principles, suggesting that first we must decide which principles are relevant; second, how they interact and the weight given to each; and finally, we need sensitivity in deciding what response is appropriate. **Ross** (1930/2002: 42) quotes **Aristotle** concerning the role of human judgement in ethical decisions: 'The sense of our particular duty in particular circumstances, preceded and informed by the fullest reflection we can bestow on the act in all its bearings, is highly fallible, but it is the only guide we have to our duty.'

Critiques of principlism

Principlism has been critiqued on many accounts. The first critique is that it reflects a mix of philosophical models and is thus not a unified approach. This leads to a lack of clarity in how to prioritise when principles lead to contradictory actions. Principles thus risk being a justificatory list of possibilities to appeal to once a decision has been made. Clouser and Gert (1990) suggest that the problem with principles being merely checklists is twofold: first, that it is assumed that the principles are firmly established and justified and so one feels secure in presuming to apply them; and second, that the agent will not be aware of the real grounds for the ethical decision.

Principlism and the ethics of justice have been critiqued from other perspectives, as disregarding context, relationships, and not providing a strategy for response (e.g. Thompson, 2002). Furthermore, the social **intuitionist** approach points out that principlism is not the way ethical decisions are usually made in practice, with intuition forming a much greater role than the application of principles (see Haidt, 2001, 2007; McNaughton, 2000; Toulmin, 1981).

Principles are no substitute for values but can give us a structure to use or an ethical space to think about our values and ethical decisions. Of necessity in this principles reasoning model, the intuitive weighing of values is in the end a matter of individual value judgement. This was exactly what the students had decided after considering how these principles could work in practice. Fulford, Dickenson and Murray clarify that 'Principles reasoning contributes to clinical decision-making by giving us a thinking skill, a way of exploring and responding to ethical problems in practice, rather than by producing answers' (2002: 10).

Values-based practice

'Being ethics' are focused on values. Fulford et al. (2002) argue for 'values-based practice' – an approach to ethics that makes a diversity of values central. They point out that ethical codes make particular values central, and suggest that ethical thinking in healthcare should be a weaving of what they call 'quasi-legal ethics' – using codes – and 'healthcare ethics', which make the diversity of human values central (2002: 1). Quasi-legal ethics focus on regulation, rules, particular values and a scientific model of medicine. In contrast, healthcare ethics are founded on the idea of partnership, the ethical process, a respect for a diversity of values and a model of medicine that includes fact *and* values, meaning, significance, understanding, empathy, intuition and subjectivity. This represents a philosophical move away from the dominance of rationality, to include emotions and intuition.

The shift to values-based practice involves a shift from rules to process and thus will involve an enlarged role for communication skills and a framework of law that reflects not just diverse professional opinion but also diverse patient values. Communication skills will be essential to find out and understand the values of the various people involved and to negotiate solutions in any ethical decision.

Exercise

1 From the perspective of values-based practice (Fulford et al., 2002), what values do you think are important for a healthcare practitioner to hold?
2 Is it a good thing to have practitioners with a diversity of values, or should people be selected for healthcare jobs on the basis of holding certain values?
3 Do you think particular values are the right ones to hold, or do you think this is context-dependent or position-dependent?

Anne

Anne immediately decided that people wanting to work in the healthcare field should value caring, wanting to help and thinking of others. She thought that beyond these basics a diversity of values could be useful, knowing that patients would hold a diversity of values. She considered again her experience giving birth to her first child and reflected that the authoritarian, beneficent approach of her obstetrician would suit patients who wanted to trust in an expert, whereas the respecting autonomy value of her midwife would be ideal for women who believed they could trust themselves and wanted support to do this. She further noted that at different points during the birth she valued each of these approaches differently, appreciating the midwife's support of her autonomy when she felt in control and knew what her body needed, but that when she was concerned that something was wrong, she wanted someone with an expert approach who she could trust to take responsibility. She further reflected that in different cultures, approaches to childbirth would vary, with some cultures prioritising the woman's knowledge about her own body, and others prioritising the expert knowledge of medicine. Furthermore, she realised that had anything gone wrong during the birth, she would have judged whichever value she had followed at the time to be wrong in retrospect; but given that her child had been born safely in the end, she judged the midwife's approach to trusting Anne's knowledge to be correct. She also noted the dynamics of power in the healthcare system, knowing that if there had been any concerns, the obstetrician's beneficent approach would take precedence over the midwife's respect of Anne's autonomy. The tutor commented that Anne's experience of healthcare whilst giving birth was a perfect example of how context-dependent values are, depending on people, circumstances and outcomes. She thought this showed very well how value is not intrinsic and universally agreed (**Dewey**), but that we all actively ascribe value to things.

Exercise

1. What is the result of focusing on values rather than principles in health-care ethics, with respect to how to judge the 'rightness' of individual ethical decisions?
2. If we accept there is never any one 'right' answer, how do we judge the ethical decisions of others?

Rubina

Rubina thought that values-based ethics focused on different priorities among people rather than the dogmatic of principlism, which decided what should be important to people. In her experience as someone from a marginalised culture, she appreciated that a values-based approach made the differences between her culture of origin and the dominant culture explicit, without deciding which values were correct. However, she also noted that this approach left her with no answers when she tried to work out which culture to follow, and this had caused her many difficulties in trying to work out her way in life as a teenager. In retrospect, she felt that she had worked her way through this period by trial and error and decided what felt right to her in each of these cultures, and taken personal responsibility for the values by which she now lives her life, informed by both her culture of origin and the dominant culture. She reflected that perhaps she had consequently had more opportunity than people who grew up as part of a dominant culture to question and shape her own values, rather than mindlessly absorbing values as though they were the 'right' and only way to be. She values being open-minded as a result of her experiences, being aware of the relativism of her own judgements. She thought that there was perhaps more danger with people thinking there was one 'right' answer that all should follow, than in acknowledging that all judgements are relative and context-dependent.

Rubina thought that each individual made their own decisions regarding values, taking into consideration all the influences on them, which will vary from one individual to another. She wondered, given this variety in values, how she judged whether others were ethical or unethical as she was aware that she did make these judgements. She thought that she would want to hear how and why someone had made a particular decision, and that, following **Socrates**, she would value considered reflection and thought above lack of consideration. She was aware that she judged her own behaviour when she failed to stop and consider possible consequences or possible impacts on others.

Values-based practice involves a move from the absolutism of quasi-legal ethics to relativism. Yet, rather than this leading to ethical chaos, it can lead to greater personal responsibility for implementing one's values. This move also avoids the dogmatic conviction of absolutism, which can be the root of abuses.

Tom and Rubina

Tom thought that the rightness of values and behaviour could be judged by how they affect all others, suggesting that all affected should be considered and imagined as to their responses (**Rawls**). However, he did realise the values involved in trying to anticipate the impact on others, and the impossibility of impartiality in considering others. Nevertheless, he concluded that impartiality should be an aim, with increasing self-awareness of bias and individual values being used to improve the accuracy of the judgements. Rubina considered Tom's **rationalist** response and suggested that it was much easier to anticipate the impact of decisions on people she was close to, such as her family members, than on people who were strangers. This led the tutor to introduce the ethics of care as another value-based alternative to principle ethics in healthcare.

The ethics of care

Definition

Ethics of care: 'The ethics of care is a normative ethical theory; that is, a theory about what makes actions right or wrong. It is one of a cluster of normative ethical theories that were developed by feminists in the second half of the twentieth century. While consequentialist and deontological ethical theories emphasize universal standards and impartiality, ethics of care emphasize the importance of response. The shift in moral perspective is manifest by a change in the moral question from "what is just?" to "how to respond?" Ethics of care criticizes the applications of universal standards as "morally problematic, since it breeds moral blindness or indifference".'

The basic beliefs of the theory are:

1 All individuals are interdependent for achieving their interests
2 Those particularly vulnerable to our choices and their outcomes deserve extra consideration to be measured according to
   - the level of their vulnerability to one's choices
   - the level of their affectedness by one's choices and no one else's
3 It is necessary to attend to the contextual details of the situation in order to safeguard and promote the actual specific interests of those involved

(http://encyclopedia.thefreedictionary.com)

The 'ethics of justice' has been critiqued, particularly by feminists, as being focused on individuals and not concerned with humans as social and relational beings. For example the principle of justice focuses on the idea of impartiality, which ignores the different attachments we have to people in relationships, thus suggesting ethical decisions are purely rational rather than involving emotions. This approach to ethics has been criticised as an '"alienated" morality for the social and moral laws come from outside the person, rather than being regarded as an internal part of her or his very being' (Banks, 1995: 64).

Care ethics originated from Gilligan's (1982) finding that girls and women are likely to evaluate ethical dilemmas in a contextualised narrative way whereas boys and men are more likely to apply a general abstract principle. From this descriptive difference has evolved a normative feminist approach to ethics including context as a central element in moral reasoning. In contrast to the traditional focus on justice for separate individuals with an emphasis on the values of individual freedom and duty, an 'ethic of care' focuses on connectedness and relationships between people and is based on values of cooperation, communication and caring via self-reflection, acknowledgement of partiality, and situatedness. This approach leads to the ideas of conflict resolution and dispute mediation rather than judgement and reparation. Gilligan also refers to the ethics of care as the ethics of responsibility, as balancing responsibilities to self and others is central (Sherwin, 2002, 2007).

The ethics of care has been especially influential in nursing, replacing the aim of cure with care. Feminist ethical approaches to healthcare do not just critique how ethical decisions are made; they also challenge the medical model concepts of health (based on male ideals), normality (again based on male ideals) and notions of autonomy and of the authority of the clinician. Gilligan stresses the importance of being able to move between the ethics of care and of justice according to the circumstances, thus providing an addition to the ethics of justice, not a replacement.

Exercise

What do you think the ethics of care can add to the ethics of justice?

Rubina

Rubina thought that the ethics of care might clarify something for her about her disquiet with the notion of autonomy in principlism. She worried that the idea of respecting the autonomy of another could lead to a lack of care and giving all the responsibility to the other rather than working with them in a caring way to think about solutions. Feminist ethics is concerned with care without paternalism, rather than individualistic notions of autonomy.

Rubina thought that this made sense of her experience that she was never an isolated autonomous individual, but always in relationship with others. The focus on relationships in the ethics of care follows the focus in various existential philosophers on relationships such as the I–Thou relation of **Buber** or our being-with-others (**Heidegger**) in the world, as opposed to the focus in rationalist philosophy on autonomous individuals. However, Rubina was concerned not to lose the notion of autonomy completely. She noted that whilst constantly in relationships, she also felt the historical core of herself to be herself alone, pulling together all her experiences and relationships to shape her own unique identity. She did not want to lose the notion of respecting individual choice, or the awareness of dynamics of power in relationships to try and ensure the autonomy of each person to make their own decisions in relationships.

Exercise

1 How do you define 'care' and is this definition useful to judge whether you are following the ethics of care or not?
2 Can you judge whether someone else is following the ethics of care? If so, how?
3 Can the ethics of care be reduced to one principle not dissimilar to beneficence? How can you make sure that the relational rather than principled approach intended by the ethic of care is maintained?
4 Do you think an approach of principlism is more appropriate for men and the ethics of care for women, given Gilligan's feminist critique?

Anne

Anne was not sure that ethical practice could be judged by the ethics of care by anyone except herself. She was aware when she thought she cared about someone and had acted out of care, but sometimes the recipient of her care did not perceive it as such. She was particularly aware with her children, when she thought she was doing her best to care for them, that they did not agree with what she thought was good for them and did not feel at all cared for, when, for example, she tidied their bedrooms. However, she did wonder whether she needed to be clearer about her motives as she was aware that at times she did things for her own needs (such as to know the house was reasonably clean), whilst trying to justify that it was for her children. She reflected that perhaps she needed to ensure that her concept of care was relational and responsive to what the other needed as opposed to the more paternalistic principle of beneficence.

Tom

Tom considered that the fundamental value of 'care' was akin to a new principle and he was not sure that it could be indiscriminately applied and assumed to be good. He thought about Anne's example of caring for her children and reflected that most people focus on trying to care for their families, and that what was needed in the world was more care for strangers or for those most in need. He thought the value of how to be in relationships may be useful but only as an adjunct to the notion of 'rights' to protect the most vulnerable. He objected to the idea that principlism was more useful for men and care ethics for women as he thought they were both useful for everyone. He did however begin to reflect on how being a man had led him to focus on rationality, autonomy and rights, at times to the detriment of relationships.

Healthcare relationships: strangers or intimates?

The focus on relationships has led to the ethics of care being seen as an ethic of intimates rather than an ethic of strangers. In contrast, an ethic of strangers focuses on equality and impartiality in treatment of others, rather than partiality in relationships. It is debatable which of these is more appropriate to apply in healthcare ethics. Appiah (2006) acknowledges partiality in relationships and our greater obligation to those closest to us, but concludes that we can do better in responding to our ethical obligation to strangers. Brown et al. (1989) emphasise that **care ethics** is an addition to the ethics of justice, not an alternative. They clarify, saying 'The moral voices of justice and care call attention to the fact that *all* human relationships, public and private, can be spoken of *both* in terms of equality and in terms of attachment, and that both inequality and detachment constitute grounds for moral concern' (Brown et al., 1989: 142).

Exercise

1 What difficulties might healthcare professionals have in trying to make mutual decisions with patients about their care?
2 How far is it appropriate to apply the ethics of strangers to a healthcare setting as opposed to the ethics of intimates?

Rubina

Rubina considered that the power involved in the roles of healthcare workers could make it difficult to aim for egalitarian relationships and mutual decision-making. She thought that perhaps doctors could be explicit about how they saw their power and expertise to challenge patients who deferred to them, but also to acknowledge their expertise in knowledge. She hoped that there was more possibility in the role of a counsellor to work towards mutuality, as long as counsellors made sure they did not take authority in the role, and instead deferred to the client's greater knowledge of themselves. However, she reflected on the difficulty that often the counsellor would be working against client expectations of counsellor authority.

Tom

Tom reflected that the ethics of strangers was perhaps more appropriate in considering all potential clients for counselling, regarding issues of equity in access. He thought that once people became clients, counsellors should be working towards knowing the clients better to make the ethics of intimates more and more applicable. However, he noted that there would always remain an inequality and lack of reciprocity in the counselling relationship which would distinguish it from the more usual mutuality of intimate relationships.

Summary

This chapter has discussed the foundations of values and professional ethics in healthcare. 'Doing ethics' or the 'ethics of justice' were presented as the traditional approach to medical ethics. The principles were examined in detail, with discussion of the ethical responsibility necessary to apply the principles. Critiques of such a principlist approach were discussed and alternatives presented, which fall under the description of 'being ethics'. These were values-based healthcare and the ethics of care. The advantages and disadvantages of each of these approaches in practice were considered. Together these approaches offer an ethic of strangers and an ethic of intimates, both of which can be useful at different times and in different contexts in healthcare settings.

The following two chapters discuss how 'doing' and 'being' healthcare ethics are applied particularly to psychotherapy and counselling and the benefits and limitations of each approach.

FOUR Ethics in counselling and psychotherapy

Introduction

This chapter discusses the literature on ethics specifically in counselling and psychotherapy. Ethical codes or frameworks are presented and their use discussed. I explore principle ethics, virtue ethics, the ethics of care and relational ethics, and the advantages and limitations or each. The purpose of this chapter is to build on previous explorations of values and ethics in healthcare, to ask you to consider on what basis you make ethical decisions in counselling.

The BACP Ethical Framework

The British Association for Counsellors and Psychotherapists (BACP, 2013) has an ethical framework for counsellors and psychotherapists which is regularly revised. This is the association in the UK that represents the majority of counsellors and therapists, although there are alternatives such as the UKCP (the United Kingdom Council for Psychotherapy), the BPS (British Psychological Society) and COSCA (Counselling and Psychotherapy in Scotland), each with their own ethical codes or frameworks. The BACP Ethical Framework is the one which most comprehensively covers the relationship between principles and values, with the other organisations structuring their ethical codes solely according to a list of principles, although the BPS Code of Ethics and Conduct (2009) articulates a related statement of values for each principle.

The BACP Framework replaces older ethical codes, and reflects the shift from rules to an emphasis on individual responsibility for ethical thinking. Jenkins explains that therapists should use this ethical framework as a toolkit, which 'provides the conceptual underpinning, or philosophical scaffolding, for developing their own finely tuned and well-thought-out, or indeed heartfelt, responses to ethical dilemmas, in the context of their relationship with clients and colleagues' (Jenkins, 2009: 107).

The BACP Ethical Framework uses a mixed philosophical approach to ethics and refers to values, principles and personal moral qualities (or virtues). It explains the reasons for this mixed approach, saying:

> The presentation of different ways of approaching ethics alongside each other in this statement is intended to draw attention to the limitations of relying too heavily on any single ethical approach. Ethical principles are well suited to examining the justification for particular decisions and actions. However, reliance on principles alone may detract from the importance of the practitioner's personal qualities and their ethical significance in the counselling or therapeutic relationship. The provision of contextually sensitive and appropriate services is also a fundamental ethical concern. Variations in client needs and cultural diversity differences are often more easily understood and responded to in terms of values. Therefore, professional values are becoming an increasingly significant way of expressing ethical commitment. (2013: 1)

The next two sections consider principles and then virtues, both of which are considered essential in the BACP Ethical Framework.

Principle ethics

Kitchener (1984) introduces principle ethics to counselling and applies Beauchamp and Childress's (1979) model of biomedical ethics. In addition to the original principles of beneficence, non-maleficence, autonomy and justice, she suggests the additional principle of fidelity (loyalty: keeping promises, telling the truth and honouring obligations), following **Ross** (1930/2002). Kitchener and Anderson (2011: 33) trace the roots and the meaning of the principle of fidelity in healthcare ethics, arguing that this principle represents the basis of trust in human relationships. Kitchener (1984) argues, following **Hare**, for an intuitive level of moral reasoning and a critical-evaluative level. At the critical-evaluative level, she suggests that principles are useful not as absolutes, but as prima facie valid, following **Ross** (1930/2002). This means they are always considered but can be overturned by stronger ethical obligations, thus being conditional duties.

In the BACP Ethical Framework, six principles are listed but these are not advocated as rules and no method is suggested to prioritise among the principles. These principles are the five suggested by Kitchener (1984) with the addition of 'self-respect'. The BACP discusses conflicts among principles and suggests that:

> Ethical decisions that are strongly supported by one or more of these principles without any contradiction from others may be regarded as reasonably well founded. However, practitioners will encounter circumstances in which it is impossible to reconcile all the applicable principles, and choosing between principles may be required. A decision or course of action does not necessarily become unethical merely because it is contentious or other practitioners would have reached different conclusions in similar circumstances. A practitioner's obligation is to consider all the relevant circumstances with as much care as is reasonably possible and to be appropriately accountable for decisions made. (2013: 2)

Exercise

1. Consider each of the original principles in the 'ethics of justice' and the potential difficulties of applying it in counselling practice.
2. What advantages and disadvantages are there in applying these principles to counselling?
3. How useful are the additional two principles of fidelity and self-respect?

Tom – Justice

Tom looked again at the principle of justice in counselling and its implications regarding access to therapy. He decided that in counselling, justice should not mean that everyone should get the same number of sessions of counselling, as different people would need different time. Tom thought that one thing that counsellors could try and do is to consider which groups of people are not accessing their services and are thus remaining strangers, and to find ways to reach out and respond to the needs of these groups. He remembered trying to access a counselling service for one of the boys that he worked with on the youth offending scheme and being told that the boy would need more than the service could offer.

Holmes and Lindley (1989) add to this consideration of whether certain groups will benefit less from psychotherapy even when they do manage to access it. I have questioned whether the inequalities in society are perpetuated in the access and benefits of psychotherapy (Proctor, 2006).

Anne and Rubina – Beneficence and non-maleficence

Anne and Rubina looked at beneficence and non-maleficence again and the values behind these judgements. Anne remembered working with a teenager who was not spending much time doing homework and his parents considered it to be in his best interests to force him to do his homework before he was allowed to communicate with his friends on-line. They wanted Anne to persuade him in counselling of the value of school work and the adverse long-term consequences of not passing his exams. Whereas Anne empathised with his parents' worries about his future, she felt uncomfortable with being asked to agree with their values and to think she knew what would be best for him. Tjelveit (1999) draws our attention to the value judgements behind the principles of beneficence and non-maleficence, resting on a broad ethical vision of what is right. This vision or the underlying values are not specified in the ethical framework. These principles are founded in utilitarianism and have been used to mean different things in various theories, from purely pleasure, to including concepts of justice and autonomy. It is not clear whether the principles should be applied to just the client or include others in the client's life who may be affected by the client's decision (see Chapter 6 for more discussion of this issue), making these value judgements even more difficult in practice. Anne and Rubina decided that even if 'good' was defined to mean pleasure or justice this would still leave individual value judgements remaining central in applying what these terms meant for other people.

Maxine and Rubina – Autonomy

Maxine considered the principle of autonomy and again stated that she thought this principle should be prioritised in counselling. Rubina questioned prioritising this principle with a client who did not prioritise autonomy themselves but instead prioritised community or religious values.

The implications of the findings from moral foundation theory (Haidt & Kesebir, 2010) are relevant here, suggesting that ethical codes should take more account of how different values are prioritised by different individuals and various cultures. Care needs to be taken to understand the cultural relativity of all our own values and to understand the different values of others.

Moral foundation theory

Moral foundation theory identifies five foundations for morality that are each linked to an evolutionarily adaptive challenge. The five foundations are (with main emotions involved in parentheses): harm/care (compassion), fairness/reciprocity (anger, gratitude and guilt), ingroup/loyalty (pride, belongingness, rage at traitors), authority/respect (respect and fear) and purity/sanctity (disgust). Empirical research has found that people who are left-leaning politically tend to value the first two foundations (harm/care and fairness/reciprocity) above the others. In contrast, conservatives tend to value all five foundations. They note that psychologists are likely to be more left-leaning politically than the general population. Correspondingly, ethical codes for psychologists prioritise principles associated with the first two foundations and not the last three. (Haidt & Kesebir, 2010)

Rubina

Rubina decided as before that she still thought the notion of autonomy was important to respect unique individuals, but that it should incorporate a sense of being there for others too. The tutor decided that the idea of heteronomy (beginning with the other) as discussed by **Levinas** might be useful here.

Levinas and autonomy

Levinas critiques the notion of autonomy as being colonisation of all outside oneself, the 'reduction of the Other to the Same' (Levinas in Peperzak, 1993: 47–48). For Levinas, heteronomy is our primary duty, saying 'my duty to respond to the other suspends my natural right to self survival' (1981/1995: 189). Although we are free not to respond to the other, we can never invalidate the other's prior claim on us. However, this does not mean a turn away from valuing individual freedom; in contrast, Levinas claims that, 'the being that imposes itself does not limit but promotes my freedom, by arousing my goodness' (1969: 200). Peperzak further explains, 'We are in the process of uncovering a heteronomy that does not abolish the freedom of the ego but rather provides it with its most authentic meaning' (1993: 49). Furthermore, 'To realise my responsibility for the Other, I myself must be free and independent; but the sense of my selfhood is my being-for-the-Other' (Peperzak, 1993: 25). Levinas is also very clear about the limits on our ability to understand the other; he sees attempts to understand as totalising or colonising – reducing the other to our own perspective. In *Totality and infinity* (1969), Levinas explains that the infinite is absolutely other, which always overflows our capacity of thought. With heteronomy, we face the other without putting our conceptions on them and we expand and learn.

Levinas's concept of heteronomy leads us to question the primacy of the principle of autonomy in psychotherapy. Loewenthal and Snell argue that the principle of autonomy in therapy has been wrongly chosen over heteronomy, and the result has been that 'the client/patient is a bit player on the therapist's stage and as a result of therapy everyone else becomes a bit player on the client/patient's stage' (2001: 27). Instead they advocate Levinas's principle of heteronomy as an aim for the therapist and the client in psychotherapy. This involves 'being able to enjoy, to dwell, to love intimately and to meet others face-to-face, and ultimately to realise that the face of the other is the aspect of divinity open to us. ... As psychotherapists, we can be ethical only if we see the other as someone who we can serve or learn from. This is ethics as practice' (Loewenthal & Snell, 2001: 30).

Exercise

1. If we replaced the traditional ethical principle of autonomy in counselling with heteronomy, how would this be different from beneficence?
2. What are the advantages of both autonomy and heteronomy?

Tom

Tom was concerned by Levinas's idea of heteronomy, as he worried that this could leave us wide open to being exploited and commanded by others rather than decide how to live our own life. Kunz (2007) distinguishes Levinas's heteronomy from servitude or suffering abuse from the other, which he suggests would be irresponsible to the other. In contrast, obedience is listening to the legitimate needs of the other. Tom understood that Levinas was suggesting that being good to others was the purpose of life but he was not sure that he agreed this was the whole purpose for him, although he did agree that thinking of others gave his life meaning. He also felt his life had meaning and purpose from developing his own sense of self including spiritual awareness, creativity and intellectual pursuits. He did not feel comfortable totally replacing the concept of autonomy with heteronomy but wondered whether they could coexist.

Rubina

Rubina thought about the difference between heteronomy and beneficence and thought Levinas's idea of heteronomy was much more based in the experience of the other than beneficence often is. She wondered whether heteronomy replacing beneficence would be a good way of separating the idea of caring for others from paternalism, with the person in authority imagining what they think is good for the other. Instead, heteronomy really focuses on responding to the needs of the other, rather than imagining what these may be or even deciding what they should be. She liked this idea but also wondered how possible it was to correctly understand the needs of the other rather than imagine, especially given what Levinas says about infinity always overflowing the idea of the other, meaning there will always be more to the other than we can ever understand or conceptualise. Rubina also really liked the idea of heteronomy not abolishing individual freedom but giving us meaning, and felt this captured well her perspective of wanting the idea of respecting autonomy to include responding to others.

The students – Fidelity and self-respect

The students thought that fidelity was useful in terms of the importance of this in the therapy relationship. However, they wondered whether it was necessary as an additional principle or whether it could already be covered in the first four principles, as not keeping promises or being honest would likely cause harm to the client and would not respect their autonomy. Maxine particularly liked the addition of self-respect, to ensure that the focus was not solely on the service of the client in the therapy relationship and that the therapist's needs were recognised and acknowledged. They wondered whether these additional principles were trying to bring more of a relational focus to the ethical framework.

Principles or intuition in counselling?

Exercise

What are the difficulties in applying a principlist approach to ethical decisions in counselling?

Maxine

Maxine considered the difficulties in applying principles to ethics when an immediate decision has to be made. She thinks that most of the time in counselling, every ethical decision she makes in what to say to her clients will be immediate and follow intuition, and she will only be able to consider how these decisions fit with principles retrospectively. This is consistent with a social **intuitionist** approach.

Social intuitionism

Haidt (2001) argues from this perspective that we generally make moral decisions based on emotions and intuitions and then use reason as a post-hoc rationalisation or justification of our action or decision. He presents evidence to show that moral intuitions (being affect-based) come first, are more powerful, are made automatically and usually lead to our moral judgements. He argues that reason has been overemphasised and that reasoning processes are motivated by non-rational reasons such as avoiding cognitive dissonance and preserving internal coherence in one's beliefs, or preserving relationships with people by agreeing with them. Reasoning is usually 'employed only to seek confirmation of preordained conclusions' (2001: 822). This theory is consistent with arguments from neuroscience that emotion is primary (e.g. Damasio, 2000).

Tom

Tom reflected that purely following intuition could lead to unthinking discriminatory practice, and that principles could be a useful check against this, even if it is a post-hoc check.

Arendt argues that principles can also be used to guard against tyranny by individuals and to try and describe agreed-upon values.

Holmes (2001: xv) suggests that principles are too simplistic, saying 'these principles, however praiseworthy, will seem to most practitioners somehow to miss many of the key aspects of psychotherapeutic practice – not least, its confusions, uncertainties and mysteries.' Urofsky, Engels and Engebretson (2008) question the foundational prevalence of Kitchener's principle ethics in counselling. Instead, they suggest the necessity to reach out to the wider disciplines of philosophy and ethics to inform a debate on ethics in counselling and to consider whether there are more suitable ethics models than principle ethics for a relational or artistic enterprise such as counselling. They mention virtue ethics and relational ethics as promising alternatives or additions.

Virtue ethics

In contrast to the idea of duties, virtue ethics is concerned with the supererogatory (beyond necessary) or moral excellence. The difference here in application of these theories is between bottom-line ethics and aims for best practice. For virtue ethicists, what is important is motive and character, not outcome or rules for action. A virtue ethics approach to counselling is an analogous approach to values-based practice in healthcare, focusing on the values or virtues of the counsellor.

Exercise

1. What virtues or moral qualities do you think are important for a counsellor to have?
2. Should these be virtues we adopt in the whole of our lives or just when we are counselling?

The students

The students brainstormed a list of virtues that they believed counsellors should have. Anne began with empathy, compassion and curiosity and Maxine added respect, self-awareness and self-care. However, she was unsure if these were virtues or competencies. Tom prioritised fairness, and good judgement, which he believed represented inherent beliefs and abilities. Rubina added humility, openness, genuineness and trustworthiness, which she felt were some of her character traits which helped her be a good counsellor.

The BACP guidelines also follow the approach of virtue ethics in suggesting the personal moral qualities that a therapist should aim to foster. These qualities are: empathy, sincerity, integrity, resilience, respect, humility, competence, fairness, wisdom and courage (see BACP, 2013: 3).

Kitchener (1996) considers the importance of virtues as an addition to but not a replacement for principles. Kitchener and Anderson (2011) refer to the Greek concept of phronesis, translated as prudence or practical wisdom. They describe this as the motivation and ability to morally reason well and apply to real-world problems. They suggest that integrity and practical wisdom together form a good basis for morality, emphasising commitment to moral values and to use good judgement to interpret the values and principles. They also mention other virtues that are argued for in counselling, which are: respectfulness, trustworthiness and care or compassion. Adshead (2005) suggests that the most important virtues for a psychotherapist to cultivate in order to practise more ethically are courage, truthfulness and personal honesty. Beebe (2009) lists the seven cardinal virtues, originating in classical antiquity and adapted by the Christian Church, and applies them to counteract the seven deadly sins in supervision. The cardinal virtues are: justice, temperance, fortitude, prudence, faith, hope and charity.

The students were interested to find how many of the virtues they had suggested had been proposed in the counselling ethics literature or were in the BACP Ethical Framework. Tom was perplexed by the idea of 'competence' being a virtue, which he felt confused the idea of virtues as character traits, and should be better considered elsewhere in the framework. He was also somewhat alarmed by the mention of 'resilience' in the code and how this could be used to judge counsellors who struggle with their own mental health. All the students believed that the virtues they had chosen were important in the whole of their lives but suggested that it was more their personal moral choice how much these virtues led their behaviour in other relationships, whereas in the role of a therapist, these virtues *should* determine their behaviour. Casemore (2009: 30) suggests that the values and principles described in the BACP Ethical Framework should apply not just to counselling but to the whole of our lives, advocating a virtue ethics approach to developing an 'ethical way of being' in the whole of our lives.

Defining and measuring virtues

Exercise

1 Do you think it is possible to assess whether counsellors have the virtues described in the BACP Ethical Framework?
2 Are the definitions of these virtues clear and agreed upon?

The students

Tom thought that some of these virtues could be measurable if they were operationalised but that interpreting what they meant behaviourally would be highly variable and value-laden. He wondered if the existence of these virtues in someone would be most usefully established by the other in a relationship with the person, rather than self-assessment. The other students agreed that they were more valid when measured by someone else, but Rubina added that misunderstandings of intentions must also be allowed for here. Most of these qualities cannot be objectively determined, and indeed may only be usefully measured by the recipient (as Rogers [1959] emphasises in the need for the client to perceive the therapist's empathy).

> This continued a discussion about how each virtue is value-laden in how it is defined, interpreted and used. The students particularly discussed what courage could mean, and the different potential ways that a client could experience a therapist who thinks they are being 'courageous', for example as challenging, confrontational, perceptive or undermining.

Similarly, integrity is defined in many ways, each of which can be understood from various perspectives. Palmer Barnes defines integrity as 'the paradoxical combination of vulnerability and confidence that makes work on character possible' (2001: 85). Kitchener and Anderson (2011) cite Beauchamp and Childress (2001), who define integrity as a connection between moral convictions, actions and emotions, suggesting the etymology of the word from the Latin *integri* meaning wholeness. They suggest that lacking integrity involves an absence of core values. Beebe defines mature integrity as a 'developed sensitivity to the needs of the whole' (2009: 44). He suggests that virtues support integrity (MacIntyre, 1984), following the medieval church tradition.

These definitions vary widely and each can be interpreted in a variety of ways giving us a glimpse of the huge difficulties in operationalising these virtues.

Maxine

Maxine wondered about the idea of trying to operationalise virtues, and she decided that she felt something would be lost in trying to measure these character traits. She felt they represented something deep about the humanity of each person and were perhaps more spiritual than behavioural. This comment reminded the tutor of **Jaspers**' ideas about values, to inspire rather than be measured.

Exercise

1. Do you think it is possible to be a bad person but a good therapist?
2. Do you think these virtues are context-dependent or universal?
3. Given **Aristotle**'s idea that virtues must be cultivated by adopting habits that develop virtues, how do you think therapists can develop the virtues necessary to be a good therapist?

Anne

Anne thought that it was not possible to be a bad person but a good therapist. She saw a bad person as someone who is selfish or unaware of others or even purposely cruel, and decided that people like this could not be good therapists, as even if they could cultivate being 'good' or aware and caring of others in therapy, this then would not be authentic. She acknowledged that her ideas of 'good' and 'bad' were context-dependent but could not imagine a context where they would not be relevant. She wondered about whether people who were selfish and unaware could develop a virtue of caring, and thought that if they really wanted to do this but had never previously learned to, this was possible by determined ongoing awareness with feedback from others. However, she thought it was much easier to have learned these values whilst growing up by demonstration and explicit teaching, as she tries to do with her own children. She also wondered whether this could be a purpose of counselling.

All the students were doubtful as to whether virtues could be taught, and thought that counselling students should be selected by the presence of virtues, and their development could be encouraged. Kitchener (1996) notes the particular difficulty for counsellor education with the notion of virtues and whether the development of virtues can be taught or encouraged, or whether students need to be selected who already possess the appropriate character traits.

Tom

Tom thought that putting virtues into practice required reflection, motivation and commitment. He thought about the principles of Buddhism and how important meditating has been to him to maintain constant reflection about himself and others and the values by which he lives his life. He was unsure whether virtues were anything more than stable values which are important for our identity (see Chapter 1). He also wondered how much the possibility of developing virtues (particularly as described by **Aristotle**) depended on living a fairly privileged life, which would be impossible for someone who was simply struggling to survive. However, he did think that even in the struggle for survival, different people developed different strategies and values for doing so that may or may not involve developing virtues that benefit the whole community.

The students

The students summarised what they had learned about virtue ethics: they are hard to teach, they are context- and culture-specific, but they may identify something more important for ethical decisions in relationships than principles. Anne wondered whether an ethic of care should be included in the BACP Ethical Framework and whether it had something to add to principles and virtues. She questioned whether it was another variation of a virtue theory. The tutor decided this was a good time to revisit the ethics of care to apply specifically to counselling.

Ethics of care

Both principle and virtue ethics focus on the individual rather than relationships. In contrast, the ethics of care starts from the relationship. It is perhaps no surprise that counselling ethics focus on the individual as this is true of nearly all models of counselling and has led to critiques of counselling theory from feminist and cross-cultural perspectives among others (see Lago & Thompson, 1996; Proctor & Napier, 2004; Proctor et al., 2006). However, many models of counselling have developed more relational perspectives and theories in response to such critiques.

Existential philosophy traces a move from the individual to the relational and could be helpful in our consideration of relational ethics in counselling. Existential philosophy in general emphasises our intersubjectivity and being-with-others (**Heidegger**) as an essential part of our existence. **Merleau-Ponty** emphasised our interrelatedness with the world and others, seeing consciousness as between us and the world, with no sense of an isolated subject. Van Deurzen-Smith (1997) suggests that **Sartre**'s major contribution to psychotherapy was to stress the social and political dimensions of our being in the world with others. **Jaspers** emphasised our communication with others as the way to find our authenticity. **Buber** stressed that I is always in relation to It or Thou.

Ethics of care as virtue ethics

Exercise

1. Do you think the ethics of care is best seen as relational or as a virtue of one person?
2. How would this alter how the ethics of care is seen in therapy?

Maxine

Maxine thought that the ethics of care needs to account for our intimates, strangers and ourselves. She thought that the ethics of care in therapy needs to be seen as a virtue of the therapist rather than relational, as she could not expect her clients to care for her; indeed she believed that the point of therapy for her as a client was that she did not have to think about her impact on the therapist, although she also noted that as the therapy relationship developed, she developed feelings of care for her therapist. This was more apparent to her now in the training situation where she found herself feeling protective of the tutor (her ex-therapist) if other students were critical of her. However, she believed that as the therapist she would want to ensure that the client was relieved of as much of this burden of care as possible so they could really use the space for their own needs.

Anne and Rubina

Anne wondered if the development of the client's care for the therapist was a natural and good part of the process and represented growth on the part of the client. She agreed that the therapist's duty was to care for the client and not expect this care to be reciprocated but she believed that in doing this, the client may learn to care in return and in turn find more of a purpose in life.

Rubina objected to the idea that teaching clients to care should be a goal in therapy, whether this is implied or explicit. She thought that this was an example of the therapist forcing their values on the client. In contrast, she believed that the therapist's job was to care for the client and the client was free to use this care however they wanted to.

Slote (2000) advocates an agent-based view of the ethics of care, rather than a relational view, as he argues that we place a higher moral value on caring than on being cared for. This is reminiscent of the asymmetry that **Levinas** refers to, noting our duty to respond to others but not to expect the same from others for ourselves. Anne agreed that an agent-based view of the ethics of care as a virtue of the therapist might be more appropriate than a relational focus in counselling ethics. However, she was reluctant to lose the relational focus, as it made clear that the therapist's care was in response to and in relationship with, the client, as opposed to their own ideas of care. Here Levinas's notion of heteronomy was useful again, and the importance of facing the other and infinity as opposed to totalising. Rubina was clear that an ethic of care was relational and to turn it into an individual virtue meant it lost its meaning. She believed that part of it was an acceptance of our interdependence and our meaning in life being determined by our relationships with others.

Relational ethics

Bond developed the idea of 'relational trust' in conjunction with his involvement in moving the BACP Ethical Framework from a primary ethic of autonomy to that of relational trust (Bond, 2004, cited in Proctor & Keys, 2013; 2010). Bond defines this, saying: '*Trust is a relationship of sufficient quality and resilience to withstand the challenges arising from difference, inequality, risk and uncertainty*' (2007: 436, italics in original). He notes the inability to rely on rules, but the necessity for 'continual ethical mindfulness' (Bond, 2004, cited in Proctor & Keys, 2013: 424). Bond (2010) explains that relational trust is bidirectional and fits well with how clients talk about what is ethically important in therapy. Following the focus of **existential philosophy**, he places the relationship firmly central in therapy, and attention to this as primary in ethics. He explains: 'Attention to the relationship and its struggles with trust and mistrust in all its variations become an affirmation of what is meaningful in life' (2007: 437). He notes that the notion of relational trust also means that the therapist and client share the responsibility and energy for maintaining the therapy relationship.

Carroll (2011) gives an example from supervision of how in various learning loops he moved from an ethic of duty to an ethic of relational trust. Furthermore, he identified the ethic of duty as a defensive practice. He explains: 'It was quite a transformational journey as I moved towards a relational ethics of faithfulness and fidelity rather than an external ethics that kept me safe and secure' (2011: 25).

Exercise

How is an ethic of relational trust useful in counselling?

The students

Tom liked the focus in relational trust on inequality and power and ethical mindfulness. Rubina was happy to have her relational focus taken account of in counselling ethics. Anne was happy to see something akin to an ethic of care but with the responsibility clearly with the counsellor. Maxine again noted that there was not sufficient focus for her on the counsellor also being responsible for self-care, and that it perhaps needed noting that the counsellor was also a person to be noticed and thought about in the relationship. She thought a relational approach did make this more likely than a focus on what is done to the client, but still thought it needed to be spelled out that it was not all just about being of service to the client. Anne was interested in the quote from Carroll (2011) about moving from an ethic of duty to one of relational trust and how the ethic of duty was a defensive practice. The tutor decided that this was a good time to explain three approaches to ethics in counselling.

Positive ethics

Barnett (2008) suggests that there are three approaches to ethics in counselling and psychotherapy: positive or aspirational ethics, risk management, and defensive practice. Positive ethics emphasise maximising virtues. Risk management in contrast focuses on decreasing risks, and defensive practice focuses on the protection of the therapist. Barnett advocates an emphasis on positive ethics. This concurs with Murdoch, who suggests: 'Ethics should not be merely an analysis of ordinary mediocre conduct, it should be a hypothesis about good conduct and how this can be achieved' (1970/1985: 78).

Exercise

Which of these approaches do you think are important in counselling?

The students

Initially the students all agreed that they wanted to aspire to positive ethics and being the best therapists they could. However, Maxine wondered where the focus on the wellbeing of the counsellor was in this. She thought that decreasing risks and protecting the therapist also had their place, and were actually the safety nets needed to be able to then focus on positive ethics. She added that counsellors also work within a legal framework and that she believed that the practice of suing counsellors may be on the increase. She thought it was very important that counsellors considered how to protect themselves in court to be able to continue to practise, and thought this was an important function of defensive practice. See Chapter 11 for an example of considering all three approaches.

The law

Jenkins (2009) considers the relationship between the ethical framework and the law, pointing out that separate and distinct legal principles will apply in court. For example, the legal concept relating to beneficence is that of duty of care, and the legal concept related to justice is of non-discrimination. Jenkins (2007) notes that the law and therapy work with different discourses; therapy works with the subjective and ambiguous nature of individual experience, whereas the law is concerned with establishing facts. He points out that the BACP Ethical

Framework (2002) does not require therapists to obey the law but to be aware of legal obligations and be legally accountable, and notes this change from earlier BACP ethical codes where counsellors were required to work within the law. As with the change from an ethical code to framework, thus emphasising principles, values and virtues as opposed to rule-following, Jenkins also notes a 'developing diversity of ethical perspectives to be found within the law, including rights-based models and the empathic valuing of individual experience' (2007: 21).

Summary

In this chapter, our students first considered principle ethics and the application of traditional biomedical ethical principles to counselling. The limits of the rational application of principles and the role of intuitions were discussed. Then virtues, the ethics of care, and relational ethics were considered with particular reference to the BACP (2013) Ethical Framework. We have also considered the three approaches of positive ethics, risk management and defensive practice, and the relationship of the law to ethical practice.

At the completion of this section, Anne commented: 'This is all very interesting, but I'm not sure any of it will make it any clearer to me how to make an ethical decision when I am counselling.' So the next chapter will focus on the practice of making ethical decisions and the place of ethical codes in making such decisions.

FIVE Making ethical decisions

Introduction

This chapter considers various decision-making models which are suggested by authors in the counselling ethics literature. Most are stage models, listing steps to go through in order to make a decision, but others advocate dimensional models which list various dimensions to be considered in no particular order and interacting with each other. Limitations of decision-making models and ethical frameworks are then discussed, along with the necessity of ethical anxiety and responsibility for ethical practice. The division between technical and ethical questions is examined and it is argued that all decisions are ethical. Finally the dynamics of power in therapy are considered a vital part of the context to be aware of in taking ethical responsibility.

Dimensional models

Dimensional models list various dimensions or components to consider in ethical decision-making. Houser and Thoma (2013) use a hermeneutic model of ethical decision-making/reasoning (Figure 5.1). At the centre is the ethical dilemma, and they suggest that the horizon of ethical decision-making includes the parts of: the counsellor's values and identity, the client's values and identity, the supervisor's values and identity, institutional context and policy, professional codes of ethics and professional knowledge, and ethical theories and the law. As a hermeneutic model, each of the parts interacts with the others and the whole in a continuous dynamic manner.

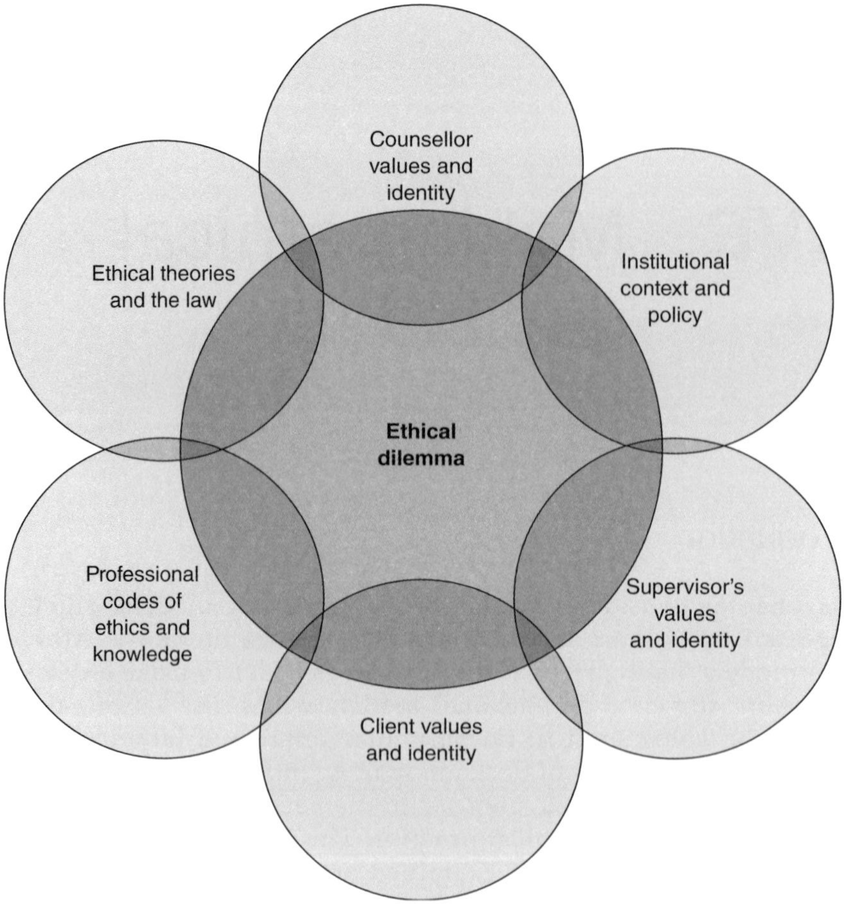

Figure 5.1 Hermeneutic model of decision-making (Houser & Thoma, 2013)

Another example of a dimensional model focuses on the counsellor's decision-making in the context of moral behaviour. Rest's (1994) components of moral behaviour are: moral sensitivity (awareness of moral implications of decisions), moral decision-making, moral motivation (evaluating competing values to motivation to act morally) and moral character (the characteristics necessary to implement a moral decision, such as courage and toughness).

Stage models

Most examples of how to make ethical decisions in the counselling literature are systematic reasoning exercises based on typical problem-solving processes involving weighing up possibilities for risk and benefit. Pope and Vasquez (2007) suggest a process of 17 steps, including consideration of the law, professional codes, research, how your feelings, biases or self-interest affect your judgement, and taking personal responsibility for your decision. Several stage decision-making models (Bond, 2010; Gabriel & Casemore, 2003; Gabriel & Davies, 2000; Pope & Vasquez, 2007; Sperry, 2007) all involve the following stages:

Stages of ethical decision-making

1 Identify and describe the problem or dilemma and consider all perspectives in the situation, identifying laws, ethical frameworks, ethical principles, organisational values and rules, and sociocultural factors involved.
2 Consult with peers or experts, exploring one's own feelings, intuitions, values, biases, self-interests and prejudices in the situation.
3 Identify possible courses of action, exploring the potential impact of each course and benefits and risks of each.
4 Using all these considerations select an action and take responsibility for justifying it and then monitor and evaluate the outcome.

Ethical dilemmas

Sperry suggests this definition of an ethical dilemma:

> Conflicts that arise when competing standards of right and wrong apply to a specific situation in counselling practice. They arise because of competing or conflicting ethical standards, because of a conflict between an ethical and a moral standard, because specific ethical standards do not address complex situations, or because other factors prevent a clear-cut application of the standard. (Sperry, 2007: 37)

The terminology of 'standards' sits within the framework of ethical codes; Sperry's language is firmly rooted in traditional principlist approaches to ethics (see Chapters 3 and 4). I offer an alternative definition within the framework of values:

Definition

Ethical dilemma: 'When there are competing or conflicting values influencing a decision or uncertainty about how to put values into practice.'

Facing ethical dilemmas can arouse ethical anxiety, which can be seen as a concomitant for taking ethical responsibility. Ethical anxiety can be considered important in the formation of moral character (Sperry, 2007: 36). Ethical anxiety and dilemmas are a continual part of counselling practice. Tools to aid ethical decision-making can only do just that and are no substitute for continual ethical mindfulness and awareness of values and how we apply principles or values in every unique situation. What is crucial is how we learn from experiences about ourselves and the nature of relationships and therapy (Bond, 1997; Holmes, 2001).

Exercise

1 Can you think of an ethical dilemma you have had working with a client?
2 How did you resolve this dilemma?
3 Are dimensional or stage models of decision-making useful to aid your thinking?

Maxine – Assessment decisions

Maxine had just started a placement in a primary care counselling service in the NHS where clients are offered up to 12 sessions. She had been allocated a client who had been on the waiting list for five months after assessment and whose husband had died a year before. At assessment it was reported that she was very down and struggling to see a future without him but she had supportive friends and she still had an active social life. When Maxine first saw her, her client reported that she was so relieved to finally be able to see a counsellor as she really needed help. She felt totally alone in the world and had also found things out about her husband that had really disillusioned her about their relationship so was questioning their life together before he died. This had brought back her experience of her parents splitting up when she was 10 years old and then finding out that her father had been having an affair. She was now wondering whether she had been sexually abused by her father although she could not remember details of events.

Maxine's dilemma was that on hearing about all the other issues that the client disclosed at this session she was worried that 12 sessions in primary care would not be enough for her and she did not know if starting to see her and then stopping could be worse than referring her on to longer-term therapy immediately. Maxine resolved this dilemma after discussing it with her supervisor on placement. She decided to have a further discussion with her client at the start of the next session, being clear that their work was limited to 12 sessions, and sharing her concerns and discussing their options.

Applying dimensional models

Maxine thought that her values and identity were relevant in that she wanted to be helpful as a counsellor but was not sure she could be in such a short time for this client. She thought that her client valued being listened to and having a space to discuss her experiences and fears, but she also thought it may be important to her client to feel that the relationship could last as long as she needed it, particularly given her recent loss. Her supervisor was also the manager of her team, and wanted individual clients to receive a good service, but also to reduce waiting lists and make sure clients who accessed the service were appropriate for that level of care and would benefit from a short-term intervention, demonstrating a good outcome. Maxine was also aware that there were fears that their service could be commissioned from somewhere else if their figures regarding outcomes and waiting lists were judged to not be good enough. She thought principles in codes of ethics were all relevant but may be competing. She thought respecting her client's autonomy was important in terms of not taking a decision out of her hands. She noted too that the principle of justice meant that she also needed to consider all the people on the waiting list, and make sure that the people who could benefit from short-term counselling use her time. She considered beneficence and whether she could know what would be good for her client, and decided this was very difficult to predict. She did not think the law was relevant but her supervisor alerted her to the possibility that if the client became clearer that she had been sexually abused by her father, she may decide she wanted to take the case to court, so any counselling work would have to be thought about in terms of the possibility of having notes or a report requested by court. Regarding moral character, Maxine was worried that her supervisor might tell her that her client should be referred on and she knew she would struggle to explain this to her client, who she predicted could be very upset particularly after waiting for this service. Concerning moral sensitivity, Maxine was pleased that she felt this situation was a dilemma that caused her anxiety about how best to respond, as she felt this demonstrated her sense of ethical responsibility.

Applying stage models

Maxine thought that the first stage was covered by the dimensional model, illustrated above. For stage two, she consulted with her supervisor, although noted that most of this had been a discussion about service requirements. She brought up her own feelings in supervision and noted her self-interest in wanting to be found useful. She also realised that she felt a little overwhelmed by her client and the issue of her not being sure about whether she had been sexually abused, and Maxine was worried about her power to influence her client in this situation. Her supervisor discussed with her whether she felt she was competent to work with the client's issues, and after discussion of the possible issues that may arise, Maxine felt more confident that she could work with the client with good supervision.

In stage three, Maxine considered her options, which she identified as:

1 Working with her client and hoping that 12 sessions were enough.
2 Referring her client on to a longer-term service and trying to advocate for her not waiting as long, given the time she had already waited.
3 Discussing the options and her concerns with her client and letting her make a decision.

Maxine was aware of her supervisor's concerns about the waiting list and knew that she favoured referring the client on, particularly as there was a voluntary sector service for women who had been sexually abused (or thought they might have been) which offered unlimited sessions. However, having met her client and hearing of her relief to be finally starting counselling, Maxine felt morally obliged to respond to this need if she could. She was aware that she felt more ethical obligation to her client than to the other people she had not yet met who were on the waiting list and who were still strangers. However, she was not happy with hoping that 12 sessions would be enough and was concerned about the risks to the client of feeling abandoned if counselling stopped at a point when she could be in the middle of working things out and possibly still very distressed. She decided that she preferred the last option as she felt it was actually impossible to judge how much time her client would need in counselling and they may find that 12 sessions would be enough. She felt this option best respected her client's autonomy and was also consistent with the principle of justice in that she would be offered the same number of sessions as everyone else on the waiting list, whilst also responsibly trying to respond to her individual needs. She thought that this option also shared the responsibility with the client of how to use the limited time they had.

In stage four, she discussed the options with her client at the next session and her client was clear that she wanted to continue working with Maxine now she had met her, and did not want to wait for another service. When Maxine reviewed how things were going with her client at their sixth appointment, her client decided that she was finding counselling very useful but she thought she would need longer after it finished, so she decided she would get in touch with the voluntary sector service for women who had been sexually abused and refer herself for further therapy. She was clear, however, that at the end of her therapy with Maxine she would be in a much better place to be able to wait for further input if necessary. She reported that it had been particularly useful to talk about life without her husband and her feelings about their life together, and doing this had made everyday life a lot easier and given her more hope for the future. Maxine felt very pleased with how her decision had worked out. She felt reassured that she had been of help to her client, who had decided to focus on the original bereavement issue in response to Maxine's concerns. She was happy that the outcome data on her client would demonstrate change and she felt that trusting her client to make this decision herself had been a really positive start to their counselling relationship. She had enjoyed working with her client and felt she would be less likely to feel overwhelmed with a client with similar issues in the future.

Limits of ethical decision-making models and ethical codes and frameworks

Decision-making models can provide a framework to follow even if each individual uses various values or interpretations of principles and therefore produces different outcomes. Codes and models cannot prevent dilemmas but can provide methods to consider the dilemmas. A framework for considering ethical decisions can help make articulating reasons for decisions easier.

It is important for counsellors to understand the principles behind codes and to think about how and when to apply them rather than use them as rules. Knapp and VandeCreek (2008) argue that understanding the moral foundations of codes helps therapists to see ethical standards less as rules imposed from outside, and more as the embodiment of shared values. Just as importantly, they suggest that 'psychotherapists who understand the moral foundations of the standards have a perspective by which to interpret and implement the enforceable standards, especially in ambiguous situations' (2008: 614). To see codes as an embodiment of shared values involves us in considering how well or not they fit with our own personal values. The difficulty here is what happens when our personal values do not fit with the values behind the codes.

Ethical responsibility

Being ethically responsible is being accountable for the decisions we make, taking responsibility for our freedom to make these choices, and being able to articulate how and why we make our decisions. Responsibility is the partner of power, and when we are in a powerful position to make decisions that concern others, taking responsibility for how we do this is essential. It is a crucial part of recognising and acknowledging our freedom to make our own choices, based on our own values.

For **Kierkegaard**, anguish is a consciousness of facing freedom; **Sartre** explains: 'Anguish is precisely my consciousness of being my own future' (1943/2003: 56). Fleeing this awareness of our freedom and ethical responsibility is for Sartre the definition of 'bad faith', an attempt to lie to oneself. For **Heidegger**, the choices we make can only be assessed according to the criteria of authenticity and resoluteness (taking on personal responsibility for the choices and making a choice knowing that guilt at missed choices is an inevitable part of the human condition).

However, this is notwithstanding the limitations we all have on this freedom, depending on the context. These dual factors of individual freedom and environmental constraints are the concerns of much existential philosophy. For existentialists, such as **De Beauvoir** (1948/1976), our task is to be always aware of both our freedom and our facticity (the constraints we have on our freedom due to our context and relationships).

Exercise

Does the existence of ethical frameworks or decision-making models facilitate or undermine ethical responsibility?

Rubina

Rubina worried that models falsely simplified the uniqueness of each ethical situation, but also thought that they had to rely on the wisdom of the practitioner considering them. She saw an ethical framework a bit like a theory in counselling – interesting to consider, but down to the wisdom and the experience of the counsellor in the application to practice. She wondered whether ways to encourage self-awareness and ethical thought in counsellors would be more useful than frameworks to apply in particular situations.

Maxine

Maxine did not find that considering ethical frameworks or following a decision-making model with her ethical dilemma had undermined her ethical responsibility. Instead, she felt it had helped her to be clearer about all the factors involved in her decision and had enhanced her responsibility by fully reflecting on her dilemma. She also felt pleased that she had made her decision and taken responsibility for it, despite her supervisor/manager favouring a different option. She thought this reflected the resoluteness with which she prioritised her own values and ethical response to her client. She did wonder how she would have felt if the situation had not turned out so positively and whether she would have been defensive in further discussions with her supervisor.

Tom

Tom wondered if it might be necessary that ethical dilemmas arose that could not be resolved by simply following codes to ensure that we all take full responsibility for our own individual responses and choices.

Anne

Anne wondered whether the existence of codes or frameworks which could be perceived as rules could have the effect of simply encouraging counsellors to cover up when they feel they have made mistakes rather than encourage learning from mistakes. She noted the threat in supervision of a supervisor reporting ethical infractions to a professional body and wondered how many supervisees refrained from talking about situations that they were unsure about as a result (see Chapter 7 for more about supervision).

Mistakes, blame or tragedies?

Responsibility is difficult when so much in relationships is unpredictable. It is impossible to know how someone else will react or respond, but ethical responsibility involves having thought about the potential impact on someone and being clear why a particular decision was made. Difficulty can arise when an action is perceived differently from how it was intended, and then it is imperative that the counsellor can explain the intention.

Exercise

Do you think someone is always responsible when something goes wrong in counselling? If not, how could complaints procedures account for tragedies?

Anne

Anne decided that of course someone is not always responsible or certainly not blameworthy when something goes wrong. She considered that relationships are unpredictable and we cannot be expected to know how someone will be affected by what we do or say or how we are. However, she did feel that counsellors have a responsibility to have considered this as far as possible and to care about their impact on clients. She thought openness to being imperfect and acknowledging and apologising for mistakes were very important, and wondered whether ethical frameworks made this more difficult. **De Beauvoir** stresses that ethics are founded on the likelihood of us getting things wrong.

Tom

Tom wondered whether the acceptance of the inevitability of mistakes and imperfection could lead to an acceptance of practice that he thought was highly dubious in counselling. He thought about counsellors choosing to use techniques that were uncommon and had no research to back them up; and possibly without both experience of applying them previously and sharing this situation with the client so they could give informed consent to be part of what he essentially saw as an experiment. He realised from this that he valued having research/evidence backing how he wanted to work, as it reassured him and potentially clients that there was a good chance of it being effective. He then realised he was unsure where the boundary lay between an ethical decision and a technical one. Whether he chooses to follow a systematic desensitisation programme with a client or challenge their unhelpful thoughts could be seen to be an ethical decision based on his values or a technical decision based on his understanding of and research into a cognitive behavioural model of therapy.

Technical or ethical questions?

The focus on evidence-based practice (EBP) in the UK is firmly on technique from the perspective of a medical model. This approach is often justified ethically, usually with the appeal to beneficence or non-maleficence. For example, Houser and Thoma suggest that 'The use of EBP may help reduce the frequency and impact of potentially harmful therapies' (2013: 191). The example they give is of the recovered memories technique, which they claim was adopted by therapists without adequate evidence, the result being unreliable memories and harm being done to people falsely accused of abusing.

Values and politics behind 'evidence'

The recovered memories technique is an astounding example of using techniques without evidence and the harm done to people falsely accused of abuse. The values and politics behind the 'false memory syndrome' debate are clear, as is the power of the people involved challenging the claims of *any* therapy clients said to have been abused, claiming that therapists have implanted memories by suggestion. The undermining of accounts of abuse given the prevalence of abuse, experienced predominantly by women and girls at the hands of men, can be seen as another example of men using their power to undermine the voices and experiences of women. This example clearly demonstrates the importance of always questioning the ethics and values behind 'evidence'.

How do we know when a decision concerning how to be as a therapist is a technical decision about effectiveness and when it is an ethical decision about doing the 'right' thing? Lomas suggests that 'There is no technique for behaving well towards another person' (1999: 66). Some suggest that we focus too much on the ethical, and that this realm should be more restricted. Garguilo asks, 'Would it not be better to focus on interventions that may be helpful or not helpful and leave the judgement of "unethical" to what is demonstrably, unequivocally, and universally damaging?' (2007: 719).

Exercise

1 Can you give an example of something that you judge to be unethical behaviour as a therapist that is unequivocally universally damaging to clients?
2 What is your evidence for this?
3 Do you judge behaviour to be unethical if it *may* be damaging? How do you decide this?

Rubina

Rubina remembered one of her clients telling her about seeing a previous therapist who had fallen asleep in her session. She thought this was a good example of therapist behaviour that she would always judge to be unethical. She justified this by saying this would be a clear contravention of the role of a therapist to pay attention to a client, whatever their model. She thought this was an ethical as opposed to a technical question as it represented underlying values about the therapist's role that would be assumed even if not formally agreed. From a consequentialist perspective, she imagined that all clients would feel personally affronted and uncared for if a therapist fell asleep. However, her client had actually not felt affronted, but instead had been worried that the therapist was tired and needed sleep, and perhaps she was too much for him. However, she thought that this proved even more how unethical this was, as therapy should be about the needs of the client as opposed to the therapist, and she believed that it is the therapist's job to not put the client in a situation where the client has to prioritise the needs of the therapist or feel bad about their own needs.

Maxine

Maxine thought that just considering behaviours that are 'universally unequivocally damaging' to be in the sphere of ethics was too limited. She thought that all decisions were actually ethical ones, including how to implement technique, relying more on the wisdom and values of the therapist than on the correctness of the implementation of the technique. She thought that her example of an ethical dilemma was clearly about ethics, although technique was relevant in terms of how she worked with certain issues with her client.

Much of the literature on ethics in psychotherapy assumes that there are behaviours which are self-evidently damaging which all will agree on, and the usual example is a therapist having a sexual relationship with a client (see Chapter 12). This focus on damage assumes that the only relevant ethical principle is of non-maleficence and avoiding harm. There are several other relevant ethical principles as well as virtues and the ethics of care. Our values and ethics influence how we understand and interpret evidence about technique and models.

I follow many previous authors in the counselling ethics literature to suggest that every decision is actually an ethical one (e.g. Grant, 2004; Schmid, 2007; Szasz, 1965/1988; Gordon 2009) especially given the contradictory evidence about effectiveness. Grant explains: 'Ethical justifications must contain premises with ethical concepts. Research cannot generate ethical concepts. Research findings, in themselves, have no implications for practice and cannot justify practice' (2004: 155). Brodley argues that therapy is fundamentally an ethical activity, and consequently, 'a therapist should place severe limits on his or her use of research in the theory and practice of therapy. Therapy, and the research applied to a therapy – both – always express the therapist's values and attitudes about persons whether the therapist is conscious of this or not' (2011b: 67).

One of the values currently reified in healthcare is that of 'efficiency', which is used to justify a focus on 'evidence-based practice'. This makes sense within a consumerist discourse of creating a product, but less sense within a discourse of process and relationships. Smith (2009) considers Aristotle's distinction between poesis (production) and praxis (action). He contends that therapy is not about production, aiming to create an end product distinct from the process, but about praxis, where the interest is in who we become through action. With praxis, questions about efficiency are widened to broader moral questions about the therapy relationship.

Therapy is a relationship, and thus an ethical response to the other is fundamental, above any ideas of technique. Here, **Levinas**'s ideas about responding to the other and approaching the other without totalising are useful as an aim (see Chapter 4). Gantt (2002) uses Levinas to suggest that psychotherapy needs to privilege responding ethically to suffering above any theory or technique. He questions the power of the client to reject the theoretical assumptions of the therapist, saying 'a client is *not* free to repudiate such interpretations and injunctions and still be judged sane within the dogmatic and totalising construction of reality tendered by any particular therapeutic approach' (2002: 76). Gantt also notes that the effect of this is to reduce not only the freedom of the client, but also the freedom of the therapist to encounter the other. He advocates for 'the freedom to have one's own theoretical and professional project overturned by the infinite mysteries of another's existence' (2002: 76). Furthermore, questions of method and technique in therapy should be subordinate to the demand for an ethical response. He concludes, 'Ultimately the call to suffer-with is ethically prior and morally superior to any method or technique. And only when psychotherapy comes to admit this ethical priority will it perhaps become a genuinely therapeutic enterprise' (2002: 83).

Power

Part of the context of making ethical decisions in a healthcare relationship concerns the dynamics of power between the healthcare provider and the recipient. The inequality of the roles of therapist and client mean the therapist has an ethical responsibility to the client which is not reciprocal. For example, the therapist must consider confidentiality with respect to the client but the client is not obliged to keep confidential what the therapist says. In Proctor (2002), I theorise the dynamics of power in therapy and identify three aspects to this power: role power, societal power and historical power. I consider the relevance to ethical practice of each, particularly emphasising the need for self-awareness to ensure any therapist feelings of powerlessness are not responded to by taking power over the client.

Aims with respect to power and therapy models

Exercise

1 What are your aims in therapy with respect to power?
2 How well do you think your chosen modality of therapy helps you fulfil this aim? Note any inconsistencies between different values or between means and ends (e.g. if the theory is to empower the client by taking power over them!).
3 How do you respond differently as a therapist from how you might respond in a social conversation? What implications might these differences have with respect to power?

Tom

Tom thought that his aims with respect to power were to prioritise the autonomy of his clients and not take any power over them. He thought about different models of therapy and how he was drawn to a cognitive behavioural approach which he saw as collaborative and respectful. He also felt that this approach treated clients as adults who could participate in an educational enterprise where infantilisation and dependence were discouraged, which he liked. However he did wonder about the effect of the expertise of the therapist and pondered how this could encourage clients to make their own decisions and trust their own expertise. Nevertheless, he did think that the conversational style that he adopted when using this approach was not dissimilar from responding in a social conversation, and he felt that he was very respectful of not asking clients to talk about areas that they were not comfortable with.

Maxine

Maxine thought that her fundamental aim with regard to power with clients was to promote their autonomy by not taking power over them. She also noted that she was concerned not to lose her own sense of power as a counsellor (power-from-within or personal power; see Proctor, 2002), or she could no longer be there for the client. She was drawn to a person-centred approach and thought that her valuing and acceptance of the client would encourage their sense of personal power and autonomy.

Role power of the therapist

Exercise

How do you deal with the role power of the therapist in your practice?

Anne

Anne thought that her aim to promote self-understanding would promote autonomy in clients, particularly in combination with her value of tentativeness and always checking things out with clients. She felt that this demonstrated her commitment to not taking power over clients. Szasz (1965/1988) emphasises the inevitability of power in psychotherapy, saying that the aim of psychotherapy is to influence people and that we need to be aware of our values which direct this influence to make them overt instead of covert. He notes, 'As a rule people influence one another to support some values and to oppose others' (1965/1988: xv–xvi). He claims that his aim in psychotherapy is to increase the patient's knowledge of self and hence increase freedom of choice.

Rubina

Rubina thought about the practicalities of counselling settings and how important it was in her organisation that the way the building is set up and the way clients are treated at every point by all involved (such as administrative staff) give them the message that they are important. She thought about a particular client she had worked with who had looked to her as an expert before she said anything, and how explicitly she had to work against this and tell her client how she saw their respective roles in counselling. She thought of another client who did not seem to understand the purpose or focus of counselling and wanted to discuss her family, and how hard she found this to deal with without taking the position of the expert telling the client how to be different. She realised that she did this when she felt powerless and vulnerable, and vowed to be more open about her concerns when this happened rather than suggesting to or instructing the clients on how they should be using counselling.

Responding to the experience of powerlessness

Exercise

Can you think of a situation when you have felt powerless in therapy or that the client has power over you? How did you deal with this? How would you have liked to have dealt with this?

Tom

Tom thought about a time when he had felt powerless as a counsellor. He had a client who took out a complaint against him to his employers. She complained that he had frightened her when he touched her arm at the end of a session and she was scared that she was about to be sexually assaulted. His employers interviewed him about this incident and he explained to them about his client's history of sexual abuse. He said that he thought any experiences with men were likely to be perceived as frightening and potentially abusive and that he believed he had done nothing to frighten her. He explained that his touch was to show care at the end of a session where she had disclosed how bad and ashamed she felt about herself and that he wanted to communicate his acceptance of her and how much he valued her. He admitted that he had misjudged how this touch would be perceived but felt her perception was due to her experiences and not related to him. His employers agreed with him that he had not behaved inappropriately and reported back to the client who was then assigned a female counsellor.

Tom considered this experience with his fellow students and discussed how upset he had felt that he had been accused of being sexually inappropriate and how much this went against his values of respect for others. He reported how powerless he had felt and how scared that his perspective would not be believed – that his employers would find him guilty and he could lose his placement and subsequent career in counselling. He realised that he had taken back power over the client by pathologising her and using his knowledge of her history to explain her perception. He felt that this went against his values and beliefs and he wished he had been able to represent his intentions without pathologising the client.

Summary

In this chapter, dimensional and stage ethical decision-making models in counselling have been presented. The effects of ethical frameworks and decision-making models have been discussed with respect to ethical responsibility. The division between technical and ethical decisions has been questioned with the suggestion that values and ethics are relevant to all decisions. The context of counselling in relation to the dynamics of power involved has been emphasised as a major dimension from which an ethical approach needs to be considered.

Rubina noted that the power dynamics inherent in the institution of counselling were one part of the context but wondered whether the wider context of the structure of society was also crucially relevant to ethical decisions. The next chapter will consider this question.

SIX Counselling, psychotherapy and society

This chapter stresses the interaction between therapy and the wider society. I ask several questions about the relevance of this interaction to our therapy practice and our lives. First, I consider if it is our responsibility to educate ourselves about the cultural contexts of a client's life. I then ask how much we should be ethically responsible to consider the impact of therapy on significant others in the client's life. Third, I ask whether or how the institution of counselling and therapy affects society as a whole. Fourth, I question the relationship between therapy and politics and the place for political activism in society as a result of our therapist role. I finally ask how the values of society impact on counselling.

Context awareness

The UKCP Ethical Code has a section on diversity and equality, and states:

> The psychotherapist undertakes to actively consider issues of diversity and equalities as these affect all aspects of their work. The psychotherapist accepts no one is immune from the experience of prejudice and acknowledges the need for a continuing process of self-enquiry and professional development. (2009: 4)

The BACP Ethical Framework lists among its fundamental values – 'Appreciating the variety of human experience and culture' (2013: 1). Under standards of practice, the following standards are listed:

- 'Practitioners should not allow their professional relationships with clients to be prejudiced by any personal views they may hold about lifestyle, age, gender, disability, gender reassignment, race, sexual orientation, pregnancy and maternity, religion or belief, marriage and civil partnership or sex.' (p. 6)
- 'The practitioner is responsible for learning about and taking account of the different protocols, conventions and customs that can pertain to different working contexts and cultures.' (p. 8)

Exercise

How much do we need to understand about the particular cultural contexts in which clients are situated?

Tom and Rubina

Tom's first thought was that this question reflected an artificial separation, as though clients could be separated from their context. Rubina agreed that the individual and the context are inseparable.

Lago and Smith, in an edited collection entitled *Anti-discriminatory practice in counselling and psychotherapy*, start from the interlinking of individual and society, saying, 'A central tenet of this book is that the individual and the society within which they are raised are inextricably intertwined' (2010: 3). They emphasise the importance of ongoing reflective practice, using supervision to address our awareness and explore our gaps or areas of denial or avoidance.

In a sense, even thinking about cultural competency as a separate issue is nonsense, trying to separate the idea of culture from our relationships with individuals within a society. This artificial separation follows the modernist preoccupation with dualisms following Descartes. Dualisms were challenged by Spinoza and these challenges were later followed by existential philosophers with their critiques of people as autonomous separate individuals. **Heidegger**, for example, stresses how being in the world is always being-with-others. Many existential philosophers (such as **De Beauvoir**, **Sartre**, **Heidegger** and **Merleau-Ponty**) emphasise the importance of each of our individual contexts and our lack of choice about where we begin our lives, referring to facticity, contingency or thrownness – words all referring to being always in a context. The emphasis in much existential philosophy on the inevitability of the influence and constraints of our situation reminds us of the importance in psychotherapy to remember that we are not working with isolated individuals, but are all part of a much bigger whole in our contexts and relations with each other. These include relations between people in different situations socially and politically, the impact of which we need to be aware of, particularly on the dynamics of power.

Bond's concept of relational trust refers to inequalities in relationships. He defines trust saying: '*Trust is a relationship of sufficient quality and resilience to withstand the challenges arising from difference, inequality, risk and uncertainty*' (2007: 436, italics in original). He believes the biggest challenges to the therapy relationship from within are those of difference and inequality. He notes the potential for differences to set people apart from each other, to enforce conformity, to elicit prejudice and cause hurt and fear. These inequalities can originate from outside the therapy relationship (in societal power and historical power) and within (role power) and (see Proctor, 2002), and can threaten the maintenance of the relationship. So for Bond, the primary ethical aim in therapy is to focus on the creation and maintenance of such a trustworthy relationship.

The students

Anne thought immediately that the most important thing here to understand different contexts was the openness of the counsellor to difference without judgement. She did not think it would be possible to understand all possible cultures that clients could come from. Maxine added the importance of the counsellor's self-awareness about their own culture to be clear what values they had and not assume they were the same for the client. Tom added that he thought it may not be desirable for counsellors to think they know about other cultures, as they may make incorrect assumptions about any one individual client, bearing in mind individual differences within cultures.

Rubina thought all the students had valid points particularly about not making assumptions, but was uncomfortable with the idea that the counsellor should not make any effort to understand other cultures. She thought that the client should not be spending their time educating the counsellor about their culture. She thought that having some knowledge about common cultures of origin and corresponding religions in particular areas could both be useful for counsellors to really understand the variety in values and different contexts and provide a useful foundation of knowledge without making assumptions about particular clients. Tom noted that for him cultural differences were not only about ethnic or religious differences. He had noticed how different cultures are reflected in the use of different language, which he thought was related to class and geography.

Cultural self-awareness

The concept of cultural competence includes cultural self-awareness (including awareness of our biases and beliefs and emotional reactions to others) and adequate awareness of both individual and group differences (Black, 2005; Pope & Vasquez, 2007). Cultural competence also includes awareness of other minoritised groups with respect to disability, sexuality, class and gender.

Exercise

1 What was your first experience of realising that someone you had met lived in a different cultural context to yours? What did this teach you about your culture? What values do you think you have in your particular culture?
2 In your personal life, what variety of cultural contexts are people situated in who you know or have known well? Consider ethnic, cultural, political or sexual minority cultures that are different from your own.
3 What gaps in your knowledge do you have from personal experience with people and how might you address these?
4 Consider a situation where you are working with a client with clearly different cultural values to your own. How might you deal with this? In what situations do you think it would be unethical to continue working with someone?

Anne

Anne noted that although she felt she had a lot of diverse contacts with people from many ethnic and class backgrounds, she had no personal friendships with lesbians or gay men. She wondered if this was because she was homophobic but did not think this was the case, just that she had not knowingly come across people. The tutor challenged her on this, and explained how heterosexism and assumptions of heterosexuality could silence people and keep lesbians and gay men away from her. Anne vowed to notice if and when she was making the assumption of heterosexuality and also thought she could start to become more aware of sexual minority cultures by reading novels and watching films.

Rubina

Rubina wondered about when she might struggle to work with someone with different values to her own. She thought it could be difficult to work with a client who was racist. She thought this situation would be easier if the racism was overt, as then she could ask the client if they wanted to work with someone else. However, if the racism was not so explicit or took a while for her to realise, the situation could be a lot trickier and perhaps some of the content of counselling would become looking at their relationship in the light of this. She wondered if she would be able to value a client who she felt hurt by in their prejudice about her, and noted that this would be a situation she would need to constantly monitor in supervision, and if she felt unable to maintain a non-judgemental relationship with the client, she would refer the client elsewhere. This reminded her of the discussion they had had earlier about the importance of shared values between the therapist and client (see Chapter 2).

The importance of the client's context led Rubina to wonder about the importance of the context of the counselling provision. She noted how different her work context seemed to be in the approach to counselling compared to other counselling contexts such as the National Health Service (NHS). For example, she noted how much more acceptable it was in her work context to meet clients wherever the client felt comfortable as opposed to having to meet in a GP surgery. The tutor agreed this was an important point and asked the other students about their thoughts on the impact of different institutional contexts on counselling.

Institutional contexts

Exercise

How much do various institutional contexts affect how the counsellor is in a therapy relationship?

Tom and Anne

Tom noted that different organisations have different policies and aims which constrain and shape the work of counsellors within them. He noted the specific constraints on confidentiality for counsellors working in a statutory setting which were different from practitioners working privately. Anne also thought that perhaps different workplace cultures could affect counsellors unconsciously and that it would be ethical to be as mindful of this as possible. She wondered whether a prison setting, for example, might lead counsellors to think more about issues of risk and their own personal safety, and aim towards decreasing risk or increasing their client's responsibility for their crimes, whereas the same counsellors would not have similar concerns or aims for the same clients in an NHS setting.

Ethical responsibility to others

Many clients experience big shifts in their life as a result of counselling, reporting changes in attitudes and values and making big life-changing decisions. Should we be interested ethically in how changes in the client affect others in their life or is that exclusively the client's responsibility? We are obliged to intervene if the client discloses something that leads us to believe that others are at immediate risk (for example if we are told that the client intends to murder or abuse someone). Is this the only time we have any ethical responsibility or concern for others?

Exercise

1. When do you ask or challenge a client about the impact of anything they are talking about on anyone else in their life?
2. Do you think counselling benefits the common good? Are there times when you are left concerned about the wider impact of counselling beyond an individual?
3. Where do you draw the line with breaking confidentiality if you think a client may harm a third person? Would this just apply to murder? What about a client who is HIV positive planning to have sex with someone else without disclosing their status? What about a client planning to put drugs in someone's drink?

Maxine

Maxine's first response was that she thought it was not the counsellor's job to think about other people in the client's life. She thought it would be impossible anyway as the counsellor only ever heard the perspective of the client. However, she was less comfortable with the idea that she would not consider others that a client was planning to harm. She wondered about a situation where a woman client who had experienced domestic violence was planning how to take revenge against the man who was violent to her. She thought that this situation would be easier for her as she would be unlikely to have any concerns or empathy for the man given what he had done. However, she imagined a situation when a male client was planning revenge against an ex-partner who had left him and in this situation she would feel very concerned for the safety of the person that he wanted to hurt. She realised she would naturally think more about the impact on people in the client's life that she identified with or she saw as vulnerable and needing protection, and thought that in these cases she would have to discuss her concerns with the client. She did wonder however whether she should be aiming to consider more *all* the people that clients talked about.

Rubina

Rubina thought that a therapist could not help but consider others in the client's life as they would be part of the client, and expressed through the client. She considered how often she referred to 'we' rather than 'I' to express her thoughts and feelings, expressing the relational origins and experiences of her thoughts and feelings. She also noted that in a therapy relationship, a new 'we' should be created that again may not be possible to separate into two I's with respect to origins of thoughts and feelings. She thought that considering parts of the client's identity that are shared with others and parts that are in conflict would be an important part of therapy, and that this would necessarily involve considering and trying to understand the perspective of significant others in the client's life and their mutual impact.

Rubina added that not only should therapists be thinking about significant others in the client's life, but that therapy as an institution should be of benefit to the community or society as a whole. However, she noted that there may be times when prioritising the client's autonomy and benefit to the community or society may be in conflict. She suspected that at these times individual autonomy would need to take precedence, but that therapists need to consider whether the provision of therapy in general is beneficial for society, and to ensure that the outcomes of therapy are not consistently to encourage individuals to become more self-focused and less concerned with the common good.

It is important to consider when or if we think about others in the client's life and the impact of the client on them. This is a situation when our biases and prejudices can play out, leading us to only consider certain people (such as those we consider vulnerable). We should check whether our values are consistent with our practice.

Impact of the institution of therapy on society

How does the existence of therapy affect relationships among us all? How does it affect other relationships in the lives of clients and therapists, and does it have an impact on all of our expectations for support within friendships and social connections?

Exercise

1 What impact does seeing a number of clients in counselling in one day have on you personally – for example on your personal relationships, on the interactions with others in your everyday life?
2 How is your decision to train as a counsellor/psychotherapist related to your gender?
3 What impact does the existence of counselling/psychotherapy have on our ability to listen to and care for each other in general?

Rubina

Rubina thought about the impact on her of spending a lot of time listening to and focusing on her clients at work. She had noticed since starting her current job that when she returned home she often needed some time by herself to be quiet or not have to respond to others before she had the energy or capacity to interact with her family in the way she wanted to. She was aware that her need for this varied, depending on her own physical health and energy and whether she had had a chance at work to sit down and reflect between clients. She had always known that having time between people would help her client work but had not previously realised the impact of this on the rest of her life, and she vowed again to ensure this was possible whenever she could.

Tom

Tom thought about how much he and his friends supported each other when any of them were upset or struggling. He remembered when he had first felt depressed and had tried to talk to a friend a little about how he was feeling about himself. His friend had tried to help with offering suggestions, but when Tom continued to talk about feeling down, he remembered that before long his friend had suggested that Tom talk to a counsellor about how he was feeling. His friend had explained that a counsellor 'might be more help than me. I just don't know what to say mate.' Tom reflected on this and wondered whether this was a negative result for society of the existence of counselling, that we don't expect friends to be able to support us to the same extent anymore as there are people paid to do that now. He thought that perhaps one result of the existence of counselling is for us to have less patience with friends who need support but also for people who do not have counselling training to feel more deskilled and worried about how to support someone as a result of this skill being professionalised.

Tom was perturbed by the idea that the existence of therapy could be bad for society with the effect of deskilling the general public from supporting each other. However, he noted that he had generally seen counselling as having political aims with respect to trying to liberate individuals from the effects of oppression. He noted that the ideal of us all supporting each other in communities was rather idealistic and probably had never described many communities, or perhaps only for certain people who were accepted within dominant cultures. He reflected that there were many perspectives from which the existence of counselling could be considered.

Anne

Anne was sure that her gender was of big relevance to her wish to become a counsellor, both in terms of her being socialised to listen and care and in terms of her position now as a mother looking for flexible caring work. She reflected on how her career decision to train as a counsellor had led her to increase her caring roles in her life which were already her main focus. However, she did think that at least as a counsellor, her ability to care was being recognised and being valued, in that hopefully she would be paid for this role.

In an earlier work I have discussed the possible impact of therapy on our expectations to care for each other emotionally as citizens as opposed to professionalising this activity, saying:

> I wonder about the impact on my personal relationships of my focus and attention and emotional energy given to my clients in therapy. Would I be better off working harder at creating the best truly mutual relationships possible in my personal life rather than making the best of the limited relationships within therapy? Is this the general impact of the existence of therapy in society – that we can all let go of the responsibility to create healing mutual relationships with people and leave this to therapists? (Proctor, 2010a: 56)

I have also questioned whether the existence of therapy has an impact on gender relations, relieving women of their traditional burden of emotional nurturance, or reinforcing these pressures, as the majority of counsellors are women (Proctor, 2010a, 2010b).

Part of our ethical responsibility is to consider the wider impact on our relationships and on society of being a therapist.

Therapy and politics

Is therapy a political activity or should it be apolitical? How is the political context relevant to practice?

Exercise

1. How do you think the values/purpose of counselling fit with your political values?
2. How much do you think the profession of counselling should be involved in politics?

Anne

Anne initially felt uncomfortable with the idea of counselling being political. She thought that therapists could be of all political persuasions as long as they possessed fundamental values of caring about people. She worried that if institutions such as the BACP got involved in politics, this could not possibly represent all therapists and that some would be alienated, thus leading to a profession representing only certain political views. As our clients come from all contexts and political persuasions, she thought that a diversity of political perspectives was important for the counselling profession. Therefore she thought it should be a duty of organisations such as BACP to be apolitical. She remembered that moral foundation theory (see Chapter 4) had shown how counselling ethical codes prioritise the two principles of harm/care and justice associated with left-wing political perspectives, and that people with left-wing political views are less likely to understand the right-wing perspective which prioritises all five moral foundations. This echoed her experience when disclosing conservative political views, where she often encountered judgement, and she thought that those with left-wing views believed that being conservative meant she was unconcerned about matters of equality, which was not the case for her.

Tom

Tom responded that he did not think it was possible for BACP to be apolitical, as not taking a political stance resulted in colluding with the status quo and failing to challenge inequalities. He believed that there were basic findings from the profession of therapy, such as psychological distress commonly being a consequence of oppression, and the psychological impact of violence and abuse, which are political issues that can be spoken about in a political arena. He believed the values behind this were usually those of equality and respect for autonomy, which were values that could be supported by all sides of the political spectrum, based on moral foundation theory, so he did not think there was a danger in alienating counsellors. He did think there were certain common values involved in counselling such as those in the ethical frameworks that all have political implications and that these should not be denied but embraced and made explicit.

In Proctor (2004, 2006), I agree with Tom that counselling cannot be apolitical. I define political as follows: 'Politics involves looking at society and groups of people, of speaking out about how our world is organised and resources distributed. It involves inequalities between people in this distribution and in opportunities and how this is dealt with. Fundamentally it is rooted in sociology rather than psychology, studying society and groups of people and their relationships rather than internal psyches' (Proctor 2006: 2). Psychotherapy is inherently a political activity, and this represents our dual role, with respect to our responsibilities to our clients, to others and to society at large.

Tom

Tom also thought that particular political environments or values would provide particular contexts for counselling and influence how we practise. He noted that practising therapy in the context of a political valuing of individualism (in the 1980s) would probably look different from practising therapy in the context of the values of community (in the 1960s).

Owens, Springwood and Wilson (2012) consider the context of consumerism and the potential conflicts between consumerist values and those of therapy. They argue that, 'Therapy, at its best, fosters negotiated, shared meanings and collaboration towards human growth. Consumerism, at its worst, breeds competition, rivalry and an envy of others' (2012: 4). Therapy can be presented as a commodity to be bought or sold, and this can bring tensions for therapists and clients practising therapy within a consumer context.

Rubina

Rubina noted that we have already established that the divide between individuals and their context is false and so agreed that counselling had to be political.

Schmid (2012) suggests that all psychotherapy is political. He argues that we develop as humans in community and this is the original definition of 'political' in Ancient Greece (see **Classical Greek philosophy** in Appendix C). Poole emphasises the interconnection between all our ethical decisions, our identity and the shaping of the world. He explains: 'The thinker has to decide not only what is right and wrong but also what he wants to *become* by deciding this matter this way rather than that way. In deciding what he wants to become, he decides indirectly what he wants the world to become' (1972: 145). In this way, thinking is inevitably political.

Summary

This chapter has looked at the relevance of the wider context within which we practise counselling. The inseparability of the client from their context was noted and the consideration of others in the client's life was discussed. The institution of psychotherapy within society was debated with respect to the consequences for individual therapists and society of its existence. Finally, I argued that politics is also relevant to therapy and whatever we do cannot be apolitical. We need to ensure, in the focus in therapy on the individual client, that we are always aware of the world outside the therapy dyad and the continuous mutual impact between the two. All our decisions in life have political implications and it is ethically responsible to consider these.

Anne noted the complexity of ethical thinking in counselling, with its principles, ethical frameworks and ethical decision-making models, considering the context and politics, and she wondered how it was possible to know whether someone is taking ethical responsibility? The next chapter will consider the concept of 'ethical mindfulness' to see if this could be useful to answer Anne's question.

SEVEN Ethical mindfulness

Introduction

How do we maintain ethical mindfulness as counsellors and psychotherapists? How do we take responsibility for being ethical with resoluteness (**Heidegger** and **Sartre**)? What can we do to fulfil our aspirations to be the best ethical practitioners that we can be? How do we judge ethical competence in ourselves and others? The concepts most often mentioned as keys to developing ethical competence are the importance of self-awareness, self-care and supervision.

Personal and professional struggles

Exercise

1. When are you likely to struggle to attend to a client? Common examples are tiredness, distress and boredom. There may be particular common themes in your life that dull this alertness, or particular clients with whom you find it harder to fully concentrate.
2. How do you know when this is happening? Can you predict it before seeing a client?
3. When you notice this reduced alertness, what strategies do you have to improve your concentration, or how do you act?
4. What self-care strategies do you have to restore your focus at these times?

Rubina

Rubina remembered working with a client who described a relationship and a situation very similar to that of her sister when she was in a violent relationship. She had found it hard to focus on her client and found herself thinking about her sister and what she had been through, and making judgements about what her client should do based on her sister's experiences. She had realised this and discussed it in supervision. Her supervisor had suggested she spend some time before meeting this client, reminding herself of the uniqueness of this client and the differences from her sister – to focus her attention on this client, to notice with her client when she lost attention, and to actively refocus on her client. She found it helpful at these times to focus all her senses on her experience of being with her client, noticing all aspects of how she looked, sounded, smelt, and on her emotions as well as the content of what she was saying. This concentrated noticing enabled her to restore her focus on her client.

Tom

Tom thought about a particular client where he had often felt bored and struggled to hold any kind of interest in what she was saying. His client was a girl in the probation service who he judged to be very superficial and rarely talking about anything that he felt had any significance. He found himself drifting off when he was supposed to be talking with her or trying to direct the conversation to topics that he thought had more significance. He had discussed this in supervision and realised how judgemental he had been and resolved to try harder to understand what this client was trying to talk to him about and why. He realised he had judged her as being not very intelligent and therefore having nothing interesting to say, and realised the high value he placed on his own intelligence and how he judged others by this value. Since this realisation, he began to question the idea of a unitary intelligence; he decided that there were many types of intelligence and resolved to find the intelligence in everyone he met. He also began to realise that he was more likely to judge girls and women as being less intelligent, and resolved to think more about this.

Anne

Anne thought about when her children were young and she remembered feeling constantly exhausted and preoccupied. She remembered how hard she had found it meeting up with friends and being interested in their lives. She reflected that this was a time in her life where she did not think she would have had the capacity or emotional competence to be a counsellor and she would have known this by her feeling too overwhelmed by her own life to focus on others. She thought she would have had no choice but to have stopped work at this point if she had been a counsellor then.

Self-awareness

A commitment to ongoing self-awareness is a key to taking ethical responsibility. One purpose of this is to be aware of our own vulnerabilities and triggers of certain feelings and behaviours in relationships, so we can be more aware of how we are with clients in therapy. However, the unpredictability of relationships and limits to how much we can be aware of ourselves and others make ethical responsibility particularly difficult.

Proctor and Keys stress the importance of self-awareness in ethical practice by 'being as aware as we can be of the struggles inherent in the ethical decision-making process, by being open to the range of influences on the process, by being prepared to be challenged and change, and by trying to articulate the process as clearly as we can' (2013: 423). We ask how we know we are ethical practitioners, concluding, 'It is in the ongoing openness to others through questioning and exploration – with clients, in supervision and in personal and professional development – that we can trust that we are practising ethically' (2013: 431).

Youngson and Green (2009) give a rationale for personal development, which is a commitment to developing self-knowledge and self-awareness. 'One of the key issues in forging and understanding human relationships is a clear knowledge of what one is bringing to that relationship and how one is affecting that relationship. Therefore it is crucial ... that individuals make a commitment to developing self-knowledge and self-awareness, in order to make and maintain relationships of quality' (2009: 155). For Pope and Vasquez (2007: xiv), ethical practice requires 'active, careful, informed, persistent and comprehensive questioning'. This questioning is particularly essential in areas where we think we are certain. 'Ethical awareness is a continuous active process that involves constant questioning and personal responsibility' (see Pope and Keith-Spiegel, 2008: 640).

The limits to our self-awareness are regularly noted in moral philosophy and particularly emphasised with the notion of the unconscious in psychodynamic therapy. Poe (1840) declared:

> All experience, in matters of philosophical discovery, teaches us that, it is the unforeseen upon which we must calculate most largely.

Before Socrates, **Plato** had Meno capturing this quandary, asking:

> How will you go about finding that thing the nature of which is totally unknown to you?

The idea of self-awareness can be critiqued as relying on a notion of a fixed self. But instead, the notion of the idea of reflexivity in research can be more useful, as an awareness of the 'constantly changing sense of our selves within the context of our changing world' (Etherington, 2004: 30).

Concepts to describe responsible ethical awareness

Various concepts are used in the counselling literature to describe responsible ethical awareness. Emotional competence, phronesis or practical wisdom and ethical mindfulness are all used to refer to a commitment to self-awareness and applying this knowledge practically in relationships.

Exercise

What concepts do you think are most useful to describe responsible ethical awareness and practice?

Definition

Emotional competence: Knowing oneself as a flawed human being (Pope and Brown, 1996). This involves self-knowledge, self-acceptance and self-monitoring. It involves knowing your own emotional strengths and weaknesses, your needs and resources, and your abilities and limits in offering therapy. It involves using this knowledge to create self-care strategies to restore and maintain our emotional competence, and an ongoing process of monitoring the need for change in these strategies as ourselves and our lives change.

Maxine

Maxine thought that the concept of ethical competence suggested a fixed thing that you either possessed or did not, and seemed to be a cognitive concept which she did not think accurately represented the nature of ethical awareness. She thought a concept was needed to represent the *dynamic* nature of ethical awareness.

Assessing ethical competence

How do we assess our own competence to work and our limitations? What criteria do we have for deciding we are not competent to take the responsibility of being a therapist? If we are very tired, poorly, traumatised, bereaved or upset, when do these conditions compromise our capacity to make decisions as a therapist? How do we assess a colleague's fitness to practise? Or how do we assess the competence of a supervisee? Shillito-Clarke (2000a) discusses the nature of the supervisor's role to judge competence and argues that any concerns need to be discussed with the supervisee. She notes the difficulty here with differences in theoretical orientation, the importance of the supervision relationship and the supervisor's ability to facilitate the counsellor's own development. If concerns are not resolved and the supervisory relationship ceases, she notes that ultimately the supervisor has no control over the counsellor's future work even if they believe the counsellor to be incompetent or unethical.

Definition

Phronesis/prudence: Rather than applying rules to situations, 'ethical reasoning is embedded in the actual experiential and practical circumstances of life'. It is developed through ethical thinking and through experience (Owens et al., 2012: 11).

Owens et al. (2012) advocate the concept of practical wisdom, from **Aristotle**'s idea of phronesis or prudence. They describe this as the ability to hold potentially competing values and demands, not losing sight of any of the considerations, aiming to be open about a decision and discuss the implications non-defensively with the client, and discussing the decision in supervision. They note the safety in discussing decisions in supervision, particularly in the context of most complaints concerning 'relatively trivial-seeming incidents which the therapist ... missed or glossed over' (2012: 10).

Maxine

Maxine was still unhappy with phronesis as a concept, thinking that it emphasised cognitive processes too much, and rational understanding rather than self-awareness.

Tom

Tom wondered whether the concept of mindfulness from Buddhism could be useful to think about ethical awareness, and remembered that Bond (2004 in Proctor & Keys, 2013) had used this concept in the context of relational trust (see Chapter 4).

Definition

Ethical mindfulness: Mindfulness is an ongoing process of maintaining as much as possible a calm awareness of one's bodily functions, sensations (feelings), objects of consciousness (thoughts and perceptions) and consciousness itself. Mindfulness is a Buddhist concept and when applied to ethics could entail this ongoing mindfulness in the service of awareness of self and impact on others in relationships (Smith, 2012).

Maxine

Maxine liked Tom's idea of ethical mindfulness and thought that this might cover the sense of dynamic self and relational awareness that she was looking for.

Self-care

Self-care refers to our ability as counsellors and psychotherapists to not just focus on being of service to clients, but to also be able to look after ourselves. It acknowledges our needs and changing capacities and the necessity of our being able both to monitor this (through self-awareness) and to attend to our own needs outside therapy, on an everyday basis and in response to crises. It also includes some awareness of the possibility that practising as a therapist can take a toll on us that we need to be aware of and attend to.

Exercise

What ongoing strategies do you have for self-care to bolster ethical competence, or increase the likelihood of ethical mindfulness?

Tom and Maxine

Tom reflected that he had worked hard on self-care to maintain his optimal mental health since his experiences with psychiatry. He thought that personal meditation and his activities with his local Buddhist community were the most essential part of his self-care. He also tried to eat well and exercise regularly. Maxine thought that she had recently realised that most important to her self-care was her friendships. She really valued her small network of close friends who she could talk to about whatever she was feeling and rely on honest feedback. She also used yoga to care for her body and mind, which helped her think more often about eating healthily.

Dunnett (2009) discusses how we recognise good psychological wellbeing in ourselves and others, and notes the personal preferences involved in this judgement. He found in his research with counsellors that this concept resides in a cluster of factors: 'good sense of self', 'good relationships', 'strategic capacities', 'engagement with the world' and 'experience and expression of affect'. He noted, however, that it is precisely when our wellbeing is deteriorating that our capacity to judge ourselves also declines. He notes that, 'The self-aware counsellor needs the same level of attunement to self which he exercises in regard to his clients. Self-regulating and self-nurturing activity needs to be in place if the professional is to live a life characterised by energy, satisfaction and openness to experience' (2009: 128). He stresses the personal individual nature of self-care strategies. Tjelveit and Gottlieb (2010) discuss self-care with respect to identifying vulnerability and developing resilience.

The BACP Ethical Framework (2013) lists the sixth principle as 'Self-respect: fostering the practitioner's self-knowledge and care for self'. It explains:

> The principle of self-respect means that the practitioner appropriately applies all the above principles as entitlements for self. This includes seeking counselling or therapy and other opportunities for personal development as required. There is an ethical responsibility to use supervision for appropriate personal and professional support and development, and to seek training and other opportunities for continuing professional development. Guarding against financial liabilities arising from work undertaken usually requires obtaining appropriate insurance. The principle of self-respect encourages active engagement in life-enhancing activities and relationships that are independent of relationships in counselling or psychotherapy. (2013: 3)

Furthermore, under 'Care of self as a practitioner', the Ethical Framework specifies:

- Attending to the practitioner's well-being is essential to sustaining good practice.
- Practitioners have a responsibility to themselves to ensure that their work does not become detrimental to their health or well-being by ensuring that the way that they undertake their work is as safe as possible and that they seek appropriate professional support and services as the need arises. (2013: 9)

This sixth principle was added to the earlier British Association of Counselling Code of Ethics (1992) to become the Ethical Framework of the BACP (2002). Unlike the previous principles, which focused on clients and the therapy relationship, this new principle focuses on counsellors as people with our own needs. Counselling requires that the counsellor's need for care and nurturance is suspended in counselling in the service of the client. Thus, counsellors' nurturance needs must be met outside therapy relationships. Dunnett (2009) considers the impact of client behaviour on therapists (including secondary traumatisation from listening to clients' traumatic expriences) and suggests that we must find ways to be aware of, acknowledge and deal with this impact in a way that also considers the needs of the client. Some authors emphasise the importance of support from networks of colleagues and organisations and the importance of supervision as a place to consult about self-care and offer personal support (Bond, 2010; Dunnett, 2009). Dunnett (2009) suggests that when the counsellor's values are at odds with those of the organisation, strategies of individual self-care are critical. Owens et al. (2012) suggest that self-care and client care are inseparably linked, that we are unable to care for clients without caring for ourselves. They suggest that beyond self-respect, we should practise self-compassion.

Anne

Anne reflected on how little she had thought about caring for herself, especially since having children, focusing almost exclusively on looking after her children and her husband. She resolved that she needed to think much more carefully about how to look after herself to make sure she had the capacity to be a counsellor. She realised that her attitude to herself was that she should be able to cope with anything, which is why she felt so guilty feeling unable to care for her father before he died. However, she realised that this attitude was neither helpful to her nor what she wanted to teach her children, and resolved to develop a much more compassionate attitude towards her own needs.

Supervision and continuing professional development

Supervision is another key part of ethical responsibility to aid and enhance self-awareness in dialogue with another. Continuing professional development (CPD) reflects an ongoing commitment to developing competence and questioning practice. As noted above, the BACP Ethical Framework includes the following statement in the principle of 'self-respect': 'There is an ethical responsibility to use supervision for appropriate personal and professional support and development, and to seek training and other opportunities for continuing professional development' (2013: 3). The UKCP Ethical Code states: 'The psychotherapist commits to an on-going process of professional and personal enquiry and challenge, commonly referred to as "Continuing Professional Development"' (2009: 6, para 5.6).

Under 'Supervising and managing', the BACP Ethical Framework further suggests:

- Supervisors and managers have a responsibility to maintain and enhance good practice by practitioners, to protect clients from poor practice and to acquire the attitudes, skills and knowledge required by their role. (2013: 7)

Supervision is also mentioned as an essential part of CPD. Points under 'Maintaining competent practice' include:

- All counsellors, psychotherapists, trainers and supervisors are required to have regular and on-going formal supervision/consultative support for their work in accordance with professional requirements.
- Regularly monitoring and reviewing one's work is essential to maintaining good practice. It is important to be open to, and conscientious in considering, feedback from colleagues, appraisals and assessments. Responding constructively to feedback helps to advance practice. (2013: 5)

Similarly, the UKCP Ethical Code states: 'The psychotherapist accepts responsibility to ensure that they are competent and have sufficient supervisory arrangements and other necessary support to enable them to meet their psychotherapeutic obligations to any client' (2009: 6, para 5.7).

Purpose of supervision

Exercise

1. What is the purpose of supervision?
2. Do you discuss your clients or yourself in relation to your work in supervision, or both?
3. Do you think there is a clear distinction between supervision and personal therapy?

Rubina

Rubina thought that the purpose of supervision was to try and protect clients from poor practice, by there being a check on the practice of a counsellor by someone usually with more experience. However, she thought it was probably only as useful as the supervisee was honest and used the supervision with integrity. She reflected that it was entirely possible for therapists to carefully present the best parts of their work in supervision for fear of reprisal and thus gain very little from the process. She also thought supervision was useful for supervisees to debrief after particularly traumatic sessions so they could offload things they had been told that they had found distressing.

Supervision can only be effective to the extent that the supervisee feels able to disclose and discuss difficulties in therapy relationships and show personal vulnerability. Wosket (2009) emphasises the quality of the relationship in the supervisory relationship. She suggests that the relationship quality will determine whether ethical issues emerge and how much supervisees disclose their ethical concerns. West (2003) sees supervision as part of the culture of counselling and psychotherapy. He suggests there are big limits to the process of supervision, saying: 'The idea that supervision practice can be viewed in terms of the construction of a professional culture, in which certain areas of experience are largely disallowed, provides a promising means of understanding, and investigating, the supervision process' (2003: 126). He suggests that fear of not being liked, or judged or reported, means that supervisees avoid ethical dilemmas. He also uses the examples of touch and spirituality as areas that supervisees report to be difficult to discuss in supervision and so often avoided. This concurs with my suggestion (Proctor, 2002: 36) that assisted self-exploration can become policing.

However, supervision is usually the only place that counsellors can reflect on the private activity that we undertake, particularly given the necessity to hold client disclosures confidentially, so it is important to consider how we can make the best use of it to maximise ethical responsibility. Beebe (2009) discusses the virtues required in supervision. Syme (2000) argues that supervision is the only structured quality control available to the profession. She argues that supervision is a place to learn, an opportunity to learn more about the client through the parallel process, and a place to offload distressing information to prevent the counsellor doing this with family or friends, which would compromise confidentiality. Finally, supervision is a place where the supervisor can pick up abusive or unhealthy practice by the counsellor, with the supervisor monitoring competence and the level of functioning of the supervisee. She stresses the importance of counsellors, being open to their own and others' assessment of their competence and being prepared to take action.

The importance of supervision in counselling follows from a **social intuitionist** perspective (see Chapter 4), as new intuitions are far more likely to be activated in conversation with another than in private reflection. Haidt (2001) emphasises the importance of discussion with others to trigger new intuitions in future situations, and argues that new thinking is much more likely to arise from intersubjective discussion than in private reflection. This could be one of the purposes of supervision with respect to moral decision-making.

Anne

Anne thought an outside person would always be useful in psychodynamic practice to help the psychotherapist reflect on their own countertransference reactions and spot any transference dynamics that the therapist had missed. Given the inevitable limits to our self-awareness, she thought this check from another more experienced practitioner was essential to good practice.

Psychodynamic practice in particular emphasises the usefulness of a third person outside the therapy relationship to reflect on the therapy process, particularly to notice the therapist's gaps, self-interest or identification with the client. McFarland Solomon (2010) discusses the ethical attitude in psychoanalysis and suggests that supervision is important to achieve 'triangulation' or the emergence of a third position beyond the therapy dyad. She explains – 'To the extent that this triangular space created by supervision is necessary to the hygiene of the analytic couple ... supervision has an ethical as well as a clinical and a didactic role to play in all analytic and therapeutic work, notwithstanding the years of experience of the practitioner' (2010: 331). This process of re-visioning gives the therapist a chance to look anew at the relationship and avoid or find a way out of a trap of only seeing a client from a particular theoretical or personal perspective.

Maxine

Maxine thought that the distinction between supervision and therapy may not be clear. Whereas she understood the focus in supervision to be client work, she thought that she may often be discussing how her client work had affected her and what it had brought up for her in her own life, which she thought was an essential part of supervision in terms of increasing self-awareness. She thought that her explorations of how she was affected by her clients and how her history and life affected her responses to her clients could cover very similar material to therapy. However, she thought that in supervision she would be prioritising what impacted on her client work to improve that.

There are different perspectives in the literature about the distinction between supervision and personal therapy. Hess (2008) suggests it is unethical to use supervision for the supervisee's personal therapy and ethical to prioritise time for discussion about client work. However, Tudor and Worrall (2007) suggest that the boundary between supervision and personal therapy is not clear and that personal and professional are inseparable, leaving what is open for discussion for negotiation between supervisee and supervisor. Tudor and Worrall (2007: 2), from a person-centred perspective, note that mandatory supervision is justified by the 'protection of clients' and the promotion of 'good practice', but they note there is little evidence to demonstrate the efficacy of supervision for clients. They argue that supervision should be centred on the person of the supervisee, not the client, and they challenge the idea of the supervisor's responsibility for the client. Tudor suggests that the supervisor being responsible to protect the client is a dangerous idea, leading to 'defensive, avoidant and paranoid supervisees – and narcissistic or paranoid supervisors!' (2007: 31). In contrast he suggests that supervision can be a place where ethical responsibility for harm, safety and protection is shared and supervisees can be open about their practice.

Tom

Tom thought that he might want different things from supervision at different points in his development as a counsellor. At different times and stages he thought he may value education, restoration, normalisation and empathy. He also noted the importance of ongoing CPD and reflected that his changing developmental needs would also be met by his seeking out diverse CPD opportunities to increase his competence. He reflected on the importance of ethical mindfulness to be aware of what his needs were at any point.

Choice of supervisor

Exercise

1 What do you look for in your choice of supervisor and what would you aim to be as a supervisor?
2 How helpful is it for supervision to be hierarchical, with the supervisor being expected to be more competent and experienced and the supervisee to learn from them?

Tom

Tom thought that he would seek a supervisor whose practice he emulated and he believed to be an ethical and a competent practitioner. He also thought that he would want a supervisor with experience in the particular area of work that he was involved in. As a supervisor, he thought that he would want to feel competent and experienced in the area of work of his supervisee.

Anne

Anne thought that she would like a supervisor who shared her values and was caring of her as a person as well as her clients. She thought it was most important that she could trust her supervisor to value her and not judge her so she could bring mistakes and be open about her concerns. She thought that she would most likely feel this with a supervisor who was humble and went out of her or his way to demonstrate care and concern. She also realised that she would want a supervisor that she judged to be able to take care of her- or himself so Anne would not feel the need to. As a supervisor, she would aspire to be caring, respectful, open and humble, being tentative with suggestions or advice, and not wanting to undermine the autonomy or development of a supervisee.

We may need different things at various stages of our development as psychotherapists. Good supervisors are alert to our changing needs. Heru (2006) discusses the idea of the optimal supervisory relationship and suggests that supervisors need to vary the balance of empathy and nurturance, with encouragement of autonomy depending on the needs of the supervisee. She emphasises the aims of establishing strong alliances and managing conflicts in supervision, which fits with Bond's (2007, 2010) ethics of relational trust.

There are many purposes involved in supervision as well as the supervisory relationship itself which all require ethical responsibility. Kaiser (1992) identifies four elements in the supervisory relationship which she discusses in the framework of ethics. These elements are: the process of accountability, the need for promoting the supervisee's personal awareness, the importance of establishing trust, and issues of power and authority. With regard to trust, Kaiser (1992) emphasises the importance in the supervisory relationship of respect, safety to make mistakes without judgement, empathy and clear communication. She maintains that trust is developed with a supervisor who is 'willing to go as far as is necessary in her exploration of the supervisee's work ... and willing to share her own emotional responses' (1992: 286). She notes that the supervisor is responsible for addressing problems and tensions in the supervisory relationship, telling the truth and treating the supervisee with integrity.

Maxine

Maxine thought that if she felt intimidated by the superior knowledge of a supervisor this would not be helpful for her, particularly not to feel comfortable to share mistakes. She thought that what was most important was that the supervisor was aware of the dynamics of power in supervision and respected her as a counsellor and encouraged her own ideas and practice.

Addressing the power dynamics in supervision is essential to clarity regarding accountability and developing trust in the relationship. Owens et al. (2012) discuss the importance of supervision or 're-visioning' to help us think about our clients. They use re-vision rather than supervision to emphasise a seeing with or alongside rather than the hierarchical nature of over-seeing that supervision usually refers to. Tyler and Tyler suggest a bill of rights for supervisees as ideals, including their right to choose an appropriate supervisor wherever possible. They suggest that focusing on the rights of supervisees means that 'the supervisee is empowered to express expectations, make decisions, and be a more active participant in the supervisory process' (1997: 87).

Summary

This chapter has focused on the necessary ingredients for counsellors and psychotherapists to be continually involved in a process of ethical mindfulness. Our students have discussed the concepts of ethical competence and mindfulness and their usefulness. We have looked at the importance of self-awareness, self-care and supervision and their place in upholding the principle of self-respect listed in the BACP Ethical Framework (2013). An ongoing commitment to be open and articulate about, to consider and challenge our practice in dialogue with others is essential to taking ethical responsibility as a therapist.

Are the ways we take ethical responsibility different depending on our model of therapy? We have seen examples in this chapter of how the focus of supervision may vary depending on the model, with psychodynamic models emphasising a third perspective, and person-centred models emphasising facilitation of the supervisee. The next chapter will consider the relevance of model of therapy to ethical responsibility.

PART THREE

Practice issues

EIGHT Values and ethics in models of therapy

Introduction

The range of approaches that fall under each main model of therapy is phenomenal, and they put into practice a range of values and philosophical approaches. This raises an issue of informed consent for therapists and clients. If a therapist attempts to describe their approach as cognitive behavioural therapy (CBT) or psychodynamic therapy for example, each could mean a wide variety of possibilities concerning how the therapist works. However, the range of value bases inherent in each approach are rarely discussed, and merit some consideration by practitioners, particularly in terms of whether the value base of each approach is consistent with the personal value base of the therapist and indeed the client.

This chapter considers the value bases of four approaches to therapy as examples, each illustrated by one of our students. These are: psychodynamic therapy, person-centred therapy, existential therapy and cognitive behavioural therapy. Owing to the different aims and value bases of each model, particular scenarios may present ethical questions in one model and not others. Certain aims or values in a particular model may conflict with certain ethical principles in certain situations. Particular ethical questions or issues for each of these models are presented as examples, with our students considering how they would address these issues.

Informed consent

Adshead discusses the difficulty of informed consent in psychotherapy, when the course of therapy is not predictable, saying, 'Psychological change in a person may have moral and political implications for him, which cannot be foreseen' (2005: 484). She suggests that 'the therapist then has to be thoughtful about maintaining the integrity of the psychotherapeutic process in itself, so that the therapy itself is an ethical process' (2005: 484). She discusses whether psychoanalytic therapists should warn patients of the possibility of unconscious transference enactments, and suggests that patients should be warned that psychotherapy 'is not always comfortable, and that many patients feel worse before they feel better' (2005: 478). However, she adds that patients should also be told that not everyone gets better with psychotherapy, and it is down to the therapist's clinical skills to distinguish between these two possibilities. Here she makes a clear move away from patient autonomy towards the authority of the therapist and their beneficence. She also addresses the difficulty of applying the principle of non-maleficence, to do no harm, to psychotherapy, when therapy may cause people distress.

The idea that clients feel worse before they feel better in therapy has been questioned by outcome studies where clients are monitored each session. Clients who start to deteriorate on symptom outcome measures usually continue to deteriorate rather than later improve. The consequence of this finding is that monitoring client feedback each session in therapy is useful (or even ethically imperative) and that deterioration should be seen as an alert to be discussed with the client (see for example Green & Latchford, 2012).

Language and metaphors

The language used by each model tells us something about the values behind each approach to counselling. Tudor and Worrall (2006) consider the importance of language and how it defines our reality, and compare the metaphoric language used by Rogers with that of Freud. Rogers frequently uses organic metaphors, representing his focus on growth, whereas Freud's metaphors are mechanical. They argue that the different use of language reflects the inherent different values and beliefs about humanity that each hold. They appeal to us to examine our metaphoric language to ensure that it is consistent with our values.

Values intrinsic to models of therapy

Exercise

What theoretical approach(es) are you particularly attracted to and are the values behind the approach(es) consistent with your personal values?

Anne – Psychodynamic therapy

Anne had decided that she was particularly interested in psychoanalytic theory, both to inform her ideas about emotional corrective relationships and to offer interpretations that could foster insight and understanding in her clients. She thought that the focus on the therapy relationship in attachment theory, object relations theory and relational psychoanalysis fitted with her values and reflected her prioritisation of relational ethics rather than the autonomous individual.

She liked the idea of having something to offer, with respect to offering understanding through interpretation, and she was also intellectually stimulated by much of the psychoanalytic literature, realising how little intellectual stimulation she had had for a long time.

She appreciated the focus on the value of self-awareness, particularly to understand countertransference, but was worried about the concept of the unconscious, wondering if she would ever feel aware enough of her own unconscious to feel responsible as a therapist. However, she decided that she could only do her best to be committed to her own self-awareness, both through her own therapy and self-analysis and by being open to feedback from others. She decided that a good ethical principle for her with clients was to always be tentative and invite feedback as much as possible, making sure she listened and took on board her clients' perception of her as they may well be aware of things in her of which she is unaware. She thought that this principle fitted the approach of relational psychoanalysis (Aron, 1996) well, emphasising mutuality but asymmetry in the roles of therapist and client.

Rubina – Person-centred therapy

Rubina identified the values in person-centred therapy of holism, seeing the person in context and trusting the person. She was particularly drawn to the value of respecting autonomy and consequent non-directivity in classical person-centred therapy. From this followed a core value of non-authoritativeness by the therapist, which she liked (see Proctor, 2002; Rogers, 1977).

However, she was aware that however much she tried not to direct her clients, she always had an influence and this was inevitable in a relationship. Nevertheless, for her this principle still felt important to constantly draw her attention to the dynamics of power in therapy and to work against her power to influence, and to explicitly encourage her clients to trust their own experiences and expertise.

She liked the value of holism and seeing the person in context, not reducing people to isolated individuals or to parts of individuals, but seeing us all as whole people and part of a much bigger whole. She thought that this focus fitted her communitarian and religious values very well.

She considered the values expressed by the therapist attitudes of congruence, unconditional positive regard and empathy. Proctor and Keys (2013) argue that the values underpinning these attitudes are: self-awareness, courage, openness, honesty, truthfulness, integrity, care, respect, love, humility and mutuality. Rubina felt all these values expressed well her aims in relationships. She thought mutuality was important in terms of respecting and trusting the client, but she also wanted to remember the inequality in the relationship.

Maxine – Existential therapy

Maxine was interested in the ideas of existential philosophy and existential therapy. She identified the values implied in existential therapy of holism, authenticity, acceptance (of all facets of existence and experience) and relationality. She particularly liked the value of trusting our own experience in existential therapy. She liked the value of seeing us all in our entirety and as always in relationship.

Maxine thought that the questions raised and descriptions of existence in existential philosophy spoke personally to her and fitted her experience of being human. However, she was aware that she was clearer about how these ideas helped her to think about her own life than she was in how they would help her with clients. She decided that the value of authenticity was entirely consistent with valuing personal meaning and choice, as this was how she understood the definition of authenticity. She thought these values helped her with clients to try and clarify whether they were relating their own meanings and values or those of others. She thought that her knowledge of existential philosophy was probably more useful for her own understanding and ability to stay with clients experiencing suffering, without trying to change something, than it was for the purpose of educating clients. Maxine was disappointed not to see more application of Eastern philosophical traditions within existential therapy and vowed to read up on more of this herself as she found certain Buddhist ideas to be compatible with her approach to therapy.

Tom – Cognitive behavioural therapy

Tom liked the values of rationality and empiricism in cognitive behavioural therapy (CBT). He also liked the pragmatic educational approach. Tom knew that collaboration was very important in CBT and he believed that this respected the autonomy of the client, as the purpose of it was to increase the client's independence and ability to apply the model without the therapist. He thought

CBT might be better described as education than as therapy and he thought that the practical, collaborative, educational approach could be empowering for clients.

He had personally found CBT useful in learning to be aware of his emotions and control them without medication, although he thought that his therapist was probably using skills from later developments of CBT (third wave approaches such as acceptance and commitment therapy, schema-focused therapy, compassion-focused therapy and dialectical behaviour therapy) rather than traditional CBT.

Tom thought that his therapist explaining the CBT approach to him was essential, as he did not feel that he had any ideas about how to proceed with his internal states without the ideas he was taught. However, he felt he had developed his autonomy in using the CBT techniques by trying to apply them and bringing back any difficulties or questions, which he felt were respectfully engaged with and listened to by his psychologist. Tom also thought it was important that his therapist had clearly explained the rationale for the CBT model and ensured that Tom understood it.

Particular ethical dilemmas for particular models

Exercise

What particular ethical dilemmas might need to be addressed within your particular model of therapy and how would you address them?

Anne – Psychodynamic therapy

Anne considered the possibility that a client could really object or be offended by her interpretation and accuse her of it being her own issue. Here, her understanding of how a client may defend against accurate interpretations may conflict with her relational ethics. Anne thought that her response to this would be to openly consider her own part in making this interpretation and whether it could be a result of her unconscious countertransference (self-awareness). However, she would also consider the client's hostility and try and interpret the transference to understand where this had come from. She would aim to always address the responsibility of both of them for the relationship (relational mutuality) but noted that, at times, any attempt to consider the client's part in a conflict could be met with hostility or defence. She hoped that she would always present her ideas tentatively and be ready to take responsibility for her side. She was clear there was no value in pushing an interpretation that the client did not accept, but neither did she want to accept total responsibility for the relationship for the sake of maintaining the relationship. She decided that she would always maintain awareness of her ideas concerning the client's contribution, but consider timing in offering this and responsiveness and respect if the client was defensive or hostile. She thought that ongoing hostility to transference interpretations would lead her to focus on the need for an emotionally corrective relationship with very limited and tentative use of interpretation.

Rubina – Person-centred therapy

Rubina thought that a particular dilemma from the perspective of this model could be if she did not like her client and was consequently unable to feel unconditional positive regard and empathy for her client. She thought this was likely to happen when a client had very different values from her, which could make it difficult for her to respect her client's autonomy to make their own choices. Her first thought here was that the biggest danger was if she felt guilty about her dislike and so was tempted to deny it to herself, thus compromising her congruence, honesty and integrity in the relationship.

She thought that her first response to this situation would be to be aware of it and discuss it in supervision, and then to make a concentrated effort to both be compassionate to her client and work on trying to understand whatever was hard for her to accept, understanding the person in context. She would also consider discussing her responses with the client (courage) and what she found difficult to understand and value. The only time she remembered encountering this situation was transformed when she discussed her reactions with her client. As a result of this conversation, Rubina's ability to empathise and unconditionally positive regard her client improved hugely, as the client was able to explain her attitudes and values more openly.

She also considered a scenario where this discussion could lead to her client feeling threatened, and thought that in this situation she might suggest that the client sees a different therapist who can hopefully better understand and value them. In this case, she would accept full responsibility for her failure to value and understand the client (humility) and try to be as open as possible about and responsible for her difficulties.

Maxine – Existential therapy

Maxine considered a scenario which she thought might cause an ethical dilemma with an existential therapy approach. She imagined a client who had terminal cancer who was refusing to accept her impending death but talked and acted as though she would recover shortly. Here, respecting the client's autonomy could conflict with her understanding from existential thought of accepting death rather than denying the experience. Perhaps Maxine was seeing her in a hospice and she knew with almost certainty from her knowledge of cancer or comments from staff that her client would die within a few months. Maxine felt this knowledge would be very difficult to have, knowing that the client did not want to face her death with acceptance but with denial. However, she would also be concerned from the values of existential therapy to accept all aspects of her client's experiencing, including her denial of death. At the same time, she thought she would have to communicate something about her belief in the importance of the client dealing with her anxiety and facing death so she would preserve her authenticity in the relationship. Maxine decided that supervision would be essential to help her be aware of her own theoretical and personal beliefs about death and to continue to honour her client's personal choice about how she dealt with her own death.

Tom – CBT

Tom considered the particular ethical issue in CBT of clients' distress increasing when facing their fears in exposure therapy. He wondered whether this contradicted the principle of non-maleficence, of not doing harm.

Olatunji, Deacon and Abramowitz (2009: 172) note that exposure suffers from a 'public relations problem' based on the idea that it is cruel and goes against the ethical principle of doing no harm (non-maleficence). They consider the question as to whether exposure can harm, and note that the evidence suggests that the short-term increase in anxiety leads to a long-term benefit. They suggest that a therapist's ethical reservations are generally not shared by patients, and they have found no examples of litigation. They claim that attrition rates are not high but only compare rates of various types of exposure. Tom decided that he would need to be clear with clients that increased distress was possible in the short term for the purpose of long-term gain. Then, it would be the clients' autonomous decision to decide whether they could face or risk this.

Summary

Within each major model of therapy, there are many approaches, each of which may start from slightly different value bases. The values behind approaches are a matter for informed consent for clients and it is important that we can be clear about how our values are consistent with the approaches to therapy that we use. This chapter considered the values implicit in four main approaches to therapy and how these were consistent with the personal values of our students. Each student then considered an ethical dilemma that may arise from their model of therapy being in potential conflict with an ethical value, and how they would approach it.

Whereas this chapter considered conflict between therapy models and ethical principles, the next two chapters focus on when two ethical principles are in conflict.

NINE Autonomy versus beneficence

Introduction

This chapter considers situations when the ethical principle of autonomy is in conflict with that of beneficence, when you believe that a client's choice is not good for them. The fundamental priority given to respecting autonomy is emphasised. The corresponding principle of informed consent is then discussed. Alternatives to principlism in ethics are then discussed to see if these approaches can better help us with situations where we struggle to accept a client's autonomous decision.

Autonomy

Respecting a client's autonomy is an ethical principle in most ethical frameworks concerning counselling and psychotherapy. Autonomy, personal choice and rights are central to western values, or particularly dominant White, male, middle-class western values. Holmes and Lindley (1989) point out that the importance of autonomy cannot be proved but is a matter of values, and the value of autonomy is commonly held and is central to ideas of liberal democracy. A notable exception is the professional body specifically for CBT, the BABCP (British Association for Behavioural and Cognitive Psychotherapies). The association's Standards of Conduct, Performance and Ethics (BABCP, 2009) makes no mention of client autonomy, focusing instead on the responsibility of the therapist to act in the best interests of the client, and the rationality with which the therapist makes these decisions.

Ringen (1996) suggests that autonomy includes three features: acting intentionally, acting with understanding and acting without coercion. These features are enshrined in law, particularly in the Mental Capacity Act (2005), which gives the right for all to autonomy in making decisions unless someone's capacity to be autonomous is assessed to be lacking with respect to a particular decision at a particular time.

Autonomy is a key principle in a principlist approach to ethics in counselling, from the traditional biomedical approach to ethics or the 'ethics of justice'. The notion of autonomy is integral to traditional duty theories of ethics, particularly from a deontological (**Kantian**) framework of ethics. From autonomy arises the principle of respect for the individual and the notion of dignity. Mill (1871/1998) added the notion of autonomy to Bentham's focus on pleasure in **consequentialism**, where he stressed the freedom of each individual to choose their preferences.

Conflict between the principles of autonomy and beneficence

One of the most common dilemmas cited concerning ethical principles in healthcare concerns the conflict between autonomy and beneficence, where respecting autonomy would lead the practitioner to trust the client's choice, and beneficence would involve the practitioner deciding that they thought what was best for the client. Ethical frameworks in counselling usually emphasise both principles, of respecting autonomy and beneficence, and are unclear about how to prioritise between them (except the BABCP [2009] Standards, which only mention beneficence). The BACP Ethical Framework suggests there will be times when choosing between principles will be required. They then suggest that, 'A practitioner's obligation is to consider all the relevant circumstances with as much care as is reasonably possible and to be appropriately accountable for decisions made' (2013: 2).

Exercise

1. When do you think your respect for the client's autonomy would be trumped by the principle of beneficence? Can you think of a time when this happened? What were the consequences and how did you deal with them?
2. What difficulties are there with prioritising beneficence over autonomy?

Tom

Tom thought that when he had worked with highly anxious clients he actively helped them to reduce their anxiety without asking them. He did not think they had the capacity to respond at the time when so anxious, and his aim was to reduce their anxiety enough to be able to participate autonomously in therapy again. He guessed that this was an example of beneficence being prioritised over autonomy, but he always made sure that he evaluated what he had done with the client once their capacity had returned.

Anne

Anne thought about how much she acts from the principle of beneficence rather than autonomy with her children, believing they are not old enough to know what would be best for themselves in the long term. She did wonder when this balance would change as they got older and noted how much her wish to protect them led to her thinking she knew better than them. She thought that the only way she would be convinced that they were responsible enough to be autonomous was if they made decisions that she agreed with, and noted that this left them no room to develop values that were different from hers. She vowed to try harder to discuss with them when she was overriding their autonomy and to try and understand better why they wanted to do something different from what she thought was best. She did think however that it was part of her responsibility as a parent to hold their long-term future in mind as she believed that children were developmentally unable to consider long-term consequences of their decisions. She thought this philosophy may also apply to counselling when clients did not have capacity to make decisions.

Several authors suggest that the purpose of therapy should be to increase autonomy (e.g. Adshead, 2008; Feenan, 2002; Szasz, 1965/1988). Szasz names his approach to psychotherapy 'autonomous psychotherapy', 'to indicate the paramount aim of this procedure: preservation and expansion of the client's autonomy' (1965/1988: 7). He argues that psychiatric symptoms are an expression of loss of control or freedom, so the aim of freedom should be both individual and collectivist freedom. He defines autonomy as the 'freedom to develop one's self – to increase one's knowledge, improve one's skills, and achieve responsibility for one's conduct. And it is freedom to lead one's own life, to choose among alternative courses of action so long as no injury to others results' (1965/1988: 22). Szasz wants psychotherapy to provide a model for the autonomous, non-coercive relationship. He is clear that this means the therapist does not take care of the client; the patient takes care of him- or herself. The patient is expected to 'recover' morally, by 'learning more about himself and by assuming greater responsibility for his conduct' (1965/1988: 24).

Anne

Anne liked the idea of teaching clients to take care of themselves and she decided to try and use each time she overrode her children's autonomy to ensure that she was working towards their development of autonomy in the future by teaching them about making decisions.

Maxine

Maxine considered the difficulty of prioritising respect for autonomy with a suicidal client, and thought that this could be an example of when she might prioritise beneficence instead as she could not believe that choosing to die could be an autonomous decision. Rubina pointed out that this was a good example of the values involved in deciding what is good for someone else, with Maxine's value of choosing to live taking precedence over a client who disagrees. Tom added that there may be circumstances when for particular clients who are chronically suffering, that being dead may be better for them than being alive, so respecting autonomy and beneficence would not be contradictory. Cullity (2007) agrees that given that autonomy is good for people, then beneficence and autonomy are rarely in conflict. Maxine was convinced however that suicide has such final consequences that she would always err on the side of believing that preserving life was better, and she considered how to minimise the negative effects of infringing her respect for the autonomy of the suicidal client. She decided that preventing a suicide would be an extreme situation that she would explain to the client and immediately ensure that the client's decisions were autonomous as soon as she knew they were safe.

Szasz (1965/1988) is clear in his prioritising of autonomy that there can be no situations which lead to the therapist deviating from this contract in favour of beneficence, as this would undermine therapy completely. He discusses the situation of suicide, and remains firm in prioritising the value of autonomy. He explains: 'Indeed, only if the patient is deeply convinced that the analyst respects his autonomy, including his right to take his own life, can he engage effectively in the analytic exploration and mastery of his ideas about suicide. With such understanding between patient and therapist, the analysand's communications about suicide remain the language of self-destruction which it is the analyst's task to analyse; without it, the analysand's communications become coercive messages intended to influence the therapist's conduct' (1965/1988: 175). Of relevance to all therapy models is the importance of being explicit about the therapist's intentions, to provide the frame which allows the work to be done.

In many organisational contexts (such as the NHS in the UK), counsellors will be required to override autonomy in the situation of a client disclosing plans for suicide and inform a relevant health professional. To preserve client autonomy or at least some sense of informed consent in these situations, it is imperative that clients are informed that this will happen if they disclose such plans. Cain (2002) argues that there are times for beneficence to override autonomy, claiming a place for authority based on expert knowledge within a partnership model, as opposed to paternalism, which involves a person's will being overridden. He advocates the importance of virtues for the professional with power, in particular, respect, diligence, honesty and altruistic concern.

Legal backing for the principle of autonomy

Legally, the responsibility lies with the therapist to prove that the client lacks capacity if they prioritise the principle of beneficence over autonomy. The Mental Capacity Act (2005) clarifies the issue about whether psychiatric disorders limit capacity for autonomy, stating that capacity is not a static concept to be determined once and for all for each person. Instead, the Act makes clear how dynamic and context-dependent assessments of capacity should be, so it is the responsibility of the therapist to determine lack of capacity each time they infringe the autonomy of the client.

The concept of autonomy and the following principles of informed consent and confidentiality clearly take precedence over the concept of beneficence in legal cases (see Bond, 2010; Jenkins, 2007). In healthcare, the patient has the right to determine whether they want treatment, irrespective of what the doctor believes will be best for the patient. This prioritising of the principle of autonomy can be overturned only by proof that the patient lacks the capacity to give or withhold consent to treatment (and the onus lies with the clinician to prove this in the UK very clearly since the Mental Capacity Act 2005).

Informed consent

The principle of informed consent follows from the principle of autonomy in healthcare ethics, as it is necessary for the client to have the necessary information to make an autonomous decision. The responsibility is with the clinician to ensure appropriate information is given clearly and understood by the patient to enable them to decide whether to consent to any kind of intervention.

Exercise

1. What information do you think needs to be given to clients at the start of therapy to enable them to make an informed decision whether to proceed?
2. Your values will affect how you present this information. What can you do about this?
3. Can you think of a time when you have wished in retrospect that you had given more information to a client earlier in therapy?

Tom

Tom thought that it was impossible to know in advance for each client what information they would need to make a decision about therapy. He always said something to clients about the limits to confidentiality and something about his model of therapy. He was aware that his values affected the way he presented this information but thought that he could only be as transparent as possible about how he saw therapy so clients could decide if they wanted his approach or not. Indeed, he thought it was important that his values would come out in how he explained therapy as then his values would be a part of the decision for the client.

Informed consent is a crucial issue in discussing the issue of a client's autonomy. Clients cannot be autonomous in their decision-making about therapy without information about therapy. Yet, therapy may be difficult to inform clients about in advance, depending on the model of therapy, because the process can be unpredictable, as can any relationship. Furthermore, how information is presented is never value-free and neutral.

Fisher and Oransky (2008: 576) argue that in addition to being an ethical matter, informed consent is also necessary to the efficacy of therapy, in terms of increasing the client's sense of ownership over the process of therapy. In practical terms, they emphasise the importance of language that is understandable to each individual patient.

They also mention the issue of capacity to consent, how dynamic, context-dependent and decision-dependent this may be, and the necessity for therapists to be familiar with the law on capacity (e.g. Mental Capacity Act 2005 in the UK). They suggest areas that informed consent should cover: the nature of therapy (including any potential hazards, fees or financial arrangements), the limits of confidentiality, the empirical validity of treatments, the status of the therapist (for example if in training), and viable alternative treatments.

Maxine and Anne

Maxine and Anne discussed what information needs to be given to clients to ensure informed consent, and thought this could vary depending on the amount of information a client wants and depending on the therapy relationship. They wondered whether creating a non-oppressive relationship where the client feels free to ask questions and contradict the therapist was perhaps more important than the information given. They thought that the notion of 'informed consent' came from a medical model of doing something to someone and was founded on countering paternalism rather than creating a collaborative or egalitarian relationship.

In the traditional approach to biomedical ethics, the professional gives information and formulates a plan, and the patient has access to some of the information with the power of veto over the plan. McMillan and Gillett (2002) suggest that instead the professional can share more with the patient about how they made a diagnosis and the consequent rationale for their proposed plan. They suggest that postmodern or narrative ethics are likely to give us more insight into moral dilemmas than the traditional approach to biomedical ethics.

Process, postmodern or narrative approach to informed consent

In psychotherapy, a process model of informed consent is essential rather than the idea of a stage of obtaining consent once and for all before therapy starts. Here, informed consent is both a process and a dialogue, whereby clients become increasingly informed about their therapy as it progresses (see Pomerantz, 2005). This process can be best described by a postmodern or narrative (see Sperry 2007: 69) approach, which tries to capture the lived experience of the people involved, including relations of power.

Chambers (2002) argues that every ethics case relies on a narrative of what choices are made and how. 'All stories are shaped by a particular teller for a particular purpose, for all narratives are infected by their situatedness' (2002: 70). He demonstrates how various narrative approaches are used as evidence for all particular approaches to ethics, whether that is a principled **rationalist** approach, or an **existential** relational approach.

A postmodern or **relativist** approach focuses on power differentials in moral relationships and can lead to the patient feeling more involved, in control and feeling some ownership over the plan. Brody argues the same for narrative ethics, suggesting that: 'when narratives are jointly constructed, power is shared between physician and patient, and the sharing of power constitutes an important ethical safeguard within the relationship' (2002: 133). He suggests that the power of the healthcare professional should not be denied or obscured, or even attempted to be minimised. He suggests that sharing power maximises the potential of the relationship to be healing and the chance of increasing the patient's sense of mastery, which is also healing. He emphasises the importance of the patient being able to tell their story of their illness and have this understood, and then shared meaning being made with the physician.

Anne

Anne thought about a client she was currently working with – a 12-year-old boy who was in foster care. She had felt really positive about the development of their therapy relationship, particularly given that he had been assessed as having attachment difficulties. However, she had been shocked and upset when she had informed him that she would not be able to see him for two weeks as she would be on holiday. He was furious and shouted that she had told him she would see him every week, and then stormed out of their session. She reflected that she wished she had been clearer at the start about potential breaks in their weekly contract and had predicted the importance of this for him. She reflected that a narrative or postmodern approach to ethics would be most useful to understand this issue in the context of his life story and her power to be there or not for him as all adults in his life had previously had.

Cultural and historical context of value of autonomy

The origin of the word autonomy was in Ancient Greece where city states were granted autonomy to allow a degree of self-government. The notion of autonomy does not mean isolation or avoidance of dependency, but often the interdependence implied in the original use of the word is missed in the focus on the autonomous self.

The understanding of autonomy as independence and the valuing of this is far from universal and the prioritisation of this value can result in the new authority of the ethicist rather than the values of the patient (Fulford et al., 2002). Blackhall, Murphy, Frank, Michel and Azen (2002) found that Korean-Americans and Mexican-Americans were less likely than European-Americans and African-Americans to believe that the patient should be told the truth about the diagnosis and prognosis of a serious illness and more likely to believe that the family should be told. However they also note wide variation within cultures, and conclude that healthcare professionals need to ask patients about how they want to handle information about their illness, and argue that rather than this abandoning commitment to individual autonomy, it means 'broadening our view of autonomy so that respect for persons includes respect for the cultural values they bring with them to the decision-making process' (Blackhall et al., 2002: 195).

Rubina

Rubina liked the idea of respecting autonomy to include meaning respecting cultural values. She thought about one of her clients who had been clear that she wanted Rubina to guide the counselling sessions and give her advice in how to deal with her anxiety. Initially, Rubina tried to explain to her client why she was not an expert as a counsellor and how she thought counselling could help by giving her a space to make her own decisions. However, after discussion in supervision, she then realised she was acting from the principle of beneficence rather than respecting the client's autonomy, and moved to acknowledging her client's request for direction and advice. She tried to take this responsibility, but only whilst sharing options with her client and making clear that any suggestions may or may not be helpful; they would find out when the client tried them if she wanted to. She found that her client really appreciated this approach and, at review, she said that she now understood Rubina's original description of counselling being a space to help her make decisions, as she felt that was what she had done in discussion, with Rubina.

Western moral philosophy and autonomy

Rationalist philosophy

The concept of autonomy is embedded in much of the modernist tradition of western moral philosophy. **Kant** sees our most fundamental ethical duty as respect for autonomy. Kant's concept of autonomy reflects the individualist modernist conception of being human which persisted into the twentieth century. The modernist concept of autonomy sees others as obstacles to our freedom. Autonomy is a foundational principle in most rationalist philosophy following Kant. Other contract theorists (such as Locke, Hume, Hobbes and Rousseau) similarly emphasised the importance of contracts to prevent our autonomy being encroached on by others. Rights theory is a branch of **contractarianism** which is still at the root of much of our current legal system.

However, **Habermas** (1993) questions Kant's individualist concept of autonomy. He claims that autonomy is intersubjective, arguing that we cannot draw conclusions in private reflection, only in consensus achieved in argumentation under sufficiently propitious conditions. Parker (2007) uses the deliberative democratic approach to healthcare decisions, following this model of intersubjective autonomy.

Existential philosophy

In **existential philosophy**, the emphasis on autonomy remains, but less associated with rationality than with authenticity, or the notion of us all having the freedom to choose how to be. This freedom is seen as limited in different ways by various philosophers. **Nietzsche**, **Heidegger** and **Sartre** saw others as being potential limits to our freedom, from whose influence we must guard ourselves.

In contrast, many existential philosophers emphasise the interdependency involved in autonomy and freedom. **Jaspers** emphasised existential communication with others as a way to develop our own authenticity. **Buber** contends that the essence of being human is to be in relation with another human, recognised as another subject. For **Levinas**, to ask about one's own being and nature is the wrong question; we must begin with the other (heteronomy). **De Beauvoir** brings together the concepts of individual autonomy (threatened by others) with self-in-relation when she describes the 'tragic ambivalence' of the human condition, 'being a sovereign and unique object amidst a universe of objects ... nothing more than an individual in the collectivity on which he depends' (1948/1976: 7). She prescribes that, 'To attain his truth, man must not attempt to dispel the ambiguity of his being but, on the contrary, accept the task of realising it' (1948/1976: 13). Thus, she focuses both on autonomy and how it is threatened by us becoming objects to other subjects, *and* on homonomy (belonging) and our dependence on others.

Exercise

1 How do the approaches of existential philosophers to autonomy modify your understanding of this principle in counselling?
2 Should the principle of autonomy be replaced by that of heteronomy as Levinas might suggest? What might the differences be?

Rubina

Rubina thought that Habermas's understanding of autonomy being intersubjective made sense of working with the client who she had just considered, with respect to the question of autonomy. She also thought that the relationship was important, where she was another subject with ideas and thoughts, which Buber's ideas of an I–Thou relationship described. She thought that Levinas's principle of heteronomy would lead to the same conclusions as focusing on the client's autonomy, as in each case she would begin with a focus on the client and what they wanted, as opposed to what she believed they wanted or was best for them.

Maxine

Maxine thought about Levinas's concept of heteronomy in the context of the importance for her of autonomy. She was initially concerned that heteronomy could be oppressive when it was not reciprocated in a relationship and wondered particularly about the dangers for women of prioritising heteronomy, and responding to the needs of others before thinking about themselves. However, she wondered if the two principles could be combined by emphasising the importance of each person *choosing* to prioritise heteronomy and respond to another as a result of an autonomous choice of values and meaning. Nevertheless she thought there were dangers in heteronomy of neglecting one's own needs. She wondered about the influence of Levinas's male gender on his security to start from the other, from the context of his male privilege. She thought that she felt much more comfortable with a relational approach, considering both in the relationship, rather than autonomy or heteronomy.

Anne

Anne wondered whether starting from Levinas's principle of heteronomy would have helped her with the client she had just considered who had been angry at her going on holiday. This could have led her to focus more clearly on his needs and to respond earlier to his need for consistency and predictability in relationships.

Applying various philosophical approaches to the autonomy-versus-beneficence dilemma

Widdershoven (2002) discusses a classic case in the debate between autonomy and beneficence. The case is of Donald Cowart, who was severely injured in a gas explosion and begged the doctors to stop treatment of his burns and allow him to die. The doctors refused to discontinue treatment and he recovered and became a lawyer, but remained indignant that he had not had the right to choose to die. Widdershoven (2002) applies principlist, phenomenological, deconstructive and hermeneutic approaches to the situation. We will consider these approaches in an analogous therapy situation.

Exercise

A client seeks long-term therapy and wants to focus on his long-standing wish to die. He explores his feelings in therapy, including his anger at the injustice of life and how unfairly resources are distributed, his powerlessness to influence these issues that matter to him, and ultimately his sense of futility about life. He cannot find any meaning in his own or anyone else's life, having rejected any kind of religious or spiritual beliefs. He believes that humans are a brief mistake in evolution who will soon thankfully cease to exist, at which point the planet will continue its development without so much interference. The client explicitly contracts to work for two years with a therapist, at which point he wants to make a decision to kill himself if he feels no different. During therapy, the therapist develops deep respect for his client's thoughtfulness about life and the world and feels very sad at the thought that his client may choose to end his life rather than contribute to the world. After 18 months of work, the client decides that he wants to plan to kill himself and use the rest of the time with the therapist to discuss the ramifications of this decision and say goodbye.

1 What would you do as a therapist with this client and why?
2 How might different philosophical approaches to ethical decisions help you work with this client in therapy?

Maxine and Anne – Principlism

Maxine thought initially from the principle of autonomy that the therapist should respect the client's autonomous decision (assuming he had capacity to make the decision) and let him die if he chooses this option. However, she was aware that if she was the therapist, this would have been a really hard decision to take and she suspected she would have tried to use her power to persuade him or help him to find the value of his continued life. She thought that it should be generally accepted that the role of health-care workers including therapists is to promote and preserve life and that patients should not expect these values to be overridden.

Anne thought that she would be interested to explore more about the client's history and whether his childhood experiences had led them to see life so negatively. She was aware that if the client was unwilling to explore this, she would not feel happy to support his autonomous decision to end his life.

In applying principlism, the principle of autonomy should be prioritised over beneficence based on the belief that the client had the capacity to make a rational decision to prefer death to life.

Maxine – Phenomenological approach

Maxine thought that with a client who wanted to die she would want to see this as a temporary crisis and she would aim in counselling to help the client re-find meaning in life. A phenomenological perspective, which focuses on the meaning given by the client, would see this case as an existential crisis, and his wish to die as a response and engagement to the situation he finds himself in. The ethical response from this perspective is to help the patient restore his relation to his situation and thus come to grips with it. This would assume that in exploring his situation, other options would become available.

Rubina – Deconstructive approach

Rubina was interested in the power of the therapist to decide how to respond to the client's wish to die. She reflected that the client could easily make a decision to kill himself without involving the therapist at all. She was also interested what others in the client's life thought about his decision and what the client thought about the impact on others of his life or death. She wondered if the therapist could involve a wider conversation including important others in the client's life, with awareness of the dynamics of power involved.

Rubina thought the deconstructive approach was a useful way to describe her approach with her client who wanted expert direction in counselling. Rather than persist with her powerful perspective on what counselling should be, she made space for her client's request and they developed an approach together that responded to both their needs.

A deconstructive approach focuses on the battle of power between the will of the client and of the therapist. Heidegger emphasises the impossibility of the process of uncovering and challenging truth and trying to pin it down. Instead he suggests that we need to make room for other accounts by listening and becoming attentive. This approach was developed further by **Derrida** in the notion of deconstruction, the aim of which is to make room for the other (Derrida, 1967/1997). Thus the deconstructive approach to this dilemma would be to listen to each perspective without trying to use power to persuade, but this does not lead to any clear guidance of what then to do. This would also involve supervision or wider consultation to seek further perspectives on the situation.

Hermeneutic approach

Similarly, a hermeneutic (see **Gadamer** in Appendix C) approach emphasises dialogue between all perspectives. In a hermeneutic approach, there is continuous dynamic influence between different relevant components. Application to this case would involve focusing on the encounter and communicative process between the client and the therapist, taking into account the dynamics of power involved. For a hermeneutic approach, truth is the result of communication and dialogue, where ideally power is not a battle but can be used positively by bringing together the powers of all involved. This dialogical style is more of a partnership, where 'Truth is ... seen as the outcome of a merger of perspectives' (Widdershoven & Weijts, 2002: 173). Again, in this approach, there is no one answer, so if the therapist and the client continued to disagree in dialogue, there would be no way to resolve the dilemma.

Rubina liked the idea of hermeneutics and for all involved to be in dialogue, to try and understand all perspectives and to try and reach consensus. She thought this approach might best describe how she worked with her client.

Summary

This chapter has discussed ethical dilemmas involving the competing principles of respecting autonomy and beneficence. The importance of prioritising respecting autonomy in ethics and law was noted. The corresponding notion of informed consent and its application to counselling have been explored. The relevance of moral philosophy to the notion of autonomy has been presented and the application of various philosophical perspectives to resolving such dilemmas has been considered. Our students explored which philosophical perspectives they found useful in their own practice and thought about their values in relation to these principles.

Maxine noted that one big issue in considering the competing principles of respecting autonomy and beneficence was that of breaking confidentiality. We shall consider this specifically in the next chapter.

TEN Confidentiality

Introduction

One frequently discussed example of the dilemma between the competing principles of autonomy and beneficence in practice is the therapist's decision to break confidentiality. This chapter will discuss the legal context of this decision and particular circumstances in which it is likely to occur. The importance of capacity will be presented.

Definitions and legal meanings of confidentiality

Definition

Confidentiality: 'the principle in medical ethics that the information a patient reveals to a health care provider is private and has limits on how and when it can be disclosed to a third party.' (http://medical-dictionary.thefreedictionary.com/confidentiality)

There are several definitions of confidentiality in the therapy literature, each focusing on a different aspect of the obligation to keep what a client says secret. Younggren and Harris define confidentiality as 'the secret-keeping duty that arises from the establishment of the professional relationship psychologists develop with their clients' (2008: 589). Mordini (2002) states that confidentiality involves defining private and public zones and defining the boundaries between these zones. He further suggests that it is about how the patient can control information flow about themselves. Adshead suggests that the principle of confidentiality may be better understood as: 'the *principle of informed consent to disclosure*' (2005: 478, italics in original). She suggests that it is the patient's strongest defence against gossip.

Confidentiality is both an ethical and a legal principle. Jenkins states that, 'Confidentiality provides a cornerstone for effective therapeutic practice, both as a pragmatic measure to build trust and rapport, and as an expression of ethical principles supporting the client's right to autonomy and self-determination' (2007: 128). Jenkins (2007) notes that, legally, confidentiality in therapy is a legitimate expectation from a client, whether or not it is explicitly stated in a written or verbal contract. He states that when a therapist decides to break confidentiality, it is expected that they discuss this with the client first unless the situation is urgent.

There are several reasons why a confidentiality agreement can be breached in law. Jenkins (2007) lists these: when the information is trivial, when it is already in the public domain, or when it is in the public interest (as defined by courts). Bond (2010) adds the condition of the client giving their consent to disclosure. Public interest covers situations such as preventing harm to others, but also covers situations where confidentiality should be maintained to protect the function of a body which requires the confidentiality of disclosed material for its function (such as child protection/safeguarding services needing to protect the confidence of people who report suspected abuse). He emphasises that therapists in the UK are *not* under a specific obligation to warn third parties of risk and that warning third parties of a client's HIV/AIDS status, for example, would be breaking client confidentiality, which Jenkins (2007) suggests would probably currently not be supported by the law. However, disclosing confidential information because of risks to others could be decided to be in the public interest, and Bond (2010) notes that courts have found in favour when a doctor disclosed information to prevent serious risk to others. Bond (2010: 180) also notes the increasing tendency to prosecute people who knowingly put others at risk of HIV infection, and considers informing a third party at risk of HIV infection from a client could be a defensible last resort. Bond (2010: 160) recommends consideration of various factors in these circumstances. These situations are complex and case law and guidance must be consulted. For example, see Philllips and Poulton (2013).

Concerning a client's risk of suicide, Jenkins clarifies that a therapist cannot be held responsible for failing to prevent its occurrence or not warning third parties; however 'to break confidentiality in order to prevent or reduce the risk of suicide would not necessarily put the therapist in jeopardy' (2007: 125). However, Bond (2010) stresses the importance in law of respecting autonomy and notes that an autonomous decision to end one's life would be respected in law, unless the client could be diagnosed with a mental illness. Jenkins (2007) and Bond (2010) state that reporting child abuse is not a legal requirement, but it may be required by an employment contract. However, it is a legal requirement to report 'terrorist activities' (see Jenkins, 2007: 115 for definition).

Over time the circumstances in which therapists can or should break confidentiality have increased and some worry about the impact of this on the practice of therapy. Others stress the importance of counsellors not making absolute promises about confidentiality. Bollas and Sundelson (1995) argue that allowing reasons to break confidentiality to multiply will result in the destruction of the private space where the client can bring all their wishes and feelings. However, Gray (2006) warns against an absolute injunction to break confidentiality, arguing that ethical decisions are more complex and we cannot make such absolute promises for the future. She argues for holding the tension, however anxiety-provoking, between keeping confidentiality against demands for information when we believe it to be right to breach confidentiality. She suggests that the important point is that when confidentiality is broken, this experience for the client must be part of the therapy to talk about and analyse.

The principle of confidentiality can sometimes be in conflict with the principle of telling the truth. This can be especially tricky when involving more than one client. For example, one client tells the therapist something about a friend and their dilemma about whether to tell the friend or not. At some point in the conversation, the therapist realises that the friend their client is talking about is one of the therapist's other clients. How can the therapist address this situation without breaking either client's confidentiality? To do this, there would be a limit about how truthful the therapist could be with either client.

The BACP Ethical Framework under 'Respecting privacy and protecting confidentiality' notes that:

- Respecting clients's privacy and confidentiality are fundamental requirements for keeping trust and respecting client autonomy. Disclosure may be authorised by client consent or the law. Any disclosures of client confidences should be undertaken in ways that best protect the client's trust and respect client autonomy.
- Exceptional circumstances may prevent the practitioner from seeking client consent to a breach of confidence due to the urgency and seriousness of the situation, for example, preventing the client causing serious harm to self or others. In such circumstances the practitioner has an ethical responsibility to act in ways which balance the client's right to confidentiality against the need to communicate with others. Practitioners should expect to be ethically accountable for any breach of confidentiality. (2013: 6)

COSCA's Statement of Ethics and Code of Practice adds to these principles specifically with regard to abiding with legal requirements - which may be different in Scotland - and confidentiality in supervision:

> A member will ensure that any information obtained about a client is kept confidential in all other professional relationships involving the member and the client. *For example: in the relationship between an organisation and its workers; or the relationship between a practitioner and her/his client-work supervisor.* (2007: 8, para 5.5, italics in original)

The UKCP Ethical Principles and Code of Professional Conduct also adds the consideration of confidentiality in the publication of client work, saying:

> The psychotherapist commits to safeguard the welfare and anonymity of clients when any form of publication of clinical material is being considered and to always obtain their client's verifiable consent in any case where the welfare or anonymity of a client may be compromised. This includes situations where a client or former client might recognise themselves in case material despite the changing of names or actual circumstances. (2009: 4, para 3.4)

Confidentiality is an area which causes therapists much anxiety (Bond, 2010) and in which therapists commonly report ethical dilemmas, particularly concerning suicide. In Clarkson's (2000) research asking therapists to describe ethical dilemmas, the most frequently mentioned issue in both therapy and supervision was that of confidentiality. Decisions about when to break confidentiality are ones that clearly involve the therapist's personal values. Even when working in settings with clear policies, values are involved in how to implement these policies in practice.

Exercise

1. Under what conditions would you consider breaking a client's confidentiality and what would your concerns be about doing this?
2. How would your decision to report concerns be affected by your belief or lack of belief in what your client is telling you? Consider a client telling you about his mother being abusive to her grandchild in the context of his anger about how she let him down as a child.

Maxine

Maxine was very worried about the limits to confidentiality and how these could be applied in practice. She reflected that if she had begun counselling whilst in the violent relationship that she was in for many years, her counsellor could have decided that the risk to her from this violence would justify breaking her confidentiality and reporting the violence to the police. She felt very strongly that if a counsellor had done this, the result would have been for her to lose any trust she had in her counsellor and also to expose her to greater risk of violence from her partner when he was confronted by the police. She had always been clear that she could not contact the police during this relationship as she could not guarantee there would be enough evidence to arrest him and that he would kill her if she reported his violence. She was also sure that the police would not believe her account as her partner was highly respected in his profession as a social worker, where he also worked closely with the police.

The students

Maxine discussed this situation with Tom at a break, not wanting to talk about her experience of domestic violence in the whole training group. Tom said that he would not have assumed domestic violence would be a reason to break confidentiality and that he would ask the tutor to clarify this. On returning to the group, the tutor encouraged a discussion about whether the students believed hearing about ongoing domestic violence would be a reason to break confidentiality. Rubina discussed the requirements within her agency of sharing risk concerns at an MARAC (Multi-Agency Risk Assessment Conference) for women experiencing domestic violence, but acknowledged that this was after the initial disclosure of domestic violence had been made and acted upon. She mentioned a time when a client of hers had disclosed that her sister was also experiencing domestic violence. Rubina had encouraged her client to urge her sister to get support but did not feel she had either the information or right to consider reporting this.

This discussion reminded Tom of the time when he had been in psychiatric hospital and had made friends with another male patient who said he had been assaulted by a member of staff whilst in seclusion. Tom remembers being horrified that his friend had disclosed this to a psychologist, who had not reported the situation or acted on his accusation. Anne commented that Tom had only heard his friend's side of the story and that he could not actually know what had happened either with the member of staff in seclusion or the details of the conversation with the psychologist. She commented that what most worried her in breaking confidentiality was the idea of acting based on just hearing the perspective of her client.

The tutor then facilitated further discussion of how students would report concerns being clear that they were reporting exactly what they had been told without making assumptions of truth. She also discussed the different contexts of various workplaces, or formats of counselling such as telephone or on-line counselling. She noted varying interpretations of reasons to break confidentiality to protect others, commenting that what she thought was important was that students had thought for themselves about when they would report concerns about risk and how they informed clients about their limits to confidentiality.

Exercise

1 One of the most common reasons why therapists override their duty to keep therapy confidential is when the client discloses suicidal intent. In what circumstances do you believe you should respect the client's autonomous right to choose to end their lives?
2 At what point would your fear for someone's safety lead you to break confidentiality and report concerns? When you hear about a child being sexually abused? When you hear about a child being smacked? How about a child being beaten with a slipper? When you hear about a man nearly killing his female partner? When you hear that your client left her elderly mother with dementia on the toilet for half an hour? Consider how much the severity of the harm and the vulnerability of the victim are factors in your decision.

Maxine

Maxine worried greatly about the idea of breaking a client's confidentiality. She thought this would be an example of prioritising beneficence over autonomy and worried about the values involved in deciding what was best for someone else. However, she was aware that if a client was suicidal she would want to override their autonomous decision to kill themselves and try and do something to keep them alive. She was aware that this reflected her personal value about the importance of life but also thought this value was fairy universal. She had not been in such a situation with a client yet, but remembered a time when a distressed friend had rung her after the breakup of a relationship, and after talking for a while Maxine had asked her how much she had had to drink as she was slurring her words and her friend had admitted she had taken an overdose. Although her friend had asked Maxine not to do anything, Maxine had rung for the emergency services and the police and ambulance had taken her to hospital. Maxine had gone to visit her friend the following weekend and had been very relieved to hear that although her friend had felt angry with her at the time and the following day and had been upset to be still alive, by the time Maxine visited, she had decided that it was a good thing she was still alive and was grateful to Maxine for calling for help. Maxine had realised that she had risked her friend continuing to be angry with her, but she felt this had been a risk worth taking as she could not live with the awareness that she could have prevented a death but had failed to. She remembered thinking at the time that if her friend had been really clear she wanted to die, she would not have telephoned her and risked her calling for help, and that if she continued being clear she wanted to die, she could always try killing herself again. She thought that if a similar situation occurred with a client in counselling, she would probably make the same decision.

Some counsellors work in contexts where there are rules about intervening in this situation, such as the NHS in England where therapists are legally bound to inform a mental health practitioner or physician if the client discloses an intention of suicide. Therapists in private practice have more leeway in deciding their own ethical position. There can be stress and an emotional toll for therapists making such decisions about life and death and taking ethical responsibility for their actions. Pope and Vasquez (2007) emphasise the stress and emotional toll for therapists of assessing risk of suicide and the impact when clients do kill themselves. Here self-care and supervision become especially important (see Chapter 7).

When we do overrule a client's autonomy to try and keep them alive, how can we do this in as respectful a way as possible? Two factors that are important in overruling the client's autonomy are explaining why this is happening to the client and taking steps to promote the future autonomy of the client.

Maxine liked the idea that her decision to override the client's autonomy in the case of suicide is to promote their future autonomy. However, she did worry that this reason could be used to justify all sorts of circumstances where therapists could override autonomy, as they could argue that the client's decision could put them at risk. She thought that a therapist deciding to tell the police about a woman being in a violent relationship could be justified by the therapist saying they were trying to promote the future autonomy of the client. She was aware that in her own case, she would have been clear that actually a therapist would have been putting her in more danger by taking this step. She thought that this was the biggest problem in prioritising beneficence over autonomy – the therapist's values would always be involved in their decision about what was best for the client and there is no objective way to know what is best for anyone.

The BACP Ethical Framework considers this situation under the title of 'Keeping trust':

> Situations in which clients pose a risk of causing serious harm to themselves or others are particularly challenging for the practitioner. These are situations in which the practitioner should be alert to the possibility of conflicting responsibilities between those concerning

their client, other people who may be significantly affected, and society generally. Resolving conflicting responsibilities may require due consideration of the context in which the service is being provided. Consultation with a supervisor or experienced practitioner is strongly recommended, whenever this would not cause undue delay. In all cases, the aim should be to ensure for the client a good quality of care that is as respectful of the client's capacity for self-determination and their trust as circumstances permit. (2013: 5)

Anne

Anne thought about when she might break confidentiality owing to her concerns about someone's safety. She realised that she would be much more likely to think about this with children as she would feel more responsible for their protection but was unsure where she would draw the line in defining child abuse. However, she hoped that if she was unsure whether a particular behaviour was abusive, those to whom she reported the situation who would be responsible for investigating would be able to decide this for her. She did think that deciding to report would be a complex decision involving weighing up the potential consequences for the client and the therapy relationship.

Capacity and confidentiality

Confidentiality becomes more complicated when working with clients who lack capacity, including children. Here, both children and parents need to be involved in informed consent. Younggren and Harris (2008) consider cases where the right of a child to confidentiality conflicts with the right of a parent to information about a child. Sometimes, conflict between interests of two different parents complicates things even further. Here, it is the therapist's responsibility to assess the capacity and best interests of the child, to argue if necessary that this overrides the right for parents to know about the child's therapy. However, Younggren and Harris (2008) and Koocher (2008) point out the importance of agreeing issues of confidentiality with all parents and children as early in therapy as possible, to try and prevent later potential threats to the ongoing therapy relationship. In therapy with couples, the client is usually considered to be the couple, thus requiring consent of both parties to disclose information outside of therapy. Similar conflicts can occur with older people who may lack capacity (owing to dementia) and their carers.

Jenkins specifically considers confidentiality with children in therapy and notes that the law respects a child's right to an independent counselling relationship, including the 'right to confidentiality, depending on their level of maturity and understanding as perceived by the adult therapist, independently of the wishes of the parent' (2007: 176). Jenkins (2010) notes the importance to children of the principle of confidentiality and suggests that counsellors may perceive constraints to high levels of confidentiality in the form of assumed duties to report child abuse, under-age sexual activity, and the need to obtain parental consent for counselling. He reassures counsellors that there is in fact 'robust support in law for counsellors providing high levels of confidentiality to young people' (2010: 263).

Exercise

How would you assess the capacity of a child who is self-harming, when determining whether to tell their parents?

Anne

Anne thought about what she would do with a child who disclosed self-harm and she reflected that this would cause her much anxiety, as she would think about how she would feel as a parent not knowing that her child was self-harming. She thought she would want to assess the potential severity of the self-harm and how much the child was aware of what they were doing, how much damage they could cause, and whether there was any suicidal intent. She thought that if she was reassured that the child understood how to keep themselves safe from serious harm, she would want to preserve the therapy relationship where the child could disclose the harm to try and use this to minimise future risk of serious harm.

The students discussed how much their individual circumstances and their personal values would affect how they would make such decisions. Tom noted he would be far more likely than Anne to identify with the young person and their rights to confidentiality and autonomy to make their own decisions without interference from their parents.

On-line counselling

Exercise

What particular issues would you need to consider concerning confidentiality with on-line counselling?

Rubina

Rubina thought that the counsellor here may not have the information to disclose risk issues, particularly if the client wants to remain anonymous. She thought it would be important in this case for counsellors to be clear about whether they could personally manage living with awareness of risks without being able to share information, as she knew she may find this too anxiety-provoking.

Goss and Anthony discuss various issues involved with on-line interventions and argue for special consideration of confidentiality issues and specialist training, as 'The conversion of verbal communication skills to its text-based, more nearly literary, equivalents, for example, requires the development of a whole new level of skills in written expression' (2009: 224). They stress the need for continuing updates in knowledge given the fast development of technology and its uses in counselling. This is one of many papers in a special issue on on-line counselling in the *British Journal of Guidance and Counselling*. They provide evidence for effectiveness and user satisfaction with computer-mediated counselling and argue that given the increased access to services this provides, it could be said to be unethical not to provide this option.

Requests for confidential information by a court

Exercise

How would you respond if a solicitor requests your notes about a client they are representing to help their court case to claim compensation for trauma as a result of a road traffic accident?

Tom

Tom thought that he would be happy as a counsellor to disclose his counselling notes if he thought they could help a client, although he would rather write a report for the purpose rather than disclose all his notes. He did think about the possibility of his notes being used for this purpose when he wrote them, and was careful to not include his opinion and just to document a summary of what his client said. He thought he would want to discuss the possible implications with his client before releasing notes and ask the solicitor if a report could be used instead.

Requests for notes from court lead us to have to think clearly about the purpose of record-keeping. Jenkins (2007) refers to the therapist legally as the 'custodian' of sensitive client information and the 'active agent' in deciding whether or not to disclose information to a third party. He considers the implications of the Data Protection Act (1998) on case notes kept by therapists, of the right of access of clients to their notes unless the therapist can justify withholding access to prevent serious harm. He notes that the ethical justification for record-keeping by therapists has often been unclear. Clearly, how counsellors keep records is an ethical decision, and we have a responsibility to preserve the confidentiality of our records as far as possible. Confidentiality also needs to be seriously considered when discussing clients in teaching or training settings or in writing about counselling for publication (see UKCP, 2009, above).

Courts and the police can order access to case notes in the public interest. Jenkins (2007) stresses that the police can have access to notes only with specific judicial authority. Courts have wider powers of access; although therapists may request the court's permission to restrict disclosure to material essential for the specific legal proceedings, they can be punished for contempt of court for refusal to surrender files. There is no concept of 'privilege' for clients' information gained in therapy in the UK as there is in some US states. Bond (2010: 161) notes the distinction between a court order and a solicitor's request, which can be refused.

Jones (2000) also considers the situation where the client, via their solicitor, requests their case notes or a report based on the counselling. Jones is clear that therapists have no obligation to respond to such requests, but that it is the therapist's responsibility to discuss with the client 'the potential consequences of taking such action on behalf of a client, such as how the information may be used by others and how it may be stored and accessed by other parties, thus further diminishing confidentiality' (2000: 22). It is the therapist's responsibility to minimise the amount of information revealed to that of particular relevance whilst still complying with the request. I would add to this the importance of the discussion as to how this may affect therapy and the therapy relationship. Bond (2010: 204–5) recommends what to consider in response to requests for reports or case notes from a solicitor.

Changing cultural and institutional expectations of confidentiality

Many counsellors now work in the context of an organisation which prioritises team working and communication between team members. Psychiatric enquiry reports frequently report lack of information sharing in multidisciplinary teams to be a contributory factor in the failure of risk prediction. Risk management and attempting to predict and prevent harm are major priorities within mental health (see Proctor, 2005). Bollas and Sundelson (1995) powerfully describe this cultural change. How much does this climate affect a counsellor's approach to confidentiality? In the UK, counsellors working in primary care or in mental health settings in the NHS are usually obliged to write their notes on a computerised system that other professionals have access to. Some systems have privacy settings where access can be restricted; others do not. This information sharing is advocated as a means to reduce risk (usually to others) but has implications for client choice (a service may be denied if clients do not agree to their records being shared). Gonsiorek (2008) warns against healthcare professionals becoming agents of the state in terms of passing on information, and the consequent deleterious effects on the healthcare relationship. He emphasises the need for therapists to ethically place the welfare of clients above the needs of the employers.

The focus on risk can easily be prioritised above client care and autonomy, and this move has been criticised by some authors. Donner et al. (2008) suggest that confidentiality should be accorded unique status as an ethical imperative in therapy. He suggests that this is no longer the case in the US: 'What began as an effort to protect children from abuse and the public from dangerous patients has resulted in an ever-larger set of exceptions to confidentiality' (2008: 372). Donner describes the current situation, saying, 'Public and private interests, mandatory reporting laws and the fear of liability attached to the possibility of a complaint about failure to protect, and continuing education courses that emphasise risk management may have diluted the value and meaning of confidentiality in the minds of many psychologists' (2008: 372). He calls upon practitioners to 'be vigilant against efforts to dilute confidential relationships and, when disclosure of confidential information is unavoidable, [they] should provide only the minimal amount of information necessary in order to preserve privacy to the fullest extent possible' (2008: 372).

Exercise

Have you noticed this change in focus in counselling settings from confidentiality to risk management? What have the consequences been for you and your clients?

Rubina

Rubina discussed the impact of the introduction of MARACs on the practice of her agency which traditionally had clearly prioritised the confidentiality of its clients. She felt that at times autonomy had been assumed with women who were still in violent situations, when they were not able to make decisions to ensure their own safety owing to loyalty to their violent partners. She welcomed the shifting priority towards safety with the introduction of MARACs and felt personally more ethically comfortable knowing that she would be sharing information about risk and not left with the individual responsibility of deciding when to act. She also felt that there was now a clearer message given to individual women about what information would be shared and with whom, which meant they could decide what to disclose in a more informed way.

Maxine

Maxine found herself getting more and more angry on listening to Rubina and decided that she had to say something in response. She told the group that she had a friend in a relationship with a violent man who disclosed to Maxine what she was experiencing. She explained that although the same rules about confidentiality in therapy did not apply in this situation of friendship, Maxine felt very strongly that to be confided in as a friend carried with it the assumption of confidentiality. Maxine would not consider breaking this trust by reporting concerns in any circumstances. She felt that Rubina's relief at not having to decide alone about when to share information amounted to running away from ethical responsibility, which Maxine found morally repugnant.

The tutor felt very uncomfortable at this point with such overt anger and judgement being expressed from one student to another. However, she also knew, from being her counsellor, about Maxine's history of being in a violent relationship, so was not surprised that this discussion had prompted such emotion in Maxine. She knew too that she was unable to reflect on this knowledge in the group as this was information that was confidential to her therapy relationship with Maxine. Instead, she reminded the group of their agreed ground rules about respecting different opinions and the impossibility of finding an absolute answer to apply to all situations and all people. She said that she thought Maxine's ideas about ethical responsibility were interesting and could begin an interesting discussion about the following of ethical codes in counselling and whether this was a demonstration or an abdication of ethical responsibility.

Exercise

1. What part would you take in the debate between Rubina and Maxine?
2. How is your evaluation of Maxine's position affected by your knowledge that the friend she is referring to is, in fact, herself?
3. If you worked for your ideal agency, what would their policy be on limits of confidentiality? What would your policy be about your limits if you worked privately?

Tom

Tom felt uncomfortable in the debate between Rubina and Maxine. He was aware that Maxine was in fact talking about herself but felt OK with her decision not to disclose this to the group. However, he was also aware that the tutor would know that Maxine was referring to herself as he knew that the tutor had been Maxine's therapist. He felt in a strange position knowing both of these things but being unable to refer to them, yet also felt that it was Maxine's right to keep all of this information to herself. His main worry was that it was the tutor who wanted to keep their former therapy relationship secret and he felt that, as the client, it should be Maxine's confidentiality that should be preserved and therefore Maxine's decision for this to be made public in the group or not. He was not convinced that Maxine would feel able to make this decision for herself rather than defer to the tutor, given the dynamics of power between them, and so thought in this situation that the tutor was lacking authenticity and resoluteness. He felt sorry for Rubina receiving Maxine's anger, judgement and lack of understanding without knowing why, but did not know what to say to support her.

Anne

Anne was clear that wherever she worked she would want to let clients know that she would break their confidentiality if she was concerned about risk of harm to them or others and particularly concerning child abuse. She was happy that she would be taking ethical responsibility for how she wanted to deal with these issues, following her clear value of wanting to protect children in particular. She did not feel that following codes was not taking responsibility, as long as she was clear with clients that this was what she was doing. She also thought that the ethical responsibility was hers in deciding how to apply codes and in justifying her decisions.

Mistakes in confidentiality

Many of us have made mistakes concerning confidentiality, for example, by discussing work about a client at a training event without permission. Even if this is anonymous, this does not ensure that particular details could not lead participants to identify or think they can identify the client. Pope, Tabachnick and Keith-Spiegel (1987) noted that over half of the therapists in their US study reported unintentionally violating their patients' confidences. Pope and Vasquez (2007) mention the most common pitfalls that can lead to violations of confidentiality, including contacting the referral source, consulting with colleagues without ensuring adequate privacy, gossip, lack of privacy and security of patient files, lack of privacy of phone calls, faxes and messages, and computers and the use of case studies in written material. They suggest that written informed consent covering issues of confidentiality is a helpful process for the therapist and client to consider and clarify confidentiality and its limits.

Best practice

Donner et al. (2008) advocate a positive ethics perspective, viewing ethics as a way to aim for the best practice, rather than avoiding rule breaking. He also gives a mandate for the importance of informed consent regarding confidentiality, and educating clients as to the risks of sharing their health information.

Exercise

Can you think of a time when you have made a mistake regarding confidentiality? How could you prevent such mistakes in the future?

Anne

Anne remembered a time when she was first volunteering as a counsellor when she needed to contact her client to rearrange her appointment, as she was poorly. When she rang, a man answered the phone who she assumed to be her client's partner and said that her client was not available. Without thinking, she left a message asking her client to call her back, just saying her name and telling him that she would have her number. Her client did not return the call and failed to attend her appointment. Anne decided to write to her client after this, apologising for her mistake in leaving a message as she felt sure that she had put her client in a difficult situation, explaining to her partner who she was. She decided from that point onwards to always check with clients about leaving messages on phones or with other people.

Conclusion

The principle of confidentiality and whether to keep or break the confidentiality of a client in therapy have been discussed in this chapter. This is a specific example of the ethical dilemma between the principles of respect for autonomy and beneficence. The legal system clearly prioritises respect for autonomy in England and Wales but various institutional contexts prioritise beneficence for the purpose of risk management. Issues of capacity, on-line practice and court requests have also been discussed, and mistakes in confidentiality have been considered. Our students discussed what values they hold which influence how they prioritise each of these principles in decisions of when to break confidentiality.

Anne noted that she saw keeping confidentiality as an essential boundary in therapy, which she noted was broken in particular circumstances. She wondered whether this would be the case for other such boundaries. The next two chapters will consider the issue of boundaries in more detail.

ELEVEN Boundaries

Introduction

In this chapter, I explore the concept of 'boundaries' in therapy, and the idea that they protect clients and/or therapists. I then discuss the choice between rigid or flexible boundaries and the possible values associated with each. Finally, I consider the distinction between boundary crossings and violations and how clear this distinction can be. The chapter ends with practice recommendations about crossing boundaries. The aim of this chapter is to ask the reader to consider their decisions about boundaries in their practice and to be clear about reasons for this and the values behind these decisions.

Definitions

There are many definitions of the concept of boundaries in psychotherapy. I shall use the term 'boundary' in its most common usage in psychotherapy and counselling – to refer to the limits of the therapy relationship.

Boundaries and protecting clients from untrustworthy therapists

Exercise

You are a therapist working in a clinic. You have just finished seeing a client who is waiting in reception for their lift home when you leave the building. Your car does not start, it is raining and you need to be home to see a client there in half an hour's time. You know your house is on your client's way home. Would you ask your client for a lift home?

Rubina

Rubina is clear that she would not ask her client for a lift as she thought it would be very difficult for them to refuse. She decided she would prefer to take a taxi despite the expense to her, as she would not want to take advantage of her position with respect to her client.

The rhetoric around boundaries is often about making services safe for clients, guarding against exploitation by the therapist (e.g. Zur, 2007: 3). Syme notes that 'the therapeutic frame offers a boundary that limits the therapist's power. This is essential when the power balance, particularly at the start of therapy, is weighted so much in the therapist's favour' (2003: 40).

In psychoanalytic literature the perils of this power imbalance are clear, where the tricky role of the unconscious in ethics is paramount. From this framework, boundaries are essential, as therapists cannot be trusted to keep their unruly unconscious in order to prevent exploitation of the client. However, Adshead notes the particular difficulty of monitoring boundaries in psychoanalytic therapy, when 'much of the pushing and crossing of boundaries in psychotherapy is done unconsciously as well as consciously' (2005: 481).

Here the traditional psychoanalytic idea of an untrustworthy mind which needs to be policed is clear. There are clear parallels with the philosophical approach of **contractarianism**, which believes that rules are necessary to curb our selfish motives and to live together in society. What is not clear in psychoanalysis is how this wayward mind could be trusted to follow rules rather than deceive itself about how the rules are being followed or when they do not apply (see Gabbard & Hobday, 2012). If therapists need rules and checks to ensure moral behaviour, one of the difficulties of this in therapy is how to ensure that therapists are following these rules, given the private nature of therapy, and the reliance in supervision on therapist self-report. Another difficulty is the lack of agreement among therapists about what these rules or boundaries should be, making a rule-based approach difficult in practice.

However, rules or contracts are part of informed consent and can make it clear to both parties what behaviour is acceptable. Szasz (1965/1988) believes the therapy contract and the boundaries described in this provide the practical considerations to make the therapeutic encounter possible. He explains that 'Every human relationship is, and must be, constrained by certain limits which can be transgressed only at the cost of destroying the relationship' (1965/1988: xii). For Szasz, an important part of the therapist not abusing the power in their role is to be clear with clients what exactly the limits of their role are so clients know what to expect.

Exercise

You are a therapist working from home and your client has just left their session. They ring your doorbell again a few minutes later saying their car has broken down, and ask if they can use your phone to call for help. It is raining. How do you respond?

Anne

Anne thinks that it would be inhumane to refuse to let a client back into the house to use the phone. However, she wonders how long the client would then remain in her home and wonders about other possible circumstances, such as her partner or children being about to come home or another client arriving and then bumping into this client. Or if she only has half an hour to eat her meal before her next client arrives, does she continue to do this whilst her client uses the phone and waits for help? She does not think that this situation could be seen as exploitative by the therapist, however, but that other possible consequences would need to be thought through and discussed.

Lott (1999) considers the particular meaning and significance that therapist acts (such as offering a hug, a cup of tea, a jumper or a hospital visit) can have in therapy, beyond any ordinary social interaction and the consequent importance of boundaries. She explains, 'Therapy is a fragile, paradoxical relationship always at risk of turning into something else – friendship, romance, the worship of devotee for guru. Boundaries can prevent this from happening. They remind client and counsellor that by being therapy, there are things that their relationship can never be, but that what it is, can be relied upon' (1999: 4). She considers dilemmas about everyday situations, and suggests that 'there are a host of situations where the delineation of a boundary is less clear, situations that fall outside the formal ethics codes and lie instead on the cusp of principles and technique' (1999: 1). She recommends that therapists need to consider these situations carefully, and explore meaning with the client. She further recommends: 'For therapists – and clients – who are struggling with boundaries, the paramount question must be: Does this serve the patient's therapeutic interests? If an act or an encounter threatens that goal, it is suspect, even if its exploitative potential is not obvious' (1999: 1).

Boundaries and protecting therapists

Neukrug, Milliken and Walden (2001) reviewed therapist misconduct complaints in the US and found that boundary violations were the most frequent complaint. However, Khele, Symons and Wheeler's (2008) report of complaints to the BACP did not uphold this prevalence. They found that complaints under the area of 'boundaries' represented only 12% of this sample, but 76% of these complaints were upheld at adjudication – a far greater proportion than in any other area. Clarkson (2000) found, in research asking therapists about ethical dilemmas, that 'dual relationships' was the third most frequently reported area, after confidentiality and concerns about a colleague's conduct.

Jenkins (2009) considers the area of working with sexual and erotic material as being particularly risky for therapists legally. He gives the example of a psychiatrist successfully sued for malpractice when making extensive use of countertransference sexual fantasy material. He states that 'Therapists working at the margins of accepted practice with sexual or erotic material are possibly ... those most at risk of professional censure and challenge in courts' (2009: 114). Not surprisingly, given the context of potential complaints and even legal action, therapists may well act defensively and self-protectively and consequently always stick to rigid boundaries.

Exercise

1. What are your usual boundaries in therapy? Consider such factors as time and place of appointments, touch, how you respond if you encounter a client outside therapy, self-disclosure, etc.
2. Consider the reasons for each of your boundaries. Do they fit with the approach of positive ethics, risk management or defensive practice? Are you emphasising one of these approaches at the expense of another? Do you have a rationale for each or are you just following rules?

Rubina

Rubina thought about her boundaries in the context of her voluntary sector work. She realised that she was very flexible and responsive to her clients' needs, seeing them if they were late for appointments and meeting them in cafes if they felt unsafe to come to her office base. She felt on the whole that her flexibility was appropriate to help her clients feel safe and to trust her but noted that on one occasion, when she had run over an appointment, she had been late for another client. Other times, she had ended up feeling really stressed trying to fit the rest of her work in. She reflected that perhaps she needed to think more about her needs and be clearer that she would not always be able to be infinitely flexible to suit her clients. She also noted that she had not really thought about defensive practice and wondered whether in her work all the danger and risk were located with the violent partners of her clients, and perhaps she was denying the potential risk to her from how her clients could perceive her. She decided to bring this issue up in a team meeting at work.

As we saw in Chapter 4, Barnett (2008) suggests that there are three approaches to ethics in counselling and psychotherapy: positive or aspirational ethics, risk management or defensive practice. Positive ethics emphasise maximising virtues. Risk management in contrast focuses on decreasing risks, and defensive practice focuses on the protection of the therapist. Barnett advocates an emphasis on positive ethics. However, I suggest that a mixture of all three approaches is necessary to account for our responsibility not just to the client's welfare, but also to the demands of the context of working and the needs of the therapist. What I think is important here is the self-awareness of the therapist to be clear from which approach they are operating at any particular time, taking responsibility for looking after themselves and their clients within particular contexts, so decisions which are made to protect the therapist are not justified by being good for the client. Supervision and personal therapy can help therapists both to improve their awareness of their own needs and to better understand their reasons for particular responses (see Chapter 7).

Tom

Tom considered how he responded when he bumped into his clients outside therapy. He had seen one of the young men he was working with in his local supermarket. First, he was careful to not acknowledge his client until his client acknowledged him, particularly as his client was with a friend. His client said hello and then introduced him to his friend as his 'shrink'. Tom felt a little embarrassed but said nothing. His client then looked in his supermarket trolley and said, 'I didn't have you down as a meat eater, but I guess even vegetarians like bacon.' Tom felt even more embarrassed but replied to his client that he was right that he was vegetarian and he had bought the bacon for someone else. The next time they met for counselling, his client said he had been wondering who he had bought the bacon for. Tom was uncomfortable with this level of self-disclosure and told his client this. He later reflected whether he should have disclosed so much in the supermarket and wondered if it would have been better to just laugh at his client's comment and move on. He thought that part of his reason for his boundaries around self-disclosure were risk management, particularly as his client had committed offences, and he did not want them to know where he lived or much about his personal circumstances. He also thought his boundary about self-disclosure was about preserving the therapy space for his client's material.

Dangers of preoccupation with risk management

Lazarus (1994) dared to critique the notion of boundaries, suggesting that the emphasis on boundaries reflects a preoccupation with risk management taking precedence over humane interventions. He argues cogently against the idea of any one rule applying to every client or every therapy relationship and advocates instead that therapists need to calculate risks responsibly in each individual situation. Included among the several published responses to his paper was one by feminist therapist Laura Brown (1994a: 277) who warns against 'ethical anarchy' but locates the problem in the abuse of the power inherent in the role of therapist, and in ethics in therapy being treated as an additional consideration rather than embedded within the theories and practices of therapy itself. She further advocates that therapists need to use ethical codes not as rules to be followed or broken, but to inform us for themes for consideration and interpretation, to inform 'a careful, thoughtful exploration of the combined ethical and clinical meanings of a behavior' (1994a: 278).

A major difficulty in discussions of 'boundaries' is the danger of therapists constraining ourselves to avoid potential abuse, but totally missing the danger of neglect. Zur suggests that a focus on conservative risk management 'can affect the quality of care negatively' (2007: 11). A refusal to be authentic and present in relationships can be experienced as abusive, and can result in harm. Heyward notes: 'It was becoming increasingly clear to me that abuse – damage, harm, violence – can result from a professional's refusal to be authentically present with those who seek help; and that such abuse can be triggered as surely by the drawing of boundaries too tightly as by a failure to draw them at all' (1993: 137). Heyward suggests the alternative of a mutually derived ethics rather than a rule-bound one, when discussing her experience of being a client where she felt harmed by a therapist drawing tight boundaries, saying, 'No professional rules or theory could have moved us through this passage safely. Only a mutual authenticity could have provided a safe passage for us both, and this was not to be' (1993: 160).

Exercise

1 How can you ensure that your boundaries do not increase your authority and power over your client?
2 How can we use the concept of boundaries in therapy to maximise the chance of protection and growth facilitation and minimise the chance of shutting out life-giving experiences?

Anne

Anne was interested in how she thought the concept of boundaries was sometimes used in psychodynamic therapy, with the therapist deciding what boundaries were good for the client. She noted here the authority in the therapist judging beneficence, which she felt uncomfortable with. She thought it was important to use the concept for therapists to be clear about their own limitations rather than decide what they thought the client needed, or the concept was in danger of being used to increase the power of the therapist over the client. She thought in her example of a client asking to use the telephone that to refuse would be neglectful and that she should not decide what would be good for the client, but that she needed to be clear about her own limitations. Thus, she could respond by asking the client to come in to use the telephone but being clear how long the client could stay depending on what else she needed to do.

Rubina

Rubina remembered a time when one of her clients also had a worker from the mental health team. Rubina had been upset by a telephone call from this worker asking Rubina why she had agreed to see her client in a crisis, and telling her it was important that she kept her boundaries about agreed appointment times, or she would be manipulated by her client. When Rubina had defended her decision to respond to her client's need, the worker had suggested that Rubina had acted unprofessionally and that perhaps her service would benefit from some training from mental health workers about boundaries and professionalism.

Sometimes, a human response is important, noting our shared humanity with our clients beyond our roles. Spinelli (2003) argues that however caring or concerned a therapist may be, this will not be enough unless the therapist is willing to be revealed as human. This approach follows the focus on the importance of relationships by existential philosophers such as **Buber** and **Heidegger**. The humanity of the therapist must be maintained for the I–Thou relationship of Buber.

Heidegger also speaks of the importance of humanity in relationships. He explains: 'As a physician one must, as it were, stand back and let the other human being be' (1987/2001: 211). If psychotherapy objectifies the human so that therapy becomes the technical concerned handling of objects, 'then the outcome of such psychotherapy cannot result in a healthier human being. In such a therapy, the human being is finally eliminated. At best, such a therapy could (only) result in a more polished object' (1987/2001: 215).

I argue that the effect of the rhetoric of boundaries is more likely to increase the likelihood of abuse or exploitation of clients by defensive practice and neglect (Proctor, 2010a). In the rhetoric of boundaries, the model is of an expert therapist, who can interpret and predict a client's needs, based on the traditional ethical principles from the ethics of justice of beneficence and non-maleficence (doing good and avoiding harm). Often a picture is painted of a client 'pushing' the boundaries of a therapist or 'resisting' the therapist's boundaries, and the usual advice given to therapists is of the danger of 'giving in' to the client. Heyward describes this experience as a client as: 'the trauma in having my passion treated as pushy and my pain as a manipulative ploy' (1993: 142).

The danger of boundaries is illustrated vividly by Bonovitz, referring primarily to intrapsychic boundaries, but just as applicable to boundaries in therapy: 'Throughout life there are boundaries that protect and facilitate growth of a vibrantly alive self. Then there are boundaries or invisible roadblocks that try to protect, but end up shutting out life-giving affective experiences so that what is left within is a starved, deadened and empty space encased in a brittle shell' (2006: 2).

Can boundaries actually serve to protect therapists rather than clients? House describes 'a certain obsession in the therapy world with "boundary speak" in recent years' (2003: 52). He claims that an obsession with boundaries in therapy 'is by no means a coincidence in terms of the professionalisation and commodification of therapy'. He suggests that this preoccupation reflects concern with status as a profession leading to a preoccupation with risk management and self-protection. Heyward agrees that 'professionalism is not simply a cultural attitude. It is an entire hierarchical system of value, status, and ultimately, of power' (1993: 201).

Another danger with the focus on boundaries concerns the mindless following of rules. The danger here is that both therapist and client can become so concerned with an external locus of evaluation that they lose touch with a sense of their own internal ability to evaluate and make decisions. Strict adherence to codes takes responsibility for the relationship away from the two people involved, leading to unthinking, unaware and therefore unethical practice (see Chapter 5 on the limits of ethical codes).

Reasons for flexible boundaries

Often boundaries are discussed as though their need has been established as fact, ignoring all the literature critiquing the concept. For example, Sarkar states that 'Setting and keeping boundaries helps professionals and patients be secure in their identities and roles' (2004: 312). However, there is also much literature advocating flexible boundaries and awareness of complexity in making decisions about boundaries. Gale questions the lack of flexibility in boundaries as rules, saying that this position implies 'that all people are somehow the same and require the same response. This is an attitude which is clearly damaging in the rearing of children and is no less so in therapy' (1999: 125). He criticises the idea of the necessity of a fixed time and place as concerning organisational convenience and dogma, and that what is important for the client is the reliability of the therapist and the attitude of care.

Instead of boundaries as rules, several authors emphasise the importance of clear negotiation and dialogue. Mearns (1997) advocates the concept of full involvement, distinct from under- or over-involvement, which is monitored in supervision, and that clear professional decisions are made about boundaries and limitations. I advocate the relational ethics of mutuality instead of the focus on boundaries, where both therapists and clients have needs and limitations that need to be negotiated within their respective roles (Proctor, 2010a).

Exercise

1 Consider the boundaries you listed in the earlier exercise. Are there particular situations that you think would justify your being flexible about these boundaries?
2 Can you think of situations with clients when you have been flexible with your boundaries? How can you evaluate the outcome of this and what did you learn from it?
3 Are there particular boundaries that you hold rigidly? Can you explain why?

Maxine and Tom

Maxine considered what she might do if she had a client who was suicidal, and she felt very worried about this idea. She thought she would feel so scared that her client might kill herself that she would offer almost anything to the client to try and prevent this. Tom said in response that he thought she was not allowing the client autonomy to choose to decide to end their own life if they want to and that this was disrespectful. Maxine agreed that whereas in theory she believed that we all have the right to make this choice, she acknowledged that this would upset her so much that she would try and prevent it for herself. She also felt that this was such an irreversible decision that she would want to protect the client from making a decision that could have later changed, so would feel justified in trying her best to prevent it at all costs. Tom wondered how much Maxine would offer to prevent this and asked her if she would look after a client in her own house to prevent this. Maxine was not sure if she would go that far but imagined that she might if the client had requested it and she really felt it would be the difference between life and death. Tom then continued to wonder how Maxine would deal with this if the client continued to feel suicidal and the immediate crisis became an ongoing situation. Maxine admitted she had not considered this scenario and acknowledged that if she had offered a lot temporarily she may feel unable to keep up with responding to this need or become resentful at how much she had offered. She resolved that in responding to clients' needs she would think carefully about how much she would offer in future and try and be clear about her personal limits.

Working with suicidal clients presents a particular scenario where therapists often renegotiate boundaries to respond to a crisis situation. Pope and Vasquez (2007: 259) discuss the context of working with clients who are suicidal and suggest that this is a time where the rigid boundaries of appointment times with no contact in between are inappropriate. They quote Farberow to advocate for a high degree of availability in these situations (1985: 9, cited in Pope & Vasquez, 2007: 260) saying, 'Providing this degree of availability to the client gives the client evidence of caring when that caring is absolutely necessary to convince that client that life is both liveable and worth living, and nothing less extreme would be effective in communicating that caring. In such cases all other considerations – dependence, transference, countertransference and so on – become secondary. The overwhelming priority is to help the client stay alive.' Similarly, Linehan emphasises the necessity of availability at these times, saying, 'Therapists often do not realise that when treating a highly suicidal client they must be available by phone and otherwise after hours: treating a highly suicidal client requires personally involved clinical care' (cited in Pope & Vasquez,

2007: 269). Pope and Vasquez (2007) conclude with the importance of ongoing attention to and assessment of the risk of suicide, and if the risk is present they recommend developing a crisis plan to reduce the risks in the environment, communicate hope and care, and most importantly, that the therapist must be willing to listen to the client and take them seriously.

Maxine

Maxine felt reassured by the idea that in situations of potential suicide the overwhelming priority is to help the client stay alive, which was in concordance with her values. However, she was still concerned about how to assess her own limits in these situations regarding how much she could offer.

Threat of suicide is an extreme example of how boundaries are dynamic and context-dependent, requiring flexible and thoughtful responses from therapists. Negotiating boundaries may lead to mistakes which need to be acknowledged and learnt from. Pope and Vasquez (2007) emphasise the therapist's responsibility to clarify beginnings and endings of therapy with a client, as a crucial issue in informed consent. They also stress the need for the therapist to clarify their availability and access to therapy to plan for anticipated needs of the client and to anticipate and plan for the self-care needs of the therapist. They stress that 'Reflexively applying a rigid set of rules about inflexible boundaries can never be an acceptable substitute for thinking through boundary issues for an individual client as clearly and carefully as possible' (2007: 205). Owens et al. (2012) suggest that ethical practice combines safety with creativity. They warn against a defensive practice response to complaints and the loss of safety that this can result in, leading to mindless rule following. Instead they advocate 'practical wisdom' to meet the demands of creative ethical practice that will inevitably include the acknowledgement of – and learning from – mistakes.

As counsellors, we are responsible for creating the conditions for responsible, safe and creative practice. Owens et al. (2012) use the language of frames to claim that boundaries should be for the purpose of taking care of the client, the therapist and the therapeutic space. They suggest that useful boundaries in practice are those of ethics, competence and supervision. The therapist needs to ensure freedom from interruptions as much as possible in the environmental frame. They emphasise the importance of clear and collaborative contracting for the contractual frame. Finally they consider the embodied relational frame and the importance again of the therapist's openness to respond explicitly to the changing needs of the client.

Tom

Tom thought about doing exposure therapy with a client from a CBT perspective, and whether meeting the client outside the office to accompany them doing whatever made them anxious would be seen as a boundary crossing.

Cognitive behaviour therapists have defended this boundary crossing using several arguments. These include arguing that the same ethical principles do not apply or that the boundary crossing is in the best interests of the client. Patterson and Gottlieb (2002) argue that most discussion of ethical principles in psychotherapy applies particularly to medium- to long-term approaches which involve transference. They argue that there is a different quality when treatment is short term and problem-focused, and that the nature of the therapy relationship is different in CBT owing to the collaborative nature, meaning the therapist is not the expert and the client can measure their own progress. The therapist is not aloof and is not an object for transference from the client but communicates directly, making a clear contract with the client about the purpose and process of therapy and goals to be worked on. They argue that this is a different context from which to judge boundary crossings. They still note, however, the importance of the principle of integrity and the importance for the therapist not to abuse the power differential in the relationship.

Olatunji et al. (2009: 177) note that temporary boundary crossings that occur for therapeutic purposes in exposure are distinct from boundary violations, and that crossings do not necessarily lead to violations. They suggest that the following points need to be considered before crossing the out-of-office boundary for exposure: that it is motivated by patient need, that it is consistent with the treatment plan, that it is 'sensitive to the patient's diagnosis, history, culture and values' (2009: 179) and that it is discussed with the patient in advance. They caution that therapists practising exposure need to be highly attentive to the issue of confidentiality when out of the office, and this should be discussed in advance with the patient. In conclusion, they argue that exposure is an effective treatment that can be carried out ethically with consideration.

Boundary crossings and boundary violations

The concept of boundaries describes usual practice in psychotherapy, but in most of the literature it is generally accepted that there are no rigid rules and there may be good reasons (or it may be unavoidable) to cross boundaries at times. An important distinction was made by Gutheil and Gabbard (1993) between boundary crossings and boundary violations, to make the distinction between a necessary or beneficial change to boundaries (crossing) and one where the therapist crosses a boundary for their own personal gain with a high likelihood of harm to clients (violation) (see Sperry, 1997, for definitions).

Boundary crossings are inevitable at times, such as chance meetings outside therapy. Good practice in dealing with boundary crossings includes trying to understand the significance or meaning for the client and discussing these situations in supervision (Adshead, 2005; and see Chapter 7 for more on supervision).

Some authors suggest that there is not a clear divide between boundary crossings and violations, or that crossings lead to violations. Sarkar (2004) argues for the 'slippery slope' hypothesis, citing Simon (1995) documenting a journey from increasing informality and social feel to therapy, and culminating in a sexual relationship. He suggests that boundaries refer to the distinction between the therapist's professional and personal identity and argues that it is the professional identity that is 'ultimately the therapeutic agent for the patient' (Sarkar, 2004: 313). He suggests that patients are naturally curious about the personal identity of the therapist and it is the therapist's responsibility not to indulge in excessive self-disclosure which would undermine their professional identity.

Others point out that boundary crossings do not necessarily lead to violations. Gutheil and Gabbard (1993) discuss the relationship between boundary crossings, violations and sexual misconduct. They describe the characteristic scenario (the 'slippery slope') of increasing boundary violations leading to sexual misconduct, but they are keen to point out that boundary crossings or even violations do not necessarily lead to sexual misconduct. They consider boundaries and crossings or violations with respect to role, time, space, money, gifts, clothing, language, self-disclosure and physical contact. They consider the various contexts and modalities in which the same behaviour could be considered benign or exploitative. They mention the difference between appropriate therapy technique and humanity or social conventions. Gutheil and Gabbard suggest that the difference between benign and harmful boundary crossings may 'depend on whether clinical judgement has been used to make the decision, whether adequate discussion and exploration has taken place, and whether documentation adequately records the details' (1993: 195).

Gutheil and Gabbard (1998) review the differences between boundary crossings and violations. They suggest that heightened awareness of the harmful consequences of violations has led to 'an excessively rigid and defensive posture' (1998: 409). They bemoan the consequences of this, saying 'While such excesses are often proffered as indicia of patient protection, the perversion of boundary theory may place professionals at risk for undeserved sanctions and may potentially harm patients themselves by frightening the professionals into rigidity in therapeutic interactions' (1998: 409). They suggest the pendulum has swung too far and there is a need to 'hasten the arrival of the pendulum to the midpoint between the extremes of boundaryless clinical practice and rigid overreaction' (1998: 410). They suggest that boundaries should not serve to create a remote and rigid way of relating, but external boundaries should provide a frame so that psychological boundaries can be crossed. They distinguish between boundary crossings (deviations from usual behaviour which do not harm the patient and are discussable) and boundary violations (which do harm and are rarely discussed and often repeated). They argue against the 'slippery slope' theory that boundary crossings necessarily lead to violations, although they note that when therapists do commit a violation, this is usually preceded by an escalation of boundary crossings. They stress the importance of context in distinguishing between violations and crossings on a case-by-case basis, guarding against the possibility of rules of forbidden behaviour to be applied across the board. Gutheil and Gabbard conclude: 'we are imperfect and often need to flounder a bit before we strike the optimal balance between intimacy and distance that is favorable between a particular patient and a particular therapist at a particular time in treatment' (1998: 414).

Crossings and violations: a clear distinction?

Exercise

1 How would you decide between a boundary crossing and a violation in your practice?
2 Could you decide in the practice of another therapist?
3 How do you decide whether a decision is technical or moral? Is there always a clear distinction?
4 Can good therapists commit boundary violations?

Anne

Anne said that she did not think the difference between a boundary crossing and a violation is clear, and it could only really be decided by the client as to whether it was helpful or harmful. She reflected on the difficulty of this in evaluating her own practice or others' practice and stressed the importance of getting the client's perspective. However, she felt that any sexual behaviour was clearly a violation and she felt that this was so obvious that it needed no justification.

Maxine and Rubina

Maxine thought that the distinction between technical and moral matters was similarly unclear, as all decisions involving technique also involve values (see Chapter 5 for previous discussion of this distinction). Rubina thought there may be some matters that are just moral as opposed to technique as no theory would justify particular behaviours on the part of the therapist. However, she agreed that all technical decisions involved values and therefore also fell into the moral sphere. Rubina wondered if intention mattered more than consequences (taking a **deontological** approach) in making the distinction between a crossing and a violation, with a violation being a lack of consideration of the client or prioritising the therapist's needs. She decided that assessing this would be important in judging the behaviour of another therapist. She also thought it was important for her to judge her own behaviour. When she responded to her client's request for an extra appointment in a crisis, her intention was to demonstrate her care and concern to her client; she was clear she had no self-interest, either in terms of wanting to see her client or to increase her figures regarding contact time, or prove anything to any of her client's other workers.

There is dispute in the literature about the distinction between crossings and violations or between technical and moral matters. A special issue of *Psychoanalytic Quarterly* discussed the matter specifically. In it Goldberg (2008a) discusses the distinction between a boundary crossing and a violation, suggesting the crucial point about a violation is that it describes a wrongdoing which is moral, as opposed to a mistake which is technical. Gabbard (2008) critiques Goldberg's suggestions that technical and moral matters can be distinguished, arguing that technical and ethical matters are always intertwined. He agrees that boundary crossings and violations are context-dependent. He concludes: 'Hence, part of clinical wisdom is knowing when boundaries must bend a bit to accommodate the patient and the treatment. In many cases, more harm is done by insistence on a rigid frame than by accommodating to contextual changes necessary to preserve the treatment' (2008: 881).

Greenberg (2008) also critiques Goldberg's arguments and suggests that the concept of boundary crossing has no usefulness, as it means such different things from different theoretical perspectives. He argues that 'error' is a relative term in psychoanalysis, depending on models and even within a model, and so predicting consequences of an intervention is impossible in any individual situation. However, he condemns this relativity with respect to moral matters. He defines a boundary violation as 'when the analyst's self-interest is so implicated that he or she is likely to be blinded to the impact of the proposed action on the patient. There are times ... in which the analyst's unexamined self-interest ... rises to such a level that increases the likelihood that the action will be exploitative' (2008: 888). He acknowledges that self-interest also leads to mistakes and that it is not always clear to distinguish between mistakes and violations. However, he suggests along with Goldberg that sexual involvement is an example which places self-interest firmly at centre stage. He suggests that in discussing potential violations, our language needs to be different. In these cases, we need to be telling ourselves that we cannot do something because our vision is too clouded and there is too much opportunity for exploitation. At these times, 'psychological reasoning cannot be determinative because there is simply no way – even in consultation with others – to distinguish reason from rationalisation' (Greenberg, 2008: 889). However, Goldberg criticises Greenberg's determination of boundary violations using the concept of self-interest as 'overly simplistic and unwise' (2008b: 918).

Anne and Tom

Anne thought it would not be possible to be a good therapist and commit a boundary violation, as she thought that the definition of a good therapist would be someone who would always think about their impact on the client and avoid exploitation. She similarly believed that good therapists were also good people and she understood this with respect to virtues. Tom questioned whether she thought it was possible for anyone to be 'good' all the time, either as a person or as a therapist, and he suggested that anyone can make a mistake, or remain unaware of self-interest. However, Anne felt that there was a qualitative distinction between a mistake and a violation, and maintained her emphasis on the virtuous therapist.

Gabbard considers whether particular therapists are more vulnerable to boundary exploitation. He suggests that we are all vulnerable at times of stress, and that stress 'may lead therapists who are ordinarily ethical into states of desperate neediness where the patient appears to offer some salvation from a state of despair' (2006: 41). He identifies common themes in therapy situations where violations occur, such as omnipotent rescue fantasies where the therapist believes that only they can save the patient, and identifies common occurrences as either lovesickness or masochistic surrender where the relationship with the patient will save either the therapist or the patient. He describes an example where a therapist offers more and more to a suicidal patient, trying to re-parent but ultimately being unable to give enough. He discusses prevention and first suggests regular consultation as he argues that we can always convince ourselves that in this particular case the departure from norms is justified.

Gabbard and Hobday (2012) note our tendency to want to distance ourselves from unethical practitioners. They state that after much experience with practitioners who have committed boundary violations, they believe it to be virtually impossible to predict prospectively which practitioners will go on to commit ethical transgressions. Nevertheless, they point to the 'them and us' and either/or tendency, saying, 'Our experience in this area over a number of years has convinced us that most members of the medical profession, when hearing of dishonest or unethical behaviour by a colleague, secretly or not so secretly wish to approach this entire topic with a binary distinction – namely, there are psychopaths and then there are the rest of us who are ethical and honest' (2012: 236). They suggest that acknowledging the near-universal vulnerability and complexity of ethical transgressions is too difficult to bear.

Practice recommendations in considering boundaries

Several authors provide useful guides or factors to think about when considering crossing a boundary with a client. One of the most commonly mentioned factors is the importance of consultation with other professionals as a check for any factors we may have missed such as self-interest. Pope and Keith-Spiegel stress that decisions about boundaries must be made in the context of a more general approach to ethics: 'Ethical awareness is a continuous active process that involves constant questioning and personal responsibility' (2008: 640). They further consider how stress can block our personal responsiveness and sense of personal responsibility and 'lull us into an ethical sleep' (2008: 640). They recommend guides to help therapists consider decisions about boundary crossings, such as Younggren's (2002) *Ethical decision-making and dual relationships.*

Brown (1994b), a feminist therapist in the USA, usefully suggests three characteristics of boundary violations which are exploitative, and advocates that therapists consider the possibility of each in making ethical decisions. These are objectifying the client, following an impulse (which does not consider the client's potential reactions to this impulse) and placing the therapist's needs paramount.

Each of these examples is an occasion where the relational principle of mutuality does not apply. I have suggested that to take the ethics of mutuality seriously is a big commitment, emotionally and politically: 'It requires clear commitment to our own self-awareness and to discussing our ethical decisions and ways of being with clients in open and mutual ways in supervision and with clients. This will not be an easy or safe process' (Proctor, 2010a: 52). Heyward also notes that 'In our most creative, deeply mutual possibilities, we become dangerous people ("dangerous" in that it threatens to transform us and the ways we work and love)' (1993: 171). Furthermore, she notes that 'People cannot live this way without strong relational networks of support and solidarity' (1993: 167).

Pope and Keith-Spiegel (2008) list seven common cognitive errors when considering boundary crossings. The first is to think that what happens outside therapy has nothing to do with therapy. The second is to think that crossing a boundary with a therapy client has the same meaning as doing the same thing with someone who is not a client. The third error is that the client will understand the boundary crossing in the same way that the therapist does. The fourth error is that a boundary crossing that was helpful for one client will also be for another. The fifth error is that the boundary crossing is an isolated event. The sixth error is that any individual therapist can envisage all relevant features to a decision without needing to consult. Finally, the seventh is that self-disclosure per se is always therapeutic.

Given that boundary crossings are inevitable, there is always the possibility of unforeseen adverse consequences. Pope and Keith-Spiegel (2008) consider what to do if a boundary crossing goes wrong. They suggest a therapist needs to be open and non-defensive, listening carefully to try and understand the situation from the client's perspective. Further, they suggest that the therapist continue to monitor and document the situation and seek consultation from colleagues. Finally they suggest that if the therapist believes they may have made a mistake, to consider apologising.

Exercise

1. What might alert you to consider that a boundary crossing could be a mistake or a violation?
2. How would you deal with this concern?
3. What could protect you in making decisions about working creatively with flexible boundaries?

Tom

Tom thought about one of his clients through the youth offending scheme. He explained that he had been concerned about how down his client was and so had texted between sessions to ask if his client was OK. His client had not replied and Tom had become increasingly concerned. Tom then tried calling his client's phone, which was then answered by someone else. Tom asked for his client and the person who answered the phone asked who he was. Tom realised that he could not answer this owing to confidentiality, so said 'just a friend' and then got to speak to his client who replied very quickly that he was OK and had to go. His client did not turn up to his next scheduled appointment and failed to respond to letters. Tom had felt very upset about this situation and felt sure that his decision to try and contact his client was the reason for him dropping out of therapy. He hypothesised that his client had been very scared that his friend who had answered his phone would work out who he was and that his client would be furious with him for putting him in this position. Tom noted that he thought this boundary crossing was a mistake as it was in response to Tom's needs for reassurance as opposed to his client's needs. He vowed to negotiate clearly in advance regarding contact between sessions in future.

Maxine

Maxine suggested that discussing boundary crossings in supervision and documenting reasons for decisions would be important to protect therapists from being blamed for unforeseen consequences of flexible working. She also thought that the most important protection for her would be to know that she was working in accordance with her values, which she had carefully considered, so if she was ever found guilty of a violation she would at least know that she had not betrayed her own values.

Anne

Anne decided that her commitment to her own self-awareness was the most important thing, bearing in mind that it would always be limited by her unconscious, so she could always make mistakes.

Summary

This chapter has discussed diverse theories and approaches to the concept of boundaries in therapy. I have questioned who boundaries protect and explored the dangers of defensive practice. I have discussed the concepts of boundary crossings and violations and whether this is a useful distinction. I hope it has enabled you to think about your position with regard to boundaries in general. The following chapter examines particular boundary issues in more depth.

TWELVE Particular boundary issues

Introduction

This chapter considers particular boundary issues in more depth. I examine specifically the issue of touch, receiving gifts, working from home, dual relationships and sexual relationships with clients and ex-clients.

Touch

Exercise

1. When might you consider or have you considered touching a client? Would you have any concerns about this? How would you deal with your concerns?
2. As a client, when would you like a therapist to touch you? When would it feel inappropriate for a therapist to touch you? Imagine or consider this from your own experience.

Anne

Anne discussed her experiences of touch when working with children and said she felt there were different issues here compared to working with adult clients. She thought that the meaning of touch would usually be different when perceived by a child compared to an adult client and that touch from a therapist would be more likely to be perceived as reassuring, comforting or caring for a child, with more potential for misinterpretation of touch as erotic between adults. As soon as she had said this, she then thought again and wondered if this distinction would necessarily be the case and wondered whether she should be more concerned about children who had experienced sexual abuse misperceiving touch as sexual.

Tom

Tom, in discussion with Anne about the differences in perception of touch in therapy between adults and children, added that he thought that dynamics of power were crucial to consider and that therapists of all clients needed to be careful as touch could be an act of authority and power. He remembered his psychiatrist patting him on the shoulder on the way out of an appointment when he was 18 years old and thinking that although he felt sure the psychiatrist had meant this as a gesture of comfort and reassurance, Tom had experienced it as authoritative and patronising.

Some authors take a position of advocating no touch in therapy, either for theoretical reasons or as defensive practice. In classical psychoanalytic practice, no touch is advocated, with the suggestion that responding to a need for touch would remove the opportunity for a client to experience and analyse the lack of this response. Gale (1999) questions this necessity for abstinence from touch in classical psychoanalytic practice. He suggests that responding to a request for touch from a client does not prevent also working through the emotions which led to the need for touch.

From a humanistic perspective, Casemore (2001: 115) states clearly that he tells counsellor students in training that they should never touch a client. He justifies this injunction by defensive practice. However, he then contradicts himself, adding, 'That is not to say that in reality clients should never be touched. There are bound to be times when it will be appropriate' (2001: 117). He further suggests that any impulse to touch a client should be carefully thought through and ideally discussed in supervision.

Others emphasize the potential benefits of touch in therapy and stress the importance of ethical responsibility in this area. Syme (2003) considers the reasons and range of responses to touch in therapy. She emphasises the importance of therapists exploring these with the client and in supervision. Yalom (2001: 187) identifies fear around touch for therapists because of the association between touch and sexual relationships. However, he entitles his chapter on the subject 'Don't be afraid of touching your patient'. In fact, he makes a point of touching clients, because of the therapeutic benefits. Bonitz (2008) discusses both the importance of avoiding exploitation and the importance of therapeutic touch, and proposes guidelines for therapists in the use of touch. These include the following: the therapist should have a clear rationale for using touch; touch should be for the client's benefit rather than the therapist's; touch should be embedded in a larger therapeutic context and within a strong alliance and used cautiously; the client should be asked for permission; the client's reactions should be monitored; and the meaning of the experience for the client should be explored. Furthermore, the therapist needs to be comfortable with touch, have training and knowledge about touch, use supervision to discuss it, and be familiar with ethical guidelines and any local regulations.

In Proctor and Keys (2013) we present an example of factors to consider when deciding whether to touch a client in a particular therapy context. Factors we consider include: the autonomy of the client; the power dynamics in the relationship and whether the client would feel able to ask for touch; the quality of the relationship and the potential for misunderstanding; the ability of the relationship to withstand and discuss any potential misunderstanding; and the therapist's emotional responses to the client in the moment in the context of the therapist's views and experiences with touch. We suggest that all these factors need to be considered in addition to awareness of ethical codes and particular institutional rules, and discussed in supervision, as well as monitoring the impact on the client of whatever decision the therapist makes. We stress the fluidity of such a decision, emphasising that the response may be different at a different time or with a different client, depending on the multitude of factors involved.

Receiving gifts

What are the ethical considerations and implications of accepting gifts from or giving gifts to clients?

Exercise

1. Have you ever been given a gift by a client? How did you respond and what was the consequence of your response? What do you think was the significance or meaning of the gift for the client and what was their perception of your response?
2. Have you ever given a gift or wanted to give a gift as a client to a therapist? If so, what was the response, or if you wanted to and did not, what did you imagine their response would be? How did this response impact on you?

Anne

Anne thought about a recent experience on a placement counselling children when one of her clients had brought a painting that he had done for her of the two of them. She had immediately accepted this gift, thanking the child and appreciating the thought and effort that had gone into creating it for her. In considering this, she became aware of how much she had responded as humanly as she would to one of her own children painting a picture for her, particularly knowing that this client had parents who were uninterested in him. However, she reflected that she had missed an opportunity to consider further with the client the meaning of this gift for him, what it represented for him and what he had hoped for in giving it to her. She also wondered if her easy acceptance and appreciation of his thought in giving her something may encourage him to give her more gifts that may cost him money, and place her in a more difficult ethical dilemma of whether to accept the gifts. However, she was glad that she had not given her client any reason to think he had done anything wrong in giving her this gift and reflected how hard it would be to question it further without this message being implied.

Rubina

Rubina reflected on her experience of wanting to give a gift to her client at the end of therapy. She described what had felt to her as a deep and meaningful connection with her client, who had reported great benefit from Rubina's care and understanding. In their work together, the metaphor of a key to unlock her inner wisdom and knowing was used a lot and was particularly meaningful to the client. Just before the end of therapy, Rubina had come across a small gold (but inexpensive) key in a jewellery shop to hang on a necklace or bracelet and immediately thought of her client, feeling that she would have loved to give it her at the end of therapy as a symbol and memory of their work together. However, she mentioned this idea in supervision and her supervisor immediately warned her of the potential for misunderstandings from the client of the meaning of this gift and recommended to her that gifts should be avoided in therapy. In thinking about it further now, Rubina thought that this had been a missed opportunity between herself and her supervisor to explore the possible meanings of this gift and possible consequences of discussing this with her client or even giving her the gift. She felt that the discussion in supervision simply alerted her to a rule that she should follow rather than enabling her to reflect ethically about her behaviour. In thinking further about it now, she wondered how to decide what would count as inexpensive, as she realised in describing the key as not expensive, that this was relative to her perception of expense; she noted that in this case her client had less money than she and may judge the key as expensive whether or not she told her how much it cost. She thought that as a result the client may be embarrassed to receive an expensive gift or think that she may owe Rubina something in response. However, Rubina decided that all of her worries about how the gift could have been perceived could have been discussed with the client and they could have considered together whether her intention (of her client feeling cared for and having a reminder of their important relationship) could be received without conflict. She did wonder whether she could have found a card with a picture of a key on it which would have felt easier to give at the end of therapy, although she was still aware that the meaning for the client and her intention in giving it would need to be discussed. She concluded with frustration that it was just so hard to spontaneously be caring in counselling!

Gifts can have many different meanings depending on the individuals involved and the therapy relationship. Some authors caution against accepting gifts, whereas others suggest taking creative ethical responsibility in response. Syme (2003) discusses the many meanings potentially involved in clients giving gifts and the dilemmas involved for therapists being part of both a personal and a professional relationship. She concludes that 'there is such richness in the language of gifts that I believe that provided the therapist is aware of the need for the therapy relationship to be non-exploitative and recognises that boundaries are being changed then the language of gifts is there to be explored creatively, not prohibited through fear' (2003: 50). Szasz (1965/1988) considers accepting gifts or favours and suggests that the analyst must not comply with social convention but instead must analyse the conduct. However, he does allow that if a patient brings a small gift the therapist may accept it so as not to make the patient feel inferior by refusing it. The ultimate value by which the therapist decides how to respond is what would increase the autonomy of the patient.

Maxine

Maxine worried about the impact on a client from a therapist refusing a gift and how embarrassed or humiliated they could feel as a result. She thought she would want to be human and graciously accept a gift with the meaning intended unless the gift was extortionate.

Every situation will be unique and requires consideration of all relevant factors and possible consequences. Brendel et al. (2007) suggest that abstract moral principles provide insufficient guidance to specific situations and propose 'clinical pragmatism'. They suggest that therapists 'focus ethical deliberations as to whether or not to accept a gift on the specific results of that decision for that particular patient in question, not merely on abstract moral principles' (2007: 44). In particular they recommend focusing on the patient's best interests and the practical result for the patient of accepting or declining the gift. They also note that the client needs to be part of this discussion. They consider the following factors in each individual context: the gift's meanings for the patient, the purpose of the gift, the type of therapy, aspects of the patient's disorder and personality, the gesture's part in the transference relationship, the patient's perceptions of the therapy, cultural expectations regarding gifts, and the patient's social and economic situation.

Working from home

Are there particular ethical implications of working from home as a therapist? Given that this is likely to involve the therapist divulging more information about themselves than if they worked in an office outside their home, can these boundary changes be helpful or harmful?

Exercise

1 What concerns might you have about working from home as a therapist? How could you deal with these concerns?
2 How would you feel about going to see a therapist in their own home?
3 Do you think working from home is an ethical issue?
4 Do you think it is the therapist's responsibility if a client sees them at home and later reports that this was damaging?

Rubina

Rubina considered the idea of working from home and thought this would exacerbate the difficulties she already has, owing to the overlapping worlds of herself and her clients. Her in-laws, who she lives with, are well-known within her community and clients visiting her at her house would compound the common focus she finds when meeting new clients of discussing connections between their respective families. She decided she feels more comfortable having some distance between her personal life and professional life by working in an office away from home, and she thought that this would give her more choice of how much to respond to questions about her personal life than if she were to work from home. On the other hand, she thought she would feel fine about seeing a therapist as a client at the therapist's home. She wondered if it would make her more interested in the therapist's personal life, but she was clear she would not ask anything as she would not want to intrude on the therapist's personal, private life.

Anne

Anne considered the idea of working from home, realising she had always assumed this would be what she would do, as it would be most convenient for her. She wondered how she would deal with confidentiality with her children and ensure no interruptions; she also thought about the lack of sound proofing on the room she had intended to use and realised that this meant her clients would potentially hear her children playing. She was ambivalent about whether this felt possible to be aware of and discuss in therapy if it seemed relevant to particular clients, or whether it would distract her and embarrass her to have to deal with information about her private family life. She decided she needed to do a lot more thinking about whether working from home was the best way forward for her.

Although working in an office at home is common practice for counsellors and psychotherapists, some authors – particularly from a psychodynamic perspective – advocate against working from home to avoid giving so much personal information about the therapist to the client and thus crossing boundaries. Maroda (2007) suggests that the defensiveness of many therapists when she questions this practice points to their feeling guilty. She begins her argument against offices at home saying, 'Because we all struggle at times with maintaining the proper boundaries, it seems reasonable to select an environment that does not blur them at the outset' (2007: 174). She suggests that therapists wanting a home office may be fulfilling the therapist's needs such as wanting to be revealed to their patients, or wanting their patients to admire or envy their lifestyle. Working from home *may* be convenient for therapists, but the therapist's needs are important too (Mills, 2007). Self-awareness about what needs are fulfilled for the therapist by this choice is essential.

Maroda is clear that she is for self-disclosure from the analyst, but that this should be at the patient's request and in their control: 'Patients naturally want to know their analysts, but the timing and nature of the pursuit of that knowledge varies enormously from patient to patient. An essential ingredient in traumatic or destabilising events is the element of control' (2007: 175). However, the patient can never have complete control over what happens in the therapy relationship, and the dynamics of this power and control are always an issue that can never be obliterated; there can be unforeseen intrusions or interruptions to therapy, wherever the therapy office is located (Mills, 2007).

Maroda (2007) questions whether clients will be able to freely disclose their reactions to being in the therapist's home, suggesting this will be potentially difficult due to the guilt of feeling that the analyst has not done this on purpose, so cannot be blamed. Gargiulo advocates making any interruptions or intrusions to the setting part of the therapy discussion, saying, 'If the analyst has not created an atmosphere in which a patient's most positive and/or negative feelings about an analyst or the therapeutic process can be talked about, then something quite essential is lacking in the process' (2007: 717). He argues that 'experimentation must be encouraged, not as an alternate to responsibility but rather as an example of professional responsibility' 2007: 718–719). He suggests we need to be more comfortable with mistakes rather than search for an idea of 'the truth'.

Working from home will have an impact on anyone else who lives with the therapist, and clients may have concerns about this. Maroda (2007) further discusses the potential effects on family members of the analyst working from home and the patient's potential worries about this. She ends with a call for therapists to question this practice, and investigate the effects of office location on complaints and malpractice suits.

Maxine

Maxine thought this debate was interesting and the issue was much more complex than she had originally thought. She had seen her ex-therapist (now her tutor) at her home and had not thought much about the impact of this on her therapy. She now realised that she probably knew more about her than she would have done if she had used an office elsewhere, in particular about her style in furnishing her house and that she has a husband and a cat. However she never met her husband and was not particularly interested in knowing anything more about her. She felt her therapist had neither been secretive about her life nor forced it on her, and Maxine had felt comfortable with where they had met. She felt her therapist had made her therapy room comfortable and soothing and that this had felt to be part of her care for her clients which Maxine appreciated. Maxine thought that working from home being convenient for the therapist did not mean this was a bad or unethical thing, and she believed it to be important for the therapist to consider their own needs to then be able to be there for the client's needs. She also reflected that working from home had probably made her therapist more flexible in responding to Maxine's requests for changes in appointments or extra appointments in a crisis, as she did not have to consider the availability of an office elsewhere. She thought this was a situation that may be beneficial to therapists and clients alike.

Dual/multiple relationships

Dual or multiple relationships occur when there are additional relationships besides the therapy relationship between the therapist and client.

Definition

Dual relationship: '... a one-to-one contracted therapy relationship between an individual in the role of "client" and one in the role of "therapist" which then overlaps into a non-therapy context or role. The overlapping occurs when there is a current therapy relationship, or before the therapy relationship has formed, or beyond its cessation. The non-therapy contact is friendship, social, sexual, collegial, financial or business oriented.' (Gabriel, 2005: 1)

The existence of a dual relationship is a major cause for complaints in therapy. Phelan (2007) examines ethical violations as grounds for membership expulsion from major counselling, psychology and social work organisations in the United States, reporting that the most common reason for expulsion between 1996 and 2006 was under the category of dual relationships, particularly those of a sexual nature.

Exercise

1 What experience do you have of multiple roles as a therapist or as a client? What were the difficulties and what helped negotiate the complexities?
2 What do you think about therapists agreeing to move to the role of supervisor with a client? What might the difficulties be with this move and how could they be negotiated?
3 What do you think about a client having the same therapist and trainer or supervisor and trainer? What might the difficulties be for client and therapist/supervisor and others in the training group? How could these be negotiated?

Maxine and Tom

Maxine decided at this stage on the course that she really should discuss her relationship with her course tutor who was previously her therapist. She felt safe enough in one-to-one discussions with Tom to disclose this, although she had not previously discussed this within the training group. She ensured that he agreed not to repeat their discussion with any other training group members or the tutor before explaining the situation. When Maxine first explained the situation, her first thoughts about the effect of this on her were positive. She said that knowing the tutor as her therapist first gave her confidence that the course would be beneficial and gave her validation that the tutor thought she would be up to being a counsellor. She reported that they had met each term to discuss the impact of their changing role and that she had never had any concerns about her tutor maintaining confidentiality concerning material that Maxine had revealed in therapy.

Tom was surprised to hear Maxine's news and considered the impact on the group about that relationship being unknown to others, and wondered whether the tutor had exhibited any favouritism towards Maxine as a result of their former relationship. Maxine felt angry at this suggestion, and was quick to defend her tutor from the possibility of being biased in this way. Tom then pointed out that Maxine's defensiveness of the tutor could also impact on her experience of the course and that perhaps it would not be helpful for her to be unable to be critical of the tutor. Maxine considered this idea and thought this may be true and wondered how much she idealised the tutor as a result of her previous therapy relationship. However, Tom continued to think about this and postulated that many of the students idealised the tutor anyway just because of her role as tutor. They discussed further and agreed that the situation was complex and could have difficulties and benefits but that what was most important was ongoing discussion about the ramifications of such a decision. Tom suggested that perhaps these discussions should take place within personal development groups, in training as there could be ramifications for the rest of the group, and Maxine agreed to discuss this possibility with the tutor. Tom privately had concerns about the power that the tutor had to influence Maxine and her inability to decide for herself if she wanted to discuss this in the group. He was unsure whether Maxine was protecting her tutor or herself from disclosing this information.

Various models and writers have different approaches to the idea of dual relationships – ranging from absolute condemnation to context-dependent, 'proceed with caution' approaches, to an emphasis on the benefits of dual relationships. Langs (2004) is clear that psychoanalytic psychotherapy requires a secure frame, and that dual relationships would severely rupture the therapy relationship. Schank, Slater, Banerjee-Stevens and Skovholt (2003) quote the American Psychological Association codes (2002), which caution psychologists against multiple relationships, 'if the multiple relationship could reasonably be expected to impair the psychologist's objectivity, competence, or effectiveness in performing his or her functions as a psychologist, or otherwise risks exploitation or harm to the person with whom the professional relationship exists' (Schank et al., 2003: 183). This is clearly from a belief about a psychologist as a scientific objective observer but usefully reminds us to consider not just harm to a client but also the ability for a therapist to continue in their role for the benefit of the client.

There is evidence that dual or multiple relationships are not rare. Anderson and Kitchener (1996) conducted a survey of psychologists to ask about non-sexual post-therapy relationships between psychologists and former patients. They concluded that psychologists are dealing with a wide variety of relationships with former patients, including friendship, social interactions, business, professional, supervisory, religious and workplace, which could be either circumstantial or intentional.

Practitioners and the literature are mixed about the ethics of such relationships, identifying potential difficulties and benefits. Reasons for seeing these relationships as ethically problematic include: the impact of special knowledge about the former client, the inability for the client to return to therapy, a power differential still existing, the possibility of confidentiality being broken, different rules negotiated in different roles, compromised professional judgement, a conflict of interests for the therapist, potentially undoing good achieved in therapy, and the continuation of transference or dependence from therapy. Reasons for seeing these relationships as not ethically problematic included: discussed and clear roles, enough time passed since termination of therapy, unplanned, confidentiality maintained, necessity to or inhumane not to change relationship, peer consultation, therapist took responsibility to maintain boundaries, and no harm was caused to the former client (Anderson & Kitchener, 1996; Hedges, 1997; Shillito-Clarke, 2000b). Furthermore, potential benefits include: greater creativity, more reflective of real life, can be therapeutic, and recognition that abuse and exploitation (not dual relationships) are the problem (Hedges, 1997; Tudor, 1999). Hedges warns of the dangers of focusing on dual relationships per se: 'The misplaced focus by licensing boards and ethics committees on dual relationships when damaging exploitation is the issue has meant that therapists can no longer simply consider what such events ... may mean to a client in the context of therapy' (1997: 235).

The dual roles of supervisor and trainer, or therapist and trainer, have been discussed in the literature, mainly in terms of the difficulties of these dual roles. Heru (2006) discusses the difficulties for supervisees in disclosing in supervision with a trainer who also has an evaluation role. Syme (2003) discusses difficulties if tutors are also therapists to students. She notes the difficulty in the tutor's evaluation role regarding the students' psychological maturity and ability to be a therapist and how this judgement would be affected by knowledge from being the students' therapist. She also notes that if the tutor is only a therapist to some students, there is a risk to these students of favouritism or being penalised. Either way, there can be an effect on the whole group. She suggests a time gap of at least a year before completing therapy and starting a course with a tutor who was the therapist, and says it is essential for the training group to know about the previous therapy relationship. She also considers the dual relationships of supervisor/therapist and suggests it is possible to change roles with attention to difference in roles, potential pitfalls, monitoring the impact and a gap between the change.

Tom

Tom thought to himself about Syme's advice on the training group knowing of a previous therapy relationship with a student and tutor and how this had not happened with his tutor and Maxine. He wondered about discussing this with the tutor directly but decided to ask Maxine's permission first.

Inevitability of dual relationships

Rubina

Rubina thought about the inevitability of dual relationships in her work, where she regularly came across her clients in social family settings. As she could predict this, she usually discussed this possibility with new clients and planned how they would deal with this, and she reassured them of confidentiality. She did not think these dual relationships were a bad thing as she experienced that often clients were more likely to trust her when they knew her position in their community, once they were reassured about confidentiality. It also meant that they did not feel it necessary to explain particular customs or values of their culture. She did think that sometimes this could be difficult for her, as she could never completely relax at social events where she may bump into her clients.

When dual relationships are inevitable, the following considerations are suggested: knowledge of codes and the law, discussions about boundaries with clients in therapy, awareness of impact on power dynamics, ongoing consultation, making sure contact outside therapy occurs in the public eye, self-knowledge and the therapist getting their needs met in relationships outside work (see Hedges, 1997; Hill, 2000; Schank et al., 2003). Hill concludes, 'Perhaps the psychotherapeutic professions should be seeking solutions to the very real ethical dilemmas of multiple relationships by pushing to be as accommodating of them as possible rather than slamming the door against them in sometimes crude and arbitrary efforts to eliminate risk' (2000: 157). Hedges (1997) advocates that panels judging therapists in these situations should be made up of expert consultants who can demonstrate advanced understanding of the complexities of dual relationships, particularly with respect to the transference/countertransference relationship.

Younggren and Gottlieb (2004) suggest a checklist of questions for practitioners to consider when contemplating multiple relationships, to protect both the client and the therapist. First, they ask whether the dual relationship is necessary; second, whether it could cause harm to the client; and third, whether it could potentially be beneficial. They then ask if there is a risk that it could disrupt the therapy relationship and finally whether the therapist is able to evaluate the matter objectively. They then list further questions to manage risk if the therapist decides to proceed with multiple relationships, concerning adequate documentation of the decision-making process, informed consent, consultation and the relevance of diagnosis and the therapy model.

Relational capacity and responsibility

Negotiating the potential benefits and pitfalls of multiple relationships takes a high level of ethical mindfulness. Gabriel (2002, cited in Gabriel, 2005) asked therapists and clients about their experiences of being in dual or multiple relationships. She found that dual relationships could have powerful beneficial or detrimental outcomes. She suggests that relational capacity is important for therapists and clients to negotiate the complexities involved in multiple relationships.

Definition

Relational capacity: 'Being robust enough to deal with relational ambiguity, conflict and stress.' (Gabriel, 2005: 137)

Whilst codes emphasise the therapist's responsibility for the therapy relationship, examples of successful dual relationships involve both therapist and client taking responsibility. Gabriel further stresses our responsibility to assess the client's relational capacity in these situations, noting that 'we need to be especially vigilant about a client's capacity to care for self in a dual relationship situation' (2005: 138). She also mentions the 'relational integrity' of both parties, which she clearly associates with intentionality.

Definition

Relational responsibility: '... both partners actively and consciously collaborated to manage the relationship'. (Gabriel, 2005: 139–140)

Gabriel further notes that relational responsibility points to the interpersonal and intersubjective nature of therapy, yet she still emphasises the therapist's responsibility to check out the client's understanding and awareness of the relationship. There is still asymmetry in the relationship - the practitioner has responsibility as the 'boundary rider' or 'process sentinel' to track the limits and ethical edges, to guard the integrity of the relationship (Gabriel, 2005: 152). Gabriel suggests that 'to be aware of "self" and "other" and to be able to distinguish these states is a critical ability for the therapist in a dual relationship' (2005: 17). Communication and awareness skills are involved, requiring ethical literacy.

Definition

Ethical literacy: '... not only a comprehensive understanding of the bases upon which decisions and actions are taken, but also a knowledge of the philosophical premises that underpin them.' (Gabriel, 2009: 17)

Gabriel (2005) uses the analogy of the ethics warrior on a quest through the unknown, and stresses that all warriors require sustenance and replenishment intellectually, spiritually and emotionally. She warns of the reflexivity and courage required, saying:

> Navigating our way through appropriate relational depth and avoiding over-involvement in the client–therapist relationship will probably require a deep understanding of self and self-in-relation. ... With the depth, intensity and mystery of I–Thou relating (Buber 1937), we will constantly tread the edges of our awareness. Perhaps it is stating the obvious to say that this demands an intensely aware and reflexive way of being in relation to self and others, as well as the courage to navigate the perimeter of our relational understanding. (2005: 34)

Maxine

Maxine liked the idea of relational capacity, responsibility and integrity, and felt that she and her tutor had been responsible in how they had negotiated the multiple roles in their relationship. She felt that the tutor had taken responsibility to check out her understanding of the relationship and the effects on her, and had been the 'boundary rider', but that Maxine had felt an involved and respected part in the negotiations.

Sexual relationships with clients

Sexual relationships with clients have always been seen as the most serious boundary violation, and ethical codes of all therapy organisations in the UK and US are clear that sexual relationships with current clients are prohibited.

Exercise

1 Do you think sexual relationships between therapists and clients are always wrong? If so, why? Which approach to moral philosophy are you using to justify your answer?
2 Can you imagine a society where sexual relationships are seen and understood differently and where sexual relationships between therapists and clients would not necessarily be wrong? If so, what would be the differences?
3 How would you judge a therapist who has a sexual relationship with a client? What do you think the consequence should be if such a complaint was upheld and why? Would the appropriate outcome vary depending on circumstances?
4 What do you think about sexual relationships between a therapist and their supervisor? Or between a therapist and their trainer or tutor?

Maxine and Anne

Maxine and Anne immediately agreed that a therapist is unethical to have a sexual relationship with a client. Maxine stated that this would be harmful and wrong – even abusive – because of the power in the position of the therapist. She considered that this could be an **intuitionist** response (it immediately feels wrong) and a **consequentialist** one (likely to lead to harm), and a **Kantian** decision (the therapist is treating the client as a means to an end for their own self-interest).

It is often assumed in the literature that all therapists will agree intuitively that sexual relationships with clients are wrong. For example, Ford states: 'It is obvious to any mental health professional that engaging in such behaviour with a client is unprofessional and unethical' (2006: 113).

Sometimes the prohibition against sexual relationships with clients is justified by the high likelihood of this resulting in harm for the client (a rule-consequentialist approach). For example, Syme (2003) defines sexual relationships with current clients as 'the absolute limit' and defines them as necessarily abusive due to the dynamics of power. She states that few therapists sexually abuse their clients, and many who do, acknowledge they did wrong and harmed their clients. She justifies this absolute prohibition by the statistics concerning the likelihood of harm to clients. The difficulty here is who decides harm and how this can be predicted. Sarkar (2004) emphasises that the Royal College of Psychiatrists (2002) is clear that harm is determined by the meaning of the behaviour to the patient and not the intentions of the therapist. In research, not all clients who have had sexual relationships with their therapists say this was harmful (although 90% do) (cited in Syme, 2003: 22).

Some argue that sexual relationships with clients go against the duty ethics of **Kant**, with the therapist using the client for their own needs. Sarkar (2004) offers a rationalist perspective on boundary violations in the philosophical tradition of Kant. He argues that boundary violations particularly involving sexual relationships are against Kant's ethical imperative, and suggests this is the reason for harm. He argues that doctors who abandon their professional relationship for their own needs fail to respect the autonomy of their patients. He asserts that due to the power imbalance, it cannot be claimed that a sexual relationship could ever be mutual; a client can only merely assent as opposed to consent and such a relationship must therefore always be about the therapist using the client for their own needs. Sarkar suggests that an occupational hazard for a psychotherapist is to be always alert for idealisation, seductiveness and neediness in the patient. He concludes that violations occur when in response to these situations therapists 'choose action over reflection' (2004: 318).

Anne

Anne added that she thought a sexual relationship between a therapist and a client is wrong owing to the transference relationship. She thought that because the context of therapy is likely to provoke strong transference feelings in the client for the therapist, the therapist would be taking advantage of this situation if they were to pursue a sexual relationship. She thought it was important in therapy to try and understand the transference, not to act on the basis of it.

Sometimes the prohibition against sexual relationships with clients is justified theoretically – usually with reference to the psychodynamic concept of transference. For example, Gabbard and Peltz argue that whether or not a patient and analyst are happy in a romantic relationship is irrelevant and that this 'in no way mitigates the exploitation of transference inherent in sexual boundary violations' (2001: 669). The difficulties here are in applying this theoretical assumption to other models of therapy (see Lazarus and Zur, 2002) and also that within psychodynamic theory, transference can occur in all relationships, not just in a therapy relationship, so many relationships could thus be defined as exploitative. Furthermore, there is variation within psychodynamic theory about how much to stress or work with the transference, as opposed to the real relationship, and it is not usually assumed that any particular interaction is always due to one or the other of these aspects of relationship. In fact, the concept of transference originated with a client's erotic feelings towards a therapist. Freud first issued the injunction against sexual relationships with clients, originally describing Breuer's client's erotic feelings towards him as transference. Even when the injunction is justified by theory, behind this is a moral philosophical justification, either of **consequentialism** or **deontology**. Potential harm is implied either directly or through an inability for therapy to continue in a useful way.

Other theoretical or technical explanations emphasise the unique context of the therapy relationship, both in terms of the likelihood of this context promoting sexual feelings and the particular context for the meaning of these feelings. For example, Owens et al. emphasise the importance of reflection in supervision on the therapist's sexual feelings towards clients, stating that, 'Because therapy is a unique relationship, sexual boundaries and erotic feelings have different meanings than in ordinary life situations. The people concerned are not "just two adults": they are adults in a relationship where everything is given meaning related to the therapeutic process' (2012: 82). Furthermore, the context of therapy is set up to promote intimacy between therapist and client, a situation only usually shared by close friends or partners. Yalom (2001) similarly emphasises the uniqueness of the therapy situation, and the likelihood of sexual feelings from clients to therapists occurring because of the level of attentiveness they receive.

Tom

Tom was interested in the idea that sexual relationships with clients were always wrong and was convinced this was due to the particular associations we have in society with sexual relationships. He wondered whether this would be different if sexual relationships did not have such an association with exclusivity, possession, power and control. If people generally felt a lot freer to have sexual encounters with people without these dynamics being involved, he wondered whether in these circumstances, sexual relationships would necessarily be so detrimental to therapy.

Maxine

Maxine could not imagine such a situation and feared that whereas some people might think these dynamics would not be involved, this could not be assumed for everyone. She thought the world would have to be a very different place for there not to be power dynamics between men and women. Tom did acknowledge that he was thinking hypothetically and that his point was that it was not sexual relationships per se that were the problem; it was the power and control that was the problem.

There have been different responses to the issue of sexual relationships between therapists and clients over time. Schoener (1989a) surveys the history of literature on sexual relationships between therapists and clients and notes the varying responses over time. Schoener (1989a) describes the increase of experimentation with physical and sexual contact and sex therapy in the 1960s and 1970s and then the backlash from feminism. He considers Chesler's (1972) chapter about women who had sexual relationships with male psychotherapists and her contention that this mirrored the patriarchal power in society, thus defining this issue as a political issue in society far beyond the ethics of the profession of therapy. From the 1970s, various prevalence studies demonstrated a sizable minority of (predominantly male) psychotherapists who stated they had had sexual relationships with (predominantly female) clients, and many knew of clients who had previously had such relationships. In most of these studies, there was a high likelihood of harm reported by either the clients or the subsequent therapists of these clients. Luepker and Schoener stress the connection with power, saying, 'Sexual involvement between client and therapist is one example of the abuse of power that occurs in some psychotherapeutic relationships' (1989: 65). Brenner notes that 'Given the fact that we usually associate boundary violations with sexual transgressions, it is important not to lose sight of the role of aggression in such cases' (2006: 50). Sexuality is often associated with issues of power and control as the rape situation makes clear, meaning that dynamics of power are crucial to consider.

Rubina

Rubina thought about sexual relationships between a therapist and their supervisor or trainer. She decided that the important issue was the dynamics of power, as Tom had pointed out. She thought that both trainers and supervisors had positions of power over supervisees or students, and therefore sexual relationships were likely to be exploitative in a similar way to those between therapists and clients.

The American Psychological Association ethical codes (2002/2010) explicitly forbid sexual relationships between evaluating supervisors and students. Heru (2006) mentions the codes set out by the American Psychiatric Association (2001), where sexual relationships between supervisors and trainees were deemed unethical if an abuse of power can occur, if the patient care is affected or if a relationship of trust is damaged. She recommends explicit discussion of sexual feelings in supervision to prevent acting on these feelings. This demonstrates the particular US context and culture of supervision, where it is seen as a training activity, not as continuing professional development, as it is in the UK. Syme (2003) considers a change from supervisory to sexual relationship in the UK context, stating that she believes there is no reason not to change after discussion and ideally consultation with another party.

Sexual relationships with former clients

Exercise

1 Do you think a sexual relationship with an ex-client is always unethical? If so, why? If not, how would you decide whether this is ethical or not?
2 How do you judge the ethics of a social relationship or friendship with an ex-client?
3 What do you think the risks could be to an ex-client of beginning a sexual relationship with their ex-therapist?
4 What do you think the risks could be to the therapist of beginning a sexual relationship with their ex-client?
5 What about the ethics of a sexual relationship between a therapist and their ex-supervisor or former tutor or trainer? How about a social relationship or friendship?

Maxine and Tom

Maxine was horrified that people could consider that sexual relationships with former clients might be ethical. In her experience of going to see a therapist, she thought that one of the factors that helped her feel safe was knowing that a sexual relationship was not possible during *and* after therapy. She felt very strongly that this should be a fixed rule and that therapists should not go into the profession if they are not prepared to follow this rule.

Schoener agrees with Maxine that 'Post-therapy romances or sexual relationships are hazardous for the client, the professional and the field of psychotherapy. ... Persons thinking of working in the field should note that being a psychotherapist ... may preclude making social or romantic contacts during the course of one's work. If you do not want to observe these limitations you should enter some other field' (1989b: 286–287). He further suggests that the lack of clarity about this issue is 'appalling'.

Tom said to Maxine that what she felt was right for her was not necessarily the case for everyone else, and he wondered if her fixity about this reflected her fear about the issue. He thought about his friendship with a nurse who he had met when he was a psychiatric patient in a community mental health team and she was a student and had done some relaxation training with him. They had chatted about attitudes to life and she had introduced him to Buddhist philosophical ideas when he had mentioned his thoughts about accepting his feelings. He had subsequently gone along to meditation classes at the Buddhist centre that she had recommended and met her there. They began to meet for coffee shortly after and became friends. He reflected that he did not feel there was a power imbalance between them now as a result of how they had originally met and that they equally discussed each of their lives. He also noted that they had not actually discussed the impact on their friendship of how they had met and he vowed to do this when he next saw her. As a result of this experience, Tom felt open-minded about social and even sexual relationships with former clients.

Maxine thought about Tom's experience and wondered how different it could have been if he had been a woman and the nurse a man. Tom noted that he was not sexually attracted to his friend who had been his nurse, but if he had been he did not think that how they had met would be a reason to not pursue a sexual relationship. He did wonder if this would be different if their genders were the opposite way round and thought this could have exacerbated the existing power dynamics due to different roles.

There is variation in how codes treat the issue of sexual relationships between therapists and former clients. The American Psychological Association (2002/2010) states that this is unethical for a period of two years after termination of therapy, which also used to be the code of the British Psychological Society (BPS). The APA adds:

> Psychologists who engage in such activity after the two years following cessation or termination of therapy and of having no sexual contact with the former client/patient bear the burden of demonstrating that there has been no exploitation, in light of all relevant factors, including (1) the amount of time that has passed since therapy terminated; (2) the nature, duration, and intensity of the therapy; (3) the circumstances of termination; (4) the client's/patient's personal history; (5) the client's/patient's current mental status; (6) the likelihood of adverse impact on the client/patient; and (7) any statements or actions made by the therapist during the course of therapy suggesting or inviting the possibility of a posttermination sexual or romantic relationship with the client/patient. (2002/2010: 14)

The BPS Code of Ethics and Conduct now states that psychologists must:

> Refrain from engaging in any form of sexual or romantic relationship with persons to whom they are providing professional services, or to whom they owe a continuing duty of care, or with whom they have a relationship of trust. This might include a former patient, a student or trainee, or a junior staff member. (2009: 22)

The BACP Ethical Framework does not have a prohibition against sexual relationships with former clients. Instead it states:

> Practitioners should think carefully about, and exercise considerable caution before, entering into personal or business relationships with former clients and should expect to be professionally accountable if the relationship becomes detrimental to the client or the standing of the profession. (2013: 6)

Similarly, the UKCP Ethical Principles and Code of Professional Conduct states:

> The psychotherapist undertakes to take into account the length of therapy and time lapsed since therapy and pay great attention

> to exercise reasonable care before entering into any personal or business relationships with former clients. Should the relationship prove to be detrimental to the former client, the psychotherapist may be called to account to the charge of a misuse of their former position as the former client's psychotherapist. (2009: 3)

COSCA's Statement of Ethics and Code of Practice states:

> 7.2 A member must not exploit a client, financially, emotionally, sexually or in any other way which does not give attention primarily to the best interests of the client.
>
> 7.3 A member's responsibility not to exploit a client extends beyond the termination of the working relationship with the client. (2007: 9–10)

The lack of clarity in ethical codes about this issue is much discussed in the literature, particularly in the US. The proposal for a complete injunction against sexual relationships with former clients causes some controversy. Schoener (1989b) notes the legal difficulties that have arisen when an outright ban has been considered, concerning an infringement of the rights of consenting adults. Bersoff (1994) argues against the ban of sexual relationships after therapy as he argues that this would go against the ethical principle of respecting the autonomy of the patient and represents a paternalistic attitude to former clients. Gabbard (1994) responds by saying that this same argument is not used against prohibiting sexual relationships with current clients and is similarly misguided in considering sexual relationships with former clients. He argues that given the evidence of a high likelihood of harm resulting to former clients in these circumstances, it would be prudent to prohibit the possibility. Gabbard and Peltz (2001) summarise the reasons for a prohibition against sexual relationships with former patients. The first reason is that transference persists beyond therapy; the second is that the power differential persists. Third, the integrity of the therapy process would be compromised if either party thought that a sexual relationship could follow termination. Fourth, many patients return for further therapy following termination.

The change from a therapy relationship to a sexual relationship can also be difficult to predict and not turn out as either party expects, given their therapy relationship. Brodley (2011a) considers the difficulty of moving from a therapy relationship into a personal relationship. She notes that clients and therapists are 'at their best' in therapy. Furthermore, 'The client's presentation of his worst characteristics is responsible, humane, critical, undefensive, and reflective in the therapy situation. Demands upon the client by the therapist are very circumscribed' (2011a: 45). She warns against therapists deceiving themselves that this relationship can hold up in other situations, and asserts that once the functional equality of therapy has gone, the inequality reasserts itself. The consequences are likely to be that 'The client loses a good therapist and is likely to get hurt when he finds he cannot hold up his end of the relationship (even if the therapist friend is not holding up his end either)' (2011a: 45). On the contrary, she suggests that it is much easier to move from being friend/lover to being in a therapy relationship as you are already aware of each other's personal limitations, and the therapy relationship can be an improvement!

The move from a therapy relationship to a sexual relationship is unpredictable in terms of its impact on both client and therapist. It is clear that it is the therapist's responsibility to prove lack of exploitation and that the unequal power relationship of therapy no longer exists in these situations. The issue of the client then being unable to return to therapy needs to be considered. There is also the potential risk of harm to the therapist if the client complains if the relationship ends (Luepker & Schoener, 1989; Schank et al., 2003). Schank et al. stress that 'These kinds of factors, therefore, make such relationships high risk' (2003: 186).

Others suggest that the change in relationship is possible without harm if care is taken. Syme (2003) mentions the problem of unresolved transference and therefore continuing inequality of power in sexual relationships between therapists and ex-clients. She refers to the likelihood of harm leading to extreme caution in considering changing relationships from a therapy relationship to a personal or sexual relationship. She does however suggest that it is possible for a therapy relationship to change to a personal and sexual one without harm to either party, and notes the possible existence of transference in all relationships.

Others suggest particular circumstances when sexual relationships with former clients are more dangerous or unethical. Gonsiorek and Brown (1989) propose that such a relationship is always unethical when: therapy is long-term and is transference-based, clients are severely disturbed or have a history of childhood abuse (due to particular vulnerability to sexual exploitation), the therapist initiates post-therapy romantic contact, or when a post-therapy relationship begins in under two years after termination of therapy. In situations other than those covered by the above exclusions, they clearly place the responsibility on the therapist to prove that no exploitation has taken place and suggest that this decision should be taken under consultation. They summarise their position saying, 'It is our belief that in most cases, post-termination sexual relationships are probably unethical and harmful to clients' (1989: 301). Schoener (1989b: 278) similarly warns against such relationships, but suggests several key factors in evaluating a post-termination relationship. These are: length and level of therapeutic involvement, power inequity remaining after treatment, the vulnerability and dependency of client and therapist, the presence of therapeutic deception, the clarity of termination, who initiated post-termination contact, discussion of pros and cons of such a relationship, whether consultation has been obtained, and consideration of the legal and professional context.

Younggren (2002) and Younggren and Gottlieb (2004) offer some potentially useful questions for therapists to ask when considering any dual relationship. They suggest that these questions help in deciding ethical practice both by minimising harm to the client and managing risk to the therapist. Questions include establishing who benefits from the dual relationship, checking the effect on therapy, and the client's consent to the dual relationship.

Rubina

Rubina did think it would be possible to move from a therapy or supervisory or training relationship to a more equal personal or social relationship if each person involved was aware of the dynamics of power and able to reflect on these and discuss them. She did not want to think that she would always be seen as a client by an ex-therapist and thought that this possibility allowed for change and growth in relationships. She thought that the main issue was the avoidance of exploitation. One of her ex-clients was now part of her closer social circle, having married one of her extended family members. They had discussed this transition and she felt this change in their relationship had been successful.

The importance of consultation and supervision is stressed for therapists to discuss such transitions (Shillito-Clarke, 2000b). Issues to explore in consultation include: the issue of confidentiality and how an ex-client would be introduced to other people in the therapist's life; considering the possibility of the relationship ending badly; and the therapist examining why this dilemma has arisen with this particular client, and if it regularly arises, why this could be the case.

Summary

This chapter has examined particular boundary issues in more depth. I considered specifically the issue of touch, receiving gifts, working from home, dual relationships, and sexual relationships with clients and ex-clients. I have focused specifically on dual relationships and sexual relationships with clients and ex-clients, because of the importance of these areas in complaints against therapists. I have suggested that often therapists' actions are assumed to be wrong without adequate consideration or justification, and I hope that this chapter will help the reader be clearer about their thoughts and feelings concerning these issues and the values which inform their decisions.

THIRTEEN Conclusion

In this book, I have tried to present the perspective that there is never any one ethical 'right' answer to any situation in counselling and psychotherapy. Rather than this ethical relativism leading to an 'anything goes' mentality, it actually leads to a greater necessity for personal ethical responsibility. Each of us is responsible for being aware of our own values and beliefs and being able to articulate their relevance in relationships. The 'students' have illustrated a variety of perspectives and dialogues between these perspectives, and we have charted the development of their ethical ideas through their own interactions with each other, their experiences in counselling and life, and their relevance to moral philosophy and academic theory in counselling. As such, I argue for pluralism, ethical mindfulness and narrative ethics, to emphasise the importance of being able to articulate a narrative of how and why we make the ethical decisions we do.

Research, writing and training

Research, writing and training are other activities which involve the same questions, considerations and awareness about self, others, values, ethics and competence. Reflexivity in research particularly emphasises the importance of ethical responsibility to take account of oneself as a researcher (see e.g. Etherington, 2004). We can ask ourselves the same questions as we would about our practice as therapists in each of these contexts: what are our aims, who do we want to be and how do we want to be in relationships with others? As with therapy, dynamics of power in each of these contexts are particularly relevant, between trainers and students and between researchers and participants. How we behave in respect to the power in these roles is always a question of ethics and values, and as with therapy, no decision about this can be justified purely technically, as behind any technical decision lie the values influencing the adoption of particular technical practices.

Our students

Exercise

1 What have you enjoyed and learned from this book about yourself and your values?
2 How are these relevant to your practice as a therapist?
3 Are there particular issues that you want to commit to addressing further in your self-development?
4 What philosophical concepts or ideas have you found most useful that you may want to research further?

Each student wrote a short reflective piece, detailing what they thought they had enjoyed and learned at the end of this module on values and ethics. To follow this spirit of dialogue and mutual learning, the tutor did the same.

Anne

Anne had realised the extent to which her identity revolved around caring for others, particularly being a mother, and how much this was related to her socialisation as a woman. However, she also valued this part of her identity and felt it reflected her values and ethics about love and care, and found the ethics of care useful to understand her approach to relationships. She liked **Kierkegaard**'s ethic of love and **Levinas**'s approach to responding to the call of the other, but felt that the **care ethics** fitted best for her, in describing preferential relationships for those close to her.

She had realised that she had not prioritised her own needs and self-care for a long time and had learned the importance of this in being a therapist. She had realised how much she expected herself to be able to cope with anything without needing anything herself. She had learned from **De Beauvoir** that at times she had lost her subjectivity in most of her relationships and vowed to regain it, and attend more to her own needs and interests, promoting her own creativity and spontaneity. She also wanted to discuss gender roles with her husband and think with him about how they could each widen their roles to role-model increased gender possibilities for their children.

In counselling, she found Bond's ideas of relational trust useful, to help her focus on looking after her own needs to be able to be trustworthy for clients. She had enjoyed thinking about her values and ethics in the context of her interest in psychodynamic theory and had found it useful to apply moral philosophy to justify her belief in tentativeness in offering interpretations, particularly **Levinas**'s injunction against totalising. She had also begun to realise how much she identified with parental concerns about children, which made it difficult for her at times to empathise with children, and she vowed to try and stop her fears for safety prevent her hearing and understanding the concerns of her own children and others that she worked with.

Maxine

Maxine clarified how crucial a value it is for her to live life free from oppression. This involved having fun and having her decisions respected and valued by others. It was equally important in her values for others, and was the bedrock of her ethical decision-making as a counsellor. She had really valued reading about the **social intuitionist** approach to ethics, and had found it validating of her experience that emotions and intuitions were far more important than logic and rationality. She thought both these priorities for her were interesting in the context of her being a woman, and her experiences of being oppressed and her emotions being invalidated. She had also begun to realise that she wanted to better prioritise her friendships with other women to make sure she did not lose their importance when she had another relationship with a man.

She found the idea of the **care ethics** and of relational trust useful to focus on relationships rather than autonomous individuals. She realised that in her priority of being free from oppression she had grown to mistrust relationships, rather than see them as growthful or life-enhancing. She maintained her belief in the importance of the counsellor being responsible for their own self-care and self-awareness, stressing the asymmetry of the therapy relationship and the importance for the client of not having to take care of the therapist. She liked the idea of putting together the concepts of ethical mindfulness with relational integrity in her approach to ethics. The relational approach also helped her to see her clients more as people in relational networks rather than isolated individuals.

She enjoyed reading **existential philosophy** to help her understand her own values and ideas, and particularly liked the idea of authenticity. She was beginning to realise how much her own values arose from her own experiences and how sometimes she was quick to anger and judge when others disagreed or threatened what she held dear. She vowed to work on this in supervision and in her own self-awareness. She was also aware what a sensitive subject suicide was for her – a situation where her most deeply held value of respecting autonomy was under threat by her belief in preserving life, or fear of feeling responsible for not saving another's life. Again, she was determined that she would be alert to this situation and make sure she spent time in supervision thinking about her responses when such situations arose.

Maxine had enjoyed working with her ex-therapist in the new setting of her being her tutor, and felt they had negotiated this change successfully while valuing their relationship. However, she had explored further how their previous therapy relationship had impacted on her experience as a student and also considered that this may have had an impact on the training group. In considering whether to tell her tutor that she might disclose this information to the training group, she was worried that this could harm her relationships with some of the other students and that perhaps her tutor would not like her to disclose this information. However, by the end of this module, she was clear that it should be her decision whether to disclose. She decided she would discuss this further with her tutor first to maintain the trust in their relationship and then discuss it in her student group the following term.

Rubina

Rubina had struggled a little with the counselling course until they got to this module on values and ethics. She had found much of the counselling theory very individualistic, with little attempt to understand the client in the context of their lives and relationships. She was heartened to discover a wealth of theory in moral philosophy and ethics that was much more relational in its focus. She struggled with the individualist focus in principle ethics but felt much more comfortable with the principles of autonomy and beneficence when she understood them in the context of existential philosophers such as **Heidegger** and **De Beauvoir**, which focused on us always in relation with others. She particularly liked **Levinas**'s concept of heteronomy (starting from the other) and thought this could usefully replace all the principles in principle ethics. Together with care ethics, she found Levinasian ethics reassuring, in terms of validating her values and priorities regarding caring for others and not beginning with herself.

She was pleased that relational approaches also resonated with the other students, and that she was not alone in this emphasis, which had often been her experience in everyday life. She was re-evaluating too the benefits of having grown up in a marginalised culture and negotiating responses to cultural messages from her family and from the dominant culture. Although this had been difficult as a teenager to work out her own identity, she now realised the benefits of the thinking she had done and the self-awareness she had gained from such close consideration of the origins of her values and clarity about her choices.

Rubina was left still feeling hurt by Maxine's judgement and anger towards her about issues of confidentiality in domestic violence. She had not felt supported by the tutor in this situation or by the other students and the result of the change of subject by the tutor had been to leave her with this hurt. Rubina did not like the awkwardness which she felt remained between her and Maxine and she resolved to speak to Maxine personally about it when they next met.

Rubina also realised at the end of this module how little she had mentioned her religious beliefs, which surprised her, given the importance of Islam to her ethics. She noted how little religion had been discussed in the module and wondered how significant this omission was. She also felt disappointed that all the moral philosophy presented was Western and she thought that they could have all benefitted from applying Eastern moral philosophy in the same way. She felt sure that this would have brought up many more discussions of the relevance of spirituality and religion to ethics and values. However, she was aware that she probably also silenced herself, given the climate of Islamophobia in society at large, and felt sad how much she kept quiet about the importance of her religion for fear of judgement and prejudice and not wanting to set herself apart from the other students. She decided she should prioritise this issue in her own self-development and that she would discuss it at work with other Muslim workers who had completed counselling courses, before considering raising the issue on the course.

Rubina was pleased about the climate and support she got where she worked, particularly having heard the thoughts and experiences from the other students in different places. She decided that the cultural context in flexibly responding to clients' needs suited her personally, despite the difficulties in her overlapping personal and professional worlds. She concluded that on balance, clients knowing of her through family connections increased their trust in her and improved counselling relationships, and she felt comfortable in being open about her personal life whilst also being clear that her focus was on her client. She did consider that perhaps if she was not so happy in her personal life or if she experienced a personal crisis that her clients learned of, this situation could perhaps become trickier, but she was confident that she would have the support and supervision she needed in her workplace to negotiate this situation if necessary.

Tom

Tom had really enjoyed the module on values and ethics as he had found it helpful to think about theories that brought together his view of himself and his political commitments. He had enjoyed thinking about justice in more detail, and valued the idea of equity rather than equality. He thought the ethics of strangers was really important to be able to consider issues of access in counselling. He had generally enjoyed the debates and learning about philosophy and wondered whether he might do a course on philosophy when the counselling course ended, as he found it useful to help understand himself and others. He was particularly interested in reading more about **Habermas**' discourse theory of morality, making rational decisions in dialogue with equal participants, and its relationship to ideal democracy and working politically. He also wanted to follow up **Jaspers**' ideas of responsibility for oneself and solidarity with others and commitment to working against oppression; he found this combination of the personal and political particularly apt.

He was quite surprised at the role he had found himself playing in the student group. He had begun the module seeing himself as an emotional person, yet had frequently found himself defending rationality and impartiality during the discussions. He had begun to realise how much his socialisation as a man had given him these values and he had started to wonder how relevant this was to his struggle with accepting or trusting his own emotions. He resolved to address this further in his own therapy.

He had been disappointed the module had not included more Buddhist philosophy, but was happy how relevant he had found it in his own thinking. He was pleased how the third wave of CBT approaches that he was attracted to valued both rationality and emotions, which fitted well with his approach to ethics.

Tom was left feeling uncomfortable at the end of this module about what Maxine had told him regarding the tutor being her ex-therapist. He felt suspicious of the tutor's reasons for not addressing this in the training group and was sad about this as he had really respected how she was in every other way as a tutor. He felt uncomfortable knowing something that he felt he could not bring up in the group, particularly when he thought it may be relevant, and really hoped Maxine would decide to disclose this information in the training group when they next met.

Tom found his experience of being a psychiatric patient invaluable in his exploration of ethics, particularly regarding his experiences of powerlessness in this context, and the difference when someone treated him with some respect. Tom was interested in the big focus on boundaries in counselling and how little he had thought about the potential for abuse in this context. He wondered whether this was due to his experiences of being exploited and seeing abuse in many guises within the psychiatric context, and knowing that the concept of boundaries was no protection at all against this. He was even more convinced that it was the attitude of the worker that mattered, and their commitment to addressing inequalities of power and valuing and respecting clients. However, he also realised that he had not thought much about power inequalities with respect to gender in relationships, and vowed to think about this much more in his own self-development.

The tutor

The tutor really enjoyed the module on values and ethics and was pleased how much the students had engaged with debates and really started to reflect on their own values and take responsibility for their own decisions, which was one of her key priorities in training. She had particularly enjoyed reading much more about Levinas than she had done previously and was convinced of the relevance of heteronomy to counselling and all relationships.

She had been interested in the varying responses from students and the relevance of their social positions to these responses. She had been interested to see the relevance of gender with Tom being the only man in the group, and noted how he had followed the male stereotype by emphasising individuality and rationality as opposed to the focus on relationships by the women. She had also noted the impact of Anne being the only parent in the group and how her self-awareness had increased with regard to the impact of this on her and what the others had learned from her experience. She had been aware of Rubina's position as the only student from a Black or Minority Ethnic group and had tried to ensure that she had taken responsibility to introduce issues of difference and inequality with respect to 'race' and culture. She hoped that Rubina had not felt this had all been left to her and that she found the group to be receptive and understanding of her position.

She thought more about how it had been for her to have Maxine as a student, having previously been her client. She was aware sometimes of more self-consciousness than usual in how she was being perceived, particularly by Maxine, and not wanting to let her down by being a worse tutor than she had been a therapist. This was not the first time she had had an ex-client as a student and she was used to holding disclosures from therapy confidentially.

However, she had found it particularly difficult when Maxine had been angry with Rubina, and she knew that the subject had touched Maxine personally. She wondered whether her protectiveness of Maxine at this point had led her to miss the impact on Rubina of this exchange. In discussing Syme's (2003) suggestion that their previous therapy relationship should be discussed within the whole training group, she wondered if she had been remiss in not suggesting this to Maxine. She had not thought this was appropriate to preserve Maxine's confidentiality but after discussing the issue in the module, she decided that when she met with Maxine to discuss the issue she would bring up the possibility to see what Maxine thought about it rather than assume she would not want to discuss this in the group. She felt confident to be able to defend her decision if she was challenged by anyone in the group and was reassured by the diversity of opinions presented when they discussed this issue in theory.

Summary

In this book, I have explored the relevance of 'doing ethics' and 'being ethics' to ethical decisions in therapy. I have emphasised the importance of a relational approach to ethics, respecting both the client and the therapist as autonomous people within relational contexts. I have suggested that dialogue, mutuality and negotiated meanings and decisions are a crucial part of ethical mindfulness and relational responsibility and integrity.

I hope this book has been a guide to help you consider your personal values and their relevance to your practice as a therapist. I also hope that it has introduced the relevance of western moral philosophy to the various approaches to ethics, to aid understanding of the foundations of ethical frameworks or codes and previous contemplation on the nature of being human and the nature of morality. I hope I have raised far more questions than suggested answers, and emphasised the role of emotions and intuition in ethical practice as well as rational critical thinking. The unpredictability of human relationships is inevitable, given the dynamic nature of being human and the limits to our awareness. I hope this book has been clear that any attempts to systematise or make rigid rules about these relationships in therapy do not do justice to this unpredictability. I hope I have inspired you the reader to embrace this unknown with excitement, curiosity and a commitment to making ethical decisions with responsibility, creativity and resoluteness.

APPENDICES

Philosophical movements and philosophers

Appendix A: Philosophical movements or concepts

Absolutism

Absolutists state that there are universal standards or principles, and attempt to explain how we can reach them.

Analytic philosophy

In traditional analytic moral philosophy, the function of theory and moral principles is to combat the selfishness of individuals thus leading to a policing role of ethics. Analytic philosophy dominated philosophy in English-speaking countries in the twentieth century, often following a focus on logic. It is contrasted with existential or continental ethics.

Care ethics

Jaggar (2000) describes the best known example of developing ethical theory beginning with the experience of women, which is the ethics of care (Gilligan, 1982). The ethics of care values emotional sensitivity, responsiveness to the needs of particular others, intimacy and connection, responsibility and trust. Although these values are generally associated with the domestic sphere, feminist ethicists following Gilligan (1982) propose that these values should become more prominent in ethical theory and in society at large. The moral subject in the ethics of care is relational, situated and embodied. An approach to moral reasoning in care ethics involves empathy, openness and receptiveness to unique others in specific situations. It involves no general principles or idea of universality.

Consequentialism

Consequentialist, utilitarian or teleological theories are a branch of **empiricist** theories, focusing solely on observable behaviour. Such theorists argue that an action is morally right if the consequences of the action are more favourable than unfavourable; thus ethics are judged purely by consequences, with motives being irrelevant. This idea originated with Bentham, and the main approach to this considers how favourable consequences are for everyone (it is also termed utilitarianism). 'Favourable' has been interpreted in diverse ways by various philosophers. Traditionally it was defined as happiness, but Mill (1871/1998) suggests that virtue, knowledge, truth or beauty should also be considered. Moore describes the principle of 'ideal utilitarianism', suggesting that consequences should be judged on all considerations that are intuitivcly recognised as good or bad, not just happiness. Mill adds to the principle of the greatest good that of justice – the greatest distribution of good or the greatest good for the greatest number. Mill (1871/1998) also suggests that, rather than each act being judged in isolation according to utilitarian principles, rules can be judged by these principles and then applied (rule-utilitarianism). So, for example, rather than deciding on each occasion whether it is right to steal something, instead the rule about whether it is right to steal or not can be judged according to the favourability of consequences and then this rule applied. Mill did however worry about the tyranny of the majority under this system, and believed that happiness was more than individual pleasure, and included cultural and spiritual happiness from seeing the happiness of others. Distribution-sensitive rule-consequentialists consider fairness in addition to wellbeing, although Hooker (2000) argues that it is unclear when unfairness trumps wellbeing. Despite this, he argues that although having two values to evaluate is messier than rule-utilitarianism, distribution-sensitive rule-consequentialism is more plausible. Critiques of consequentialism point out the difficulties of defining happiness or pleasure for another beyond a tautological definition of 'something to be aimed for'.

Contractarianism

Contract theorists (such as Hobbes, Locke, Rousseau, Hume and Kant) span **rationalists** and **empiricists**. They focus on the idea that human nature is flawed and untrustworthy and that contracts between a ruler and those ruled are necessary for mutual security against each individual following purely their own self-interests, and to curb the selfishness of human emotion. Thus they argue that each individual cannot be trusted to be moral alone and a structure of societal organisation helps to ensure morality. Contract theory is based on the idea of citizens giving consent to rulers and the moral obligation to keep to these agreements.

Deontological theories

Deontology refers to philosophy focusing on duty. Deontological philosophy focuses on motives as opposed to consequences. Kant is a deontological philosopher.

Empiricism

Locke and Hume are empiricist philosophers. For Locke, passion or emotion drives action, and reason only assesses but does not initiate action. Similarly for Hume, emotion motivates us, whereas reason informs us to consider potential consequences. Hume suggests that the basis of knowledge is in experience and observation, as in science. He describes how impressions (raw experiences or perceptions) give rise to ideas and this provides data for reasoning. Although he allows that inductive reasoning and inference are untrustworthy and can lead to errors, he holds that the most we can hope for is to eliminate mistakes by trial and error and to gain a closer approximation to the truth.

However, the distinction between **rationalism** and empiricism is not quite so clear-cut. Rachels suggests that reason also shapes and sustains attitudes and emotions: 'Thus moral judgments express attitudes, but not just any attitudes: they express attitudes that are evoked and sustained by the deliberative process' (2000: 81).

Existential/continental philosophy

Existential philosophy includes the philosophy of Kierkegaard, Nietzsche, Heidegger, Sartre, De Beauvoir, Husserl, Merleau-Ponty, Jaspers, Buber and Tillich. Existential philosophy is particularly concerned with existence as opposed to essence – the way we as whole beings encounter the world, as opposed to splitting us into component parts or studying us as universal abstract entities. Van Deurzen-Smith describes existential thinking as 'an attempt to think about everyday human reality in order to make sense of it' (1997: 1). Key themes in existential philosophy are life and death and being always in relationship.

Continental ethics describes a similar group and focus to existential philosophy, elaborated by mainly non-English-speaking European philosophers in the twentieth century. Continental ethics focuses on helping individuals to ethically flourish 'to awaken and enliven – to energise people to ethical creativity' (Schroeder, 2000: 396). Continental thinkers 'seek to produce an awakening – as if people all-too-often sleepwalk through their lives. Duties, imperatives, rules and regulations only deepen the daze (which one might call ethical death)' (2000: 396). Continental ethicists want to inspire people by higher values, and light the spark of ethical creativity.

Intuitionism

Intuition was given a central role in philosophy by Descartes, who defined intuition as 'the conception which an unclouded and attentive mind gives us so readily and distinctly that we are wholly freed from doubt about that which we understand' (1955: 7). McNaughton (2000) describes intuitionism as a species of **deontological** theories. He explains that intuitionists such as Sedgewick believe that some moral duties are 'self-evident'. He suggests that the terminology of intuitionism is misleading, as it is not used here to refer to judgements about what we are inclined to do, and intuitionism does not imply that there is a mysterious faculty by which we detect moral properties. Instead, McNaughton (2000) refers to intuitionism as the approach to rationalism that was popular in England between the two world wars, with Ross (1930/2002) being a key text to systematically describe the intuitionist theory.

Moore argued that goodness is indefinable but immediately recognisable by intuition. McMahan defines an intuition as 'a spontaneous moral judgment ... not the result of conscious inferential reasoning' (2000: 94). He argues that intuitions are immediately compelling, in a way that rational moral theory is not. Posner (1995) stresses the role of emotion as moral data, particularly the emotions of disgust and revulsion which determine what people believe to be morally wrong more than any rational argument. He argues that many situations require immediate action where deliberation is not possible, and only intuition can be relied upon. He further suggests that any moral theory without intuition is in danger of describing rules or situations that bear no relation to what we recognise as morality. MacIntyre explains the difficulty with intuitionists, saying, 'they are, on their own view, telling us only about what we know already. That they sometimes disagree about what it is we already know already only makes them less boring at the cost of being even less convincing' (1966: 254).

Phenomenology

This is the study of subjective experience and consciousness. It originated as a philosophical movement with Husserl in the early twentieth century and is an important philosophical root of humanistic and existential therapy. Intentionality is a term in phenomenology referring to consciousness *of* something, whatever consciousness is directed at. Phenomenology was developed by Heidegger and influenced **existential** philosophers such as Levinas and Merleau-Ponty.

Rationalism

Rationalist theories focus on using reason to make ethical decisions, whereas **empiricists** focus on using the information from senses. Much of philosophical debate between rationalists and empiricists is on the primacy of reason or emotion. Rationalists believe that morals and ethics are the field of reason, its role being to curb emotion, passion or self-interest. Aristotle and Plato believe that reason is the route to work out the best route to the good life. For Plato, senses are not to be trusted, as they can give us only impressions of the ideal real forms or purpose of things. Moral principles should be discovered by reason, whose role it is to guide the will to control the appetite of passions. Kant, Descartes and Spinoza are also rationalist philosophers. Kant regards empiricism, information gained from the senses, or *phenomena*, as highly suspicious evidence to use in moral decisions, saying, 'everything empirical is not only quite unsuitable, as a contribution to the principles of morality, but is even highly detrimental to the purity of morals' (1785/1994: Book 1: 34).

Relativism/postmodernism

Relativists or postmodernists suggest there is no right or wrong, purely competing accounts that we all try and justify in relationships. Relativists suggest that all may make different decisions and no account or decision can be pronounced more 'right' or 'true' than any other. Others

(Kierkegaard, Levinas, Derrida) take the lack of moral pronouncements further, suggesting that each ethical decision is a singular and new event in relation to another, and there is no status for any rules or principles to apply, but that each situation must be dealt with afresh and with responsibility. Caputo (2000) claims that situations involving ethical decisions are always unprecedented but that this does not lead to an 'anything goes' approach, but instead to more responsibility. Whereas following rules would be easier, instead: 'I must respond, be responsible, in a deep and radical way' (Caputo, 2000: 118).

Poole (1972: 116) traces back the idea of relativism to Protagoras who Plato tried to refute in Ancient Greece. Protagoras's famous quote is that each of us is the measure of all things. Poole suggests that Protagoras was referring to how each of us has a different perspective on everything. However, he does not suggest that Protagoras is advocating that all opinions and judgements are equally valid. He promotes the idea of 'deep subjectivity', where the whole is not reduced to the parts and the aim in analysis is to consider as many perspectives as possible and be clear about the criteria that we use to judge possibilities.

Any statements that are not true in all contexts at all times are relative. The relativist position can either be general ethical relativism or ethical subjectivism. In both, there are no universal ethical standards but, in ethical relativism, each society has its own and no one society can judge another as being better or worse. Montesquieu (1689–1755) first stressed the extent to which the values of an individual depend on the society to which the individual belongs. However, Montesquieu also proposes that there are eternal norms by which all societies can be judged. Ethical subjectivism goes further, saying that each individual has their own standards and we cannot judge each other.

Social intuitionism

Social intuitionism is one model which explains how reason and intuition interact and that reasoning can affect how we perceive and intuit in future situations. Haidt (2001) argues from this perspective that we generally make moral decisions based on emotions and intuitions and then use reason as a post-hoc rationalisation or justification of our action or decision. He presents evidence to show that moral intuitions (being affect-based) come first, are more powerful, are made automatically and usually lead to our moral judgements. Moral judgement is socially functional rather than truth-seeking (Haidt, 2007). Furthermore, judgements are an interpersonal process, with evaluations based on cultural norms. He argues that reason has been overemphasised and that reasoning processes are motivated by non-rational reasons such as avoiding cognitive dissonance and preserving internal coherence in one's beliefs, or preserving relationships with people by agreeing with them. Reasoning is usually 'employed only to seek confirmation of pre-ordained conclusions' (Haidt, 2001: 822).

In contrast, moral intuitions are sudden appearances of moral judgements without awareness of a reasoning process. Haidt (2001, 2007) argues that reason *can* affect moral judgements, either in rare circumstances where people can override their intuition with logic, which may happen where intuition is weak and processing capacity is strong, or in private reflection where reason can activate new intuitions. New intuitions are most likely to be activated in conversation with others, however, as an intersubjective process.

Thus the place of reasoning ability becomes much less important in moral behaviour. Emotional and self-regulatory factors are more powerful determinants of behaviour, and emotions such as empathy, shame, guilt and remorse provide motivation for moral action.

Appendix B: Timeline – List of philosophers by date of birth

469 BC Socrates

↓

428 BC Plato

↓

384 BC Aristotle

↓

301 BC Stoics

↓

...

↓

1596 Descartes

↓

1632 Spinoza

↓

1724 Kant

↓

1770 Hegel

↓

1813 Kierkegaard

↓

1844 Nietzsche

↓

1859 Dewey

↓

1877 Ross

↓

1878 Buber

↓

1883 Jaspers

↓

1889 Heidegger

↓

1900 Gadamer

↓

1905 Sartre

↓

1906 Arendt

Levinas

↓

1908 De Beauvoir

Merleau-Ponty

↓

1919 Hare

↓

1921 Rawls

↓

1929 Habermas

↓

1930 Derrida

Appendix C: Philosophers listed alphabetically

Arendt (1906–1975)

Hannah Arendt fled the Nazi regime in East Prussia in 1933 and ended up a citizen of the US. Much of her work (influenced by Husserl, **Heidegger** and **Jaspers**) concerns these experiences, examining totalitarianism and political systems. She argues for plurality and the dangers of mass society and suggests that thinking is a safeguard against evil. She argues that 'thinking could also liberate the capacity for judging particulars' (Bernasconi, 1998: 481). Rather than freedom being the will of a solitary individual, 'Freedom belongs to the sphere of human plurality, where action is inspired by principles, rather than being guided by motives, and power is a relation that springs up between people acting in concert, rather than being something that belongs to each individual as such' (Bernasconi, 1998: 482).

Aristotle (384–322 BC) see Classical Greek philosophy

Buber (1878–1965)

Unlike previous philosophy which was interested in the relation of humans to the external world of objects, Martin Buber contends that to be human is to be more than relating to objects: it is to relate to other beings. He contrasts I–It relations (treating another as an object) with I–Thou relations. Buber contends that the essence of being human is to be in relation with another human, recognised as such as a subject, or end in itself, rather than merely a means to an end or object for the first human. He discusses how each human being is formed in 'natural association' (Buber, 1923/1970: 76) with another in the mother's womb, and how from the point of birth, the infant human longs for relation, and is given time to exchange the natural association in the womb with 'spiritual association' (1923/1970: 77) in relationship. Buber emphasises in I–Thou relation: 'You no longer felt the one, limited by the other; you felt both without bounds, both at once' (1923/1970: 130).

Following **Kierkegaard**, for Buber, love is a responsibility of I for Thou. Similarly following **Kierkegaard**, there is only freedom in I–Thou relations, and from these relations comes the meaning or purpose of life. Buber appeals to the concept of God, who he terms the eternal Thou. In his I–Thou or I–You relation, Buber finds God, or 'infinity or eternity – here and now' (Kaufman, 1970: 30). As such, Kaufman claims that Buber 'succeeds in endowing the social sphere with a religious dimension' (1970: 30).

Classical Greek philosophy: Socrates, Plato and Aristotle (469–322 BC)

The three most influential Ancient Greek philosophers are Socrates, Plato and Aristotle, who all focus on the question of how to live the good life.

Socrates begins by encouraging people to question and think for themselves, to discover inner knowledge of the essence or purpose of things. Socrates thought that the good life must have reflection as part of its goodness: '*the unexamined life,* as he puts it, *is not worth living*' (Williams, 1985: 21, italics in original). Plato believes that all wrong doing is caused by ignorance, that no one would deliberately do wrong.

Aristotle stresses the importance of ethics to everyday life and who we are as people, suggesting that the purpose of enquiring into ethical matters is to become better people. Plato and Aristotle believe that *reason* is the route to work out the best route to the 'good life'. For both these Greek philosophers, reason is the territory of the educated male, who therefore has the moral justification to control and rule those lower in the hierarchy. The ultimate goal for Aristotle is in this life, of good for its own sake. His goal is termed *eudaimonia*, which includes the idea of happiness and virtue, but is a description of the state of a whole life, not a changeable emotion. Eudaimonia is found by achieving a 'reasonable and appropriate' balance between extremes. He suggests that the good citizen has virtues which are good habits we acquire which regulate our emotions, and that most virtues fall at a mean between more extreme character traits and are hard to attain. For Aristotle, the virtuous person would intuitively see what was right and wrong, rather than follow rules, as rules are inadequate to capture the wide requirements of different situations.

De Beauvoir (1908–1986)

The Second Sex was first published in France in 1949 and translated and published in English in 1953. In it Simone de Beauvoir discusses how the history of thought is men's thought and how philosophers have portrayed women, such as **Aristotle**, who believed women are lacking and defective. De Beauvoir uses the concept of the 'Other' from Hegel and the particular situation in which women are set up as Other to the One of men, particularly in that women have never been in the minority. She discusses how women have not challenged their otherness and suggests that the social conditions set up for women make it particularly hard for women to organise themselves, being dispersed among men. 'The bond that unites her to her oppressors is not comparable with any other' (1949/1997: 19).

Following Hegel's proposal of the human need for mutual recognition to become a Subject, she suggests that women need to reclaim their subjectivity. She explains, 'along with the ethical urge of each individual to affirm his subjective existence, there is also the temptation to forgo liberty and become a thing. This is an auspicious road, for he who takes it – passive, lost, ruined – becomes henceforth the creature of another's will, frustrated in his transcendence and deprived of every value. But it is an easy road; on it one avoids the strain involved in undertaking an authentic existence' (1949/1997: 21).

De Beauvoir considers our inevitable dependence on others, claiming that 'no existence can be validly fulfilled if it is limited to itself. It appeals to the existence of others' (1948/1976: 67). She describes the 'tragic ambivalence' of the human condition, with life always facing death, and of 'being a sovereign and unique object amidst a universe of objects ... nothing more than an individual in the collectivity on which he depends' (1948/1976: 7). She prescribes that 'To attain his truth, man must not attempt to dispel the ambiguity of his being but, on the contrary, accept the task of realising it' (1948/1976: 13). She points out how frightening this dependence is and notes how some people try and escape the ambiguity of this situation by trying to separate themselves from others. She argues that we are unable to escape our dependence on others or find a meaning in life not involving others, saying: 'Man can find a justification of his own existence only in the existence of other men ... I concern others and they concern me.' Furthermore, 'To will oneself free is also to will others free' (1948/1976: 72, 73).

In *The Ethics of Ambiguity*, De Beauvoir points to the idea that ethics are founded on the likelihood of getting it wrong, saying: 'the most optimistic ethics have all begun by emphasising the element of failure involved in the condition of man; without failure, no ethics. ... One does not offer an ethics to a God' (1948/1976: 10).

Derrida (1930–2004)

Jacques Derrida suggested deconstruction as a way of 'loosening the grip of the most prestigious and powerful elements of tradition. A deconstruction frees up the repressed senses, the silenced voices, the excluded and marginalised elements that succumb to the violence of tradition' (Caputo, 1998: 231). For Derrida, there is an absence of essence, and all experiences are mediated by language. Deconstruction moves from dualisms of either/or to both/and. A deconstructive approach states that merely applying a rule is a matter for administration not ethics; thus ethics is pertaining to making decisions, 'in a situation of radical *indecision* or of undecidability of the case in question in terms of any rules for judging it' (Bennington, 1998: 556). Thus, a decision must be an invention and its justification. Deconstruction gives no grounds for making decisions and mandates a lack of self-righteousness about them.

Descartes (1596–1650)

René Descartes was a key figure in **rationalism**, equating rationality with the proof of our existence in his famous 'cogito ergo sum' (I think therefore I am). He was responsible for introducing the dualism of the mind and body, claiming that each worked following different laws. This set the scene for dualist thought (as opposed to the holism of **Spinoza**) which became a cornerstone of modernist thought.

Dewey (1859–1952)

John Dewey is a pragmatist. He suggests that one should choose the system of beliefs that generates the least contradictions and works practically. All knowledge is trial and error but we have no alternative but to trust our senses and reason provisionally. It is practice that matters and theory divorced from practice is useless. In his book *Theory of Valuation*, Dewey sees goodness as the outcome of ethic valuation, a continuous balancing of 'ends in view'. An end in view is an objective potentially adopted, which may be refined or rejected based on its consistency with other objectives or as a means to objectives already held. His empirical approach does not accept intrinsic value as an inherent or enduring property of things. Dewey denies categorically that there is anything like intrinsic values and he holds the same position in regard to moral values – moral values are also based on a learning process, they are never 'intrinsic'. Instead, deliberation indirectly guides action by shaping, changing and reinforcing habits. Dewey's (1922/1988) conception of habits suggests they are results of learning from experience and shaped by our cultures. They embody our previous choices, including our choice to strengthen or alter our habits. The key is to use them to automatically do what is useful but also to reflect on whether they remain the most useful way to do something. Dewey argues that morality is a habit. Thus the aim of moral education is to make us habitually sensitive to the needs and interests of others, and to evaluate our habits to check their appropriateness in changing circumstances.

Gadamer (1900–2002)

Hans-Georg Gadamer was influenced by **Heidegger**, **Kant**, **Hegel** and Husserl as well as **Classical Greek philosophy**. He is associated with hermeneutics, which is characterised by openness to diversity. He is concerned with reflective judgement (defined by **Kant**) or phronesis (practical wisdom: **Aristotle**) as opposed to truth. According to **Kant**, determinate judgements involve the application of rules to a particular situation, whereas in reflective judgement no universal law is adequate in a particular case. Fidelity to this idea is key in Gadamer's writing where no system or method is elaborated, only the 'deep conviction that the law of interpretation is to be found in the details of each experience and in the belief that no matter how sedimented a tradition might become it is never resistant to unfolding itself and disclosing something new' (Schmid, 1998: 433).

In such unique situations, Gadamer advocates a phenomenological approach to understand the uniqueness of the situation. In these situations, the limits of conceptuality become visible. However, he contends that these situations of the finiteness of knowledge are universal, and reflective judgement is always necessary. He sees history and human affairs as a 'conversation', in which the struggle is for understanding between participants. Schmid summarises his contribution, saying: 'Gadamer's philosophical hermeneutics struggles to open and widen the possibilities of thinking today beyond those determined by philosophical conceptualisation. It is a struggle to carry on the conversation of philosophy, and, at the same time, to move beyond itself into a future' (1998: 441).

Habermas (1929–)

Jürgen Habermas (1993) presents a discourse theory of morality. He questions the foundational role **Kant** gives to individual reflection. He argues that consciousness and thought are structured by language; we are individuals through our socialisation in networks of reciprocal social relations. Thus the deliberating subject is in a social sphere of communication, and meanings are matters for communal agreement using rational autonomy. Moral judgements are not about factual truth but about communal agreement: 'truth and normative rightness are *essentially* discursive matters' (Habermas, 1993: xv). He argues that we cannot draw conclusions in private reflection, only in consensus achieved in argumentation under conditions sufficient for participation by all.

He holds onto the hope of reason in communication and democracy, defending Enlightenment rationality. Judgements must be determined in an ideal speech situation with freedom from coercion and all participating, which is of course never fully realised. Following **Rawls**, the principles of deliberation include universality: all affected can accept the consequences, and the chosen option satisfies the interests of all better than other options. All must have an impartial concern with the ends willed in common so all participants must adopt the perspectives of all involved. He preserves the role of autonomy by rejecting sources of moral authority external to the will of rational agents, although he argues that autonomy is intersubjective.

Hare (1919–2002)

Richard Hare brings together the rationalism of **Kant** and the principles of act-utilitarianism to combine critical and intuitive levels of moral thinking. He suggests that intuition leads us to prima facie principles and that critical thinking helps us to decide which facts are relevant and to adjudicate between conflicting principles. He considers the prudent (carefully considered) preferences of affected people as relevant features which need to be understood by using intuition, considering prudent preferences as those preferences that would be made given knowledge of all relevant facts to maximise future happiness. For each moral decision, he suggests the preferences of each person involved need to be considered with each person being given equal weight but taking into account the intensity of each preference, so the decision maker would always make the same decision if the same situation hypothetically arose again but the decision maker was in the position of a different affected person. As with **Rawls**, the key principle here is for each person to be treated impartially. Intuition helps us decide what principles should be used to make this critical judgement, so an intuitive principle of partiality or altruism towards those closest to us may be justified. He also suggests that this method is impossible to use in a crisis situation requiring an immediate judgement. In this situation there will be no time for the critical thinking required and intuition will necessarily determine the response. Following **Kant** he suggests one fundamental principle, which is that moral principles should be universal, which implies equal respect and concern for all. He calls his approach 'rational universal prescriptivism': 'Reason leaves us with our freedom, but constrains us to respect the freedom of others and to combine with them in exercising it' (Hare, 1981: 228).

Hegel (1770–1831)

Georg Hegel suggests that the self needs an external object to differentiate from to recognise itself; thus people need each other for awareness and mutual recognition. Here, Hegel sows the seeds for a relational model of self-development, as he believes that the mind is necessarily social, and requires recognition from another for existence. He discusses how the master–slave dialectic leads to a lack of self-consciousness for both parties. **De Beauvoir** extends this idea to the subjugation of women and the necessity for women to reclaim their subjectivity. Hegel was also notable in recognising that the view of human nature and therefore ethical philosophy are dependent upon the historical conditions of the time.

Heidegger (1889–1976)

Martin Heidegger believes in nothing beyond humans' ways of being. His most influential work is *Being and Time* published in 1927. He is concerned with the nature and temporality of being human, the knower as opposed to knowledge. He contends that how we know anything depends on its nature, and that the human being as knower draws together everything in the world that we know. The essence of the human being (or 'dasein' as he calls it) is its existence and its possibilities of various ways of being. For Heidegger, our choices cannot be right or wrong; they can only be assessed according to the criteria of authenticity and resoluteness (taking on personal responsibility for the choices and making a choice knowing that guilt at missed choices is an inevitable part of the human condition).

Being for Heidegger is at the same time *being-with-others* or how we are with each other in the world. The concept of relationship and empathy rests on the idea of two separate subjects relating to each other, but Heidegger (1987/2001: 112) notes how we are always already with each other in our being in the world.

Jaspers (1883–1969)

Karl Jaspers' approach is therapeutic, wanting to appeal to each human being to realise their genuine existential possibilities. Salamun (1998: 220) identifies the values behind Jaspers' thinking which he aims to stimulate by his philosophising. These are: courage without self-deception, composure, patience, self-possession and dignity. He adds to these attitudes the importance of: responsibility for one's actions and their consequences; respecting others, or 'existential solidarity' (Jaspers, 1932/1970: 63) with others; helping others to realise their own potential without using for one's own purpose; and finally, intellectual integrity and open-mindedness to struggle against political oppression.

Kant (1724–1804)

For Immanuel Kant, being moral means conforming to duty. Kant seeks and justifies categorical principles to be the foundation of ethics. He begins with two principles: 'Act only according to the maxim whereby you can at the same time will that it should become a universal law' (1785/1994: Book 1: 30); second, 'Act in such a way that you treat humanity, whether in your own person or in the person of another, always at the same time as an end and never simply as a means' (1785/1994: Book 1: 36). He then argues that this second imperative implies the first and so is left with the second as the fundamental categorical imperative. Thus, the categorical moral imperative is to treat others with dignity and not as instruments to fulfil our own needs. Kant has a positive view of human nature, believing that as we experience a sense of duty, we are therefore moral beings. He states that we are inherently moral agents with a sense of right and wrong. But he also believes we have imperfect wills that are compelled by self-interest which we should overcome.

Kierkegaard (1813–1855)

For Søren Kierkegaard, the purpose of human nature and the meaning of existence is to love: 'to love human beings is still the only thing worth living for; without this love you really do not live' (1847/2009: 344). Following **Kant**ian ideas of duty, he saw eternal love as a duty, and the highest form of love, to be offered to all, not in a preferential way as is erotic love or friendship. His focus is on Christianity and living an altruistic life in community, with a constant focus on the subjective experience of selfhood. He introduces the concept of authenticity, espousing maturity to involve authentic selfhood – neither following the crowd nor being absorbed in the life of the senses. For either of these immature positions, the problem for Kierkegaard is choicelessness and lack of meaning or purpose in life.

Levinas (1906–1995)

Emmanuel Levinas moves the fundamental ethical principle from **Heidegger**'s focus on autonomy (from **Kant**), to heteronomy, putting the other first. For him, to ask about one's own being and nature is the wrong question; we must begin with the other – heteronomy. Levinas critiques the notion of autonomy as being colonialisation of all outside oneself, the 'reduction of the Other to the Same' (Levinas in Peperzak, 1993: 47–8). For Levinas, heteronomy is a duty: 'my duty to respond to the other suspends my natural right to self survival' (1981/1995: 189). However, this does not mean a turn away from valuing individual freedom; in contrast, we find our freedom and authentic meaning from our ethical response to the Other. Levinas claims that 'the being that imposes itself does not limit but promotes my freedom, by arousing my goodness' (1969: 200). Furthermore, Peperzak explains, 'To realise my responsibility for the Other, I myself must be free and independent; but the sense of my selfhood is my being-for-the-Other' (in Peperzak, 1993: 25).

The Other is not just another subject like myself or just a unique other, as we are all unique, but more than this, the Other is always beyond our ability to know. Levinas is very clear about the limits on our ability to understand the Other; he sees attempts to understand as totalising or colonialising – reducing the Other to our own perspective. In *Totality and infinity* (1969), Levinas explains that the infinite is the absolutely other which always overflows our capacity of thought: 'The way in which the other presents himself, exceeding *the idea of the other in me*, we here name face.' To face the other 'is therefore, to *receive* from the Other beyond the capacity of the I, which means exactly: to have the idea of infinity. But this also means: to be taught' (1969: 51). So in heteronomy we face the other without putting our conceptions on them and we expand and learn.

Merleau-Ponty (1908–1961)

Maurice Merleau-Ponty's emphasis is on the body and our position in the world whilst being intrinsically connected to it. Moreira explains: 'Merleau-Ponty transcended the theoretical centering of phenomenology in consciousness and in the subject towards the mutual constitution between man/woman and the world' (2012: 52). She argues that Merleau-Ponty liberates psychotherapy from its focus on the inner experience of the client to the intersubjective field mutually constituted by the therapist, the client and the world. Merleau-Ponty is explicit about the relational nature of dialogue. He refers to us all as 'mundane', inhabiting the world and being inhabited by it, always being subjects and objects at the same time. For Merleau-Ponty, phenomenology brings together subjectivity and objectivity. For him, 'The world is not what I think, but what I live through. ... The phenomenological world is not bringing to explicit expression of a pre-existing being, but the laying down of being. Philosophy is not the reflection of a pre-existing truth, but, like art, the act of bringing truth into being' (1945: xviii). For Merleau-Ponty, the body is not separate from the mind, but the embodiment of our essence, the vehicle through which we perceive the world.

Nietzsche (1844–1900)

Friedrich Nietzsche follows **Kierkegaard** in his interest in human nature and consciousness, as opposed to right and wrong. From Nietzsche and through various following postmodern philosophers, the focus of ethical philosophy changed, from a discussion of how we know right from wrong, to the nature of being human. He had no time for religion, another staple ingredient in earlier philosophers' accounts of morality, and proclaimed the death of God (Nietzsche, 1896). He meant by this that God no longer inspires creativity in modern culture. He argues for nihilism – right and wrong are meaningless concepts; as is truth. He sees the foundations of humanity as sexuality, self-expression and the will to power (or moral strength). He wants us to develop ourselves as unique people with distinct talents, to go 'beyond ourselves', and brings the concept of 'Superman' to represent this idea, who embraces all of life, bringing meaning and purpose to life through the positive affirmation of all of life as it is.

Plato (428/427–348/347 BC) see Classical Greek philosophy

Rawls (1921–2002)

John Rawls was a **rationalist** who used the method of impartial observer, requiring us to think through the consequences for each person involved and decide the best course of action for all impartially. He advocates the modification of principles in response to practical problems, and terms this adjustment between principles and intuitive responses 'reflective equilibrium'.

Ross (1877–1971)

W.D. Ross followed the **rationalist** tradition of **Kant** but combined the idea of duty with that of considering consequences and intuitionism (Ross, 1930/2002). He conceives of *prima facie duties* which always count towards an action being right, tending to be a duty unless overridden by a stronger duty. He derives these duties from appealing to our reflective judgements about decisions and through intuitive induction. He prefers the term 'responsibilities' to duties and suggests actions are right in virtue of the responsibilities which bear upon the case. He lists the prima facie duties as: fidelity (keeping promises), reparation (making amends for wrongdoing), gratitude (to others for their help), justice (fair distribution of benefits and burdens), beneficence (doing good), self-improvement and non-maleficence (not doing harm).

Sartre (1905–1980)

Jean-Paul Sartre states we are always engaged in a world of values, saying 'my acts cause values to spring up like partridges' (1943/2003: 62). Behaviour acquires value through the culturally agreed social significances of acts. Sartre explains, 'Values are sown on my path as thousands of little real demands, like the signs which order us to keep off the grass' (1943/2003: 62). Much of the time, Sartre argues, we are not conscious of our freedom to choose our own values and ways of being, and when we are this brings anguish. We cannot appeal to anything to justify our values, they are purely an expression of our freedom to be unique individuals. In justifying ourselves and our own existence, we cannot get beyond our freedom to choose our own values. Sartre expresses our inability to escape this freedom, saying: 'I have to realise the meaning of the world and of my essence; I make my decision concerning them – without justification and without excuse' (1943/2003: 63).

'Bad faith' for Sartre is an attempt to fill the nothingness at the heart of our being with something other to flee from our anguish; an attempt to lie to oneself. He explains: 'Man pursues being blindly by hiding from himself the free project which is this pursuit' (Sartre, 1943/2003: 646). In contrast, 'good faith' is to acknowledge and accept our responsibility for choosing how we live our lives.

Socrates (469–399 BC) see Classical Greek philosophy

Spinoza (1632–1677)

Baruch Spinoza challenged the dualism of **Descartes**, which became foundational for western modern ways of thinking. Spinoza hypothesised only one substance, of which mind, body, people, nature and God are all one. By understanding more about ourselves in the universe, we become more active (as opposed to passive), more free and more infinite.

Stoics

Stoic philosophy began following **Classical Greek philosophy** in the Hellenistic period beginning from around 301 standard BC. The philosophy involved the transformation of emotions using reason to develop clear judgement and calm. For the Stoics, 'reason' meant not only using logic, but also understanding the processes of nature – the logos, or universal reason, inherent in all things. The aim was to maintain a will in accord with nature. The Stoics believed that each individual fits within a divine plan for the whole universe and that morals should consist in seeking to be in tune with the universe and to act with integrity to be part of the wider world soul.

References

Adshead, G. (2005) Ethics and psychotherapy. In G.O. Gabbard, J.S. Beck & J. Holmes (Eds.), *Oxford textbook of psychotherapy* (pp. 477–485). Oxford: Oxford University Press.

Adshead, G. (2008) Personal responsibility, abnormality, and ethics: psychotherapy as moral understanding. *Psychiatry, 7*(5), 225–227.

American Psychiatric Association (2001) *The principles of medical ethics.* Arlington, VA: American Psychiatric Association.

American Psychological Association (2002/revised 2010) *Ethical principles of psychologists and codes of conduct.* Washington, DC: APA.

Anderson, S.K. & Kitchener, K.S. (1996) Nonsexual posttherapy relationships between psychologists and former clients: an exploratory study of critical incidents. *Professional Psychology: Research and Practice, 27*(1), 59–66.

Appiah, K.A. (2006) *Cosmopolitanism: ethics in a world of strangers.* London: Penguin.

Aron, L. (1996) *A meeting of minds.* London: Analytic Press.

Aveline, M. (2001) Complexities of practice: psychotherapy in the real world. In F. Palmer Barnes & L. Murdin (Eds.), *Values and ethics in the practice of psychotherapy and counselling* (pp. 128–143). Buckingham: Open University Press.

BABCP (2009) *Standards of conduct, performance and ethics in the practice of behavioural and cognitive psychotherapies.* Bury: BABCP. Available from www.babcp.com

BACP (2002/revised 2013) *Ethical framework for good practice in counselling and psychotherapy.* Lutterworth: BACP. Available from www.bacp.co.uk/ethical_framework

Banks, S. (1995) *Ethics and values in social work.* London: Macmillan.

Barnett, J.E. (2008) The ethical practice of psychotherapy: easily within our reach. *Journal of Clinical Psychology, 64*(5), 569–575.

Beauchamp, T.L. (2007) The 'four principles' approach to health care ethics. In R.E. Ashcroft, A. Dawson, H. Draper & J.R. McMillan (Eds.), *Principles of health-care ethics* (pp. 3–10). Chichester: John Wiley.

Beauchamp, T. & Childress, J. (1979) *Principles of biomedical ethics* (1st ed.). New York: Oxford University Press.

Beauchamp, T. & Childress, J. (2001) *Principles of biomedical ethics* (5th ed.). New York: Oxford University Press.

Beebe, J. (2009) The integrity of the supervisor and the sins of psychotherapy supervision. In G. Heuer (Ed.), *Sacral revolutions: reflecting on the work of Andrew Samuels: cutting edges in psychoanalysis and Jungian analysis* (pp. 43–50). London: Routledge.

Bennington, G. (1998) Derrida. In S. Critchley & W. Schroeder (Eds.), *A companion to continental philosophy* (pp. 549–558). Oxford: Blackwell.

Bernasconi, R. (1998) Arendt. In S. Critchley & W. Schroeder (Eds.), *A companion to continental philosophy* (pp. 478–483). Oxford: Blackwell.

Bersoff, D.N. (1994) Explicit ambiguity: the 1992 ethics codes as an oxymoron. *Professional Psychology: Research and Practice, 25*, 382–387.

Bion, W.R. (1967/1984) *Second thoughts.* London: Karnac Books.

Black, R. (2005) Intersections of care: an analysis of culturally competent care, client centered care, and the feminist ethic of care. *Work, 24*(4), 409–422.

Blackhall, L.J., Murphy, S.T., Frank, G., Michel, V. & Azen, S. (2002) Ethnicity and attitudes toward patient autonomy. In K.W.M. Fulford, D.L. Dickenson & T.H. Murray (Eds.), *Healthcare ethics and human values* (pp. 187–196). Oxford: Blackwell.

Bollas, C. & Sundelson, D. (1995) *The new informants.* London: Jason Aronson.

Bond, T. (1997) Therapists' dilemmas as stimuli to new understanding and practice. In W. Dryden (Ed.), *Therapists' dilemmas.* London: Sage.

Bond, T. (2007) Ethics and psychotherapy: an issue of trust. In R.E. Ashcroft, A. Dawson, H. Draper & J.R. McMillan (Eds.), *Principles of healthcare ethics* (pp. 435–442). Chichester: John Wiley.

Bond, T. (2010) *Standards and ethics for counselling in action* (3rd ed.). London: Sage.

Bonitz, V. (2008) Use of physical touch in the 'talking cure': a journey to the outskirts of psychotherapy. *Psychotherapy: Theory, Research, Practice, Training, 45*(3), 391–404.

Bonovitz, J. (2006) The self and its boundaries: an introductory overview. In S. Akhtar (Ed.), *Interpersonal boundaries: variations and violations* (pp. 1–14). Oxford: Jason Aronson.

BPS (2009) *Code of ethics and conduct.* Leicester: BPS. Available from www.bps.org.uk

Brendel, D.H., Chu, J., Radden, J., Leeper, H., Pope, H., Samson, J., Tsimprea, G. & Bodkin, J.A. (2007) The price of a gift: an approach to receiving gifts from patients in psychiatric practice. *Harvard Review of Psychiatry, 15*(2), 43–51.

Brenner, I. (2006) Going over the edge – a one-person or two-person psychology? In S. Akhtar (Ed.), *Interpersonal boundaries: variations and violations* (pp. 49–60). Oxford: Jason Aronson.

Brodley, B. (2011a) Ethics in psychotherapy. In K.A. Moon, M. Witty, B. Grant & B. Rice (Eds.), *Practising client-centered therapy: selected writings of Barbara Temaner Brodley* (pp. 33–46). Ross-on-Wye: PCCS Books.

Brodley, B. (2011b) Client-centered values limit the application of research findings: an issue for discussion. In K.A. Moon, M. Witty, B. Grant & B. Rice (Eds.), *Practising client-centered therapy: selected writings of Barbara Temaner Brodley* (pp. 63–72). Ross-on-Wye: PCCS Books.

Brody, H. (2002) 'My story is broken; can you help me fix it?' Medical ethics and the joint construction of narrative. In K.W.M. Fulford, D.L. Dickenson & T.H. Murray (Eds.), *Healthcare ethics and human values* (pp. 133–140). Oxford: Blackwell.

Brown, L. (1994a) Concrete boundaries and the problem of literal-mindedness. *Ethics and Behavior, 4*(3), 275–281.

Brown, L. (1994b) Boundaries in feminist therapy: a conceptual formulation. *Women & Therapy, 15*(1), 29–38.

Brown, L.M., Tappan, M.B., Gilligan, C., Miller, B. & Argyris, D.E. (1989) Reading for self and moral voice: a method for interpreting narratives of real-life moral conflict and choice. In M.J. Packer & R.B. Addison (Eds.), *Entering the circle: hermeneutic investigation in psychology* (pp. 141–164). Albany, NY: State of New York Press.

Buber, M. (1923/1970) *I and thou.* New York: Touchstone.

Cain, P. (2002) 'Partnership' is not enough: professional-client relations revisited. In K.W.M. Fulford, D.L. Dickenson & T.H. Murray (Eds.), *Healthcare ethics and human values* (pp. 278–281). Oxford: Blackwell.

Caputo, J.D. (1998) Heidegger. In S. Critchley & W. Schroeder (Eds.), *A companion to continental philosophy* (pp. 223–236). Oxford: Blackwell.

Caputo, J.D. (2000) The end of ethics. In H. LaFollette (Ed.), *Ethical theory* (pp. 111–128). Oxford: Blackwell.

Carroll, M. (2011) Supervision: a journey of lifelong learning. In R. Shohet (Ed.), *Supervision as transformation: a passion for learning* (pp. 14–28). London: Jessica Kingsley.

Casemore, R. (2001) Managing boundaries – it's the little things that count. In R. Casemore (Ed.), *Surviving complaints against counsellors and psychotherapists: towards understanding and healing* (pp. 111–120). Ross-on-Wye: PCCS Books.

Casemore, R. (2009) Relational ethics as a way of being. In L. Gabriel & R. Casemore (Eds.), *Relational ethics in practice: narratives from counselling and psychotherapy* (pp. 23–31). London: Routledge.

Chambers, T. (2002) The literary nature of ethical enquiry. In K.W.M. Fulford, D.L. Dickenson & T.H. Murray (Eds.), *Healthcare ethics and human values* (pp. 70–75). Oxford: Blackwell.

Chesler, P. (1972) *Women and madness*. New York: Doubleday.

Clarkson, P. (2000) *Ethics: working with ethical and moral dilemmas in psychotherapy*. London: Whurr.

Clouser, K.D. & Gert, B. (1990) A critique of principlism. *Journal of Medicine and Philosophy, 15*(2), 219–236.

Cooper, M. (2008) *Essential research findings in counselling and psychotherapy: the facts are friendly*. London: Sage.

COSCA (2007) *Statement of ethics and code of practice*. Stirling: COSCA. Available from www.cosca.org.uk

Cullity, G. (2007) Beneficence. In R.E. Ashcroft, A. Dawson, H. Draper & J.R. McMillan (Eds.), *Principles of healthcare ethics* (pp. 19–26). Chichester: John Wiley.

Damasio, A. (2000) *The feeling of what happens: body, emotion and the making of consciousness*. London: Vintage.

De Beauvoir, S. (1948/1976) *The ethics of ambiguity*. New York: Citadel.

De Beauvoir, S. (1949/1997) *The second sex*. London: Vintage.

Derrida, J. (1967/1997) *Of grammatology* (G.C. Spivak, Trans.). Baltimore & London: Johns Hopkins University Press.

Descartes, R. (1955) Rules for the direction of the mind. In *The philosophical works of Descartes Vol. 1* (E.S. Haldane & G.R.T. Ross, Trans.). New York: Dover.

Dewey, J. (1922/1988) *Human nature and conduct*. Carbondale: Southern Illinois University Press.

Donner, M.B., VandeCreek, L., Gonsiorek, J.C. & Fisher, C.B. (2008) Balancing confidentiality: protecting privacy and protecting the public: unbalancing confidentiality. *Professional Psychology: Research and Practice, 39*(3), 369–376.

Dunnett, A. (2009) The role of practitioner self-care in practitioner–client relationship ethics. In L. Gabriel & R. Casemore (Eds.), *Relational ethics in practice: narratives from counselling and psychotherapy* (pp. 119–130). London: Routledge.

Etherington, K. (2004) *Becoming a reflexive researcher: using ourselves in research*. London: Jessica Kingsley.

Feenan, D. (2002) Capable people: empowering the patient in the assessment of capacity. In K.W.M. Fulford, D.L. Dickenson & T.H. Murray (Eds.), *Healthcare ethics and human values* (pp. 236–240). Oxford: Blackwell.

Fisher, C.B. & Oransky, M. (2008) Informed consent in psychotherapy: protecting the dignity and respecting the autonomy of patients. *Journal of Clinical Psychology, 64*(5), 576–588.

Ford, G.G. (2006) *Ethical reasoning for mental health professionals.* Thousand Oaks, CA: Sage.

Freud, S. (1928) *The future of an illusion.* London: Hogarth Press.

Fulford, K.W.M., Dickenson, D.L. & Murray, T.H. (2002) Introduction: many voices: human values in healthcare ethics. In K.W.M. Fulford, D.L. Dickenson & T.H. Murray (Eds.), *Healthcare ethics and human values* (pp. 1–19). Oxford: Blackwell.

Gabbard, G.O. (1994) Reconsidering the APA's policy on sex with former patients: is it justifiable? *Professional Psychology: Research and Practice, 25*(4), 329–335.

Gabbard, G. (2006) Sexual and nonsexual boundary violations in psychoanalysis and psychotherapy. In S. Akhtar (Ed.), *Interpersonal boundaries: variations and violations* (pp. 39–48). Oxford: Jason Aronson.

Gabbard, G.O. (2008) Commentary on Goldberg, A. (2008) Some limits of the boundary concept. *Psychoanalytic Quarterly, 77*(3), 877–882.

Gabbard, G.O. & Hobday, G.S. (2012) A psychoanalytic perspective on ethics, self-deception and the corrupt physician. *British Journal of Psychotherapy, 28*(2), 235–248.

Gabbard, G.O. & Peltz, M.L. (2001) Speaking the unspeakable: institutional reactions to boundary violations by training analysts. *Journal of the American Psychoanalytic Association, 49*(2), 659–673.

Gabriel, L. (2005) *Speaking the unspeakable: the ethics of dual relationships in counselling and psychotherapy.* Hove: Routledge.

Gabriel, L. (2009) Relational ethics, boundary riders and process sentinels: allies for ethical practice. In L. Gabriel & R. Casemore (Eds.), *Relational ethics in practice: narratives from counselling and psychotherapy* (pp. 9–22). London: Routledge.

Gabriel, L. & Casemore, R. (2003) *Relational ethics in practice: narratives from counselling and psychotherapy.* London: Routledge.

Gabriel, L. & Davies, D. (2000) The management of ethical dilemmas associated with dual relationships. In C. Neal & D. Davies (Eds.), *Pink therapy vol 3: Issues in therapy with lesbian, gay, bisexual and transgendered clients* (pp. 35–54). Buckingham: Open University Press.

Gale, D. (1999) The limitations of boundaries. In C. Feltham (Ed.), *Controversies in psychotherapy and counselling* (pp. 124–131). London: Sage.

Gantt, E.E. (2002) Utopia, psychotherapy and the place of suffering. In E.E. Gantt & R.N. Williams (Eds.), *Psychology for the other: Levinas, ethics and the practice of psychology* (pp. 65–83). Pittsburgh: Duquesne University Press.

Garguilo, G.J. (2007) Framing the question: psychoanalytic process, the unconscious, and home offices – an alternate perspective. *Psychoanalytic Psychology, 24*(4), 715–719.

Gilligan, C. (1982) *In a different voice: psychological theory and women's development.* Cambridge, MA: Harvard University Press.

Goldberg, A. (2008a) Some limits of the boundary concept. *Psychoanalytic Quarterly, 77*(3), 861–875.

Goldberg, A. (2008b) Response to commentaries on Goldberg, A. (2008a) Some limits of the boundary concept. *Psychoanalytic Quarterly, 77*(3), 915–920.

Gonsiorek, J.C. (2008) Informed consent can solve some confidentiality dilemmas, but others remain. *Professional Psychology: Research and Practice, 39*(3), 374–375.

Gonsiorek, J.C. & Brown, L.S. (1989) Post therapy sexual relationships with clients. In G.R. Schoener, J.H. Miligrom, J.C. Gonsiorek, E.T. Luepker & R. Conroe (Eds.),

Psychotherapists' sexual involvement with clients: intervention and prevention (pp. 289–301). Minneapolis: Walk-in Counseling Center.

Gordon, P. (2009) *The hope of therapy.* Ross-on-Wye: PCCS Books.

Goss, S. & Anthony, K. (2009) Developments in the use of technology in counselling and psychotherapy. *British Journal of Guidance and Counselling, 37*(3), 223–230.

Grant, B. (2004) The imperative of ethical justification in psychotherapy: the special case of client-centered therapy. *Person-centered and Experiential Psychotherapies, 3*(3), 152–165.

Gray, A. (2006) Confidentiality: a contribution to the debate. *British Journal of Psychotherapy, 22*(3), 363–372.

Green, D. & Latchford, G. (2012) *Maximising the benefits of psychotherapy: a practice-based evidence approach.* Chichester: Wiley-Blackwell.

Greenberg, J. (2008) Commentary on Goldberg, A. (2008) Some limits of the boundary concept. *Psychoanalytic Quarterly, 77*(3), 883–890.

Gutheil, T.G. & Gabbard, G.O. (1993) The concept of boundaries in clinical practice: theoretical and risk management dimensions. *American Journal of Psychiatry, 150*(2), 188–196.

Gutheil, T.G. & Gabbard, G.O. (1998) Misuses and misunderstandings of boundary theory in clinical and regulatory settings. *American Journal of Psychiatry, 155*(3), 409–414.

Habermas, J. (1993) *Justification and application: remarks on discourse ethics.* Cambridge, MA: MIT Press.

Haidt, J. (2001) The emotional dog and its rational tail: a social intuitionist approach to moral judgement. *Psychological Review, 108*(4), 814–834.

Haidt, J. (2007) The new synthesis in moral psychology. *Science, 316*, 998–1002.

Haidt, J. & Kesebir, S. (2010) Morality. In S. Fiske, D. Gilbert & G. Lindzey (Eds.), *Handbook of social psychology* (5th ed., pp. 797–832). Hoboken, NJ: Wiley.

Hare, R.M. (1981) *Moral thinking: its levels, method, and point.* Oxford: Oxford University Press.

Hedges, L.E. (1997) In praise of the dual relationship. In L.E. Hedges, R. Hilton, V.W. Hilton & O.B. Candhill (Eds.), *Therapists at risk: perils of the intimacy of the therapeutic relationship* (pp. 221–250). Northvale, NJ: Jason Aronson.

Heidegger, M. (1927/1962) *Being and time* (J. Macquarrie & E. Robinson, Trans.). Oxford: Blackwell.

Heidegger, M. (1977) *The question concerning technology and other essays.* New York: Harper Torchbooks.

Heidegger, M. (1987/2001) *Zollikon seminars: protocols-conversations-letters* (M. Boss, Ed., F. Mayr & R. Askay, Trans.). Evanston, IL: Northwestern Press.

Heru, A. (2006) Psychotherapy supervision and ethical boundaries. *Directions in Psychiatry, 26*(1), 79–88.

Hess, A.K. (2008) Ethical and legal considerations in psychotherapy supervision. In A.K. Hess, K.D. Hess & T.H. Hess (Eds.), *Psychotherapy supervision: theory, research and practice* (2nd ed., pp. 521–534). Chichester: John Wiley.

Heyward, C. (1993) *When boundaries betray us: beyond illusions of what is ethical in therapy and life.* New York: HarperCollins.

Hill, D. (2000) Question 34: What are the issues to consider when... it is then discovered that the pair have overlapping worlds? In C. Jones (Ed.), *Questions of ethics in counselling and therapy* (pp. 154–157). Buckingham: Open University Press.

Holmes, J. (2001) Foreword. In F. Palmer Barnes & L. Murdin (Eds.), *Values and ethics in the practice of psychotherapy and counselling* (pp. xv–xvii). Buckingham: Open University Press.

Holmes, J. & Lindley, R. (1989) *The values of psychotherapy.* Oxford: Oxford University Press.

Hooker, B. (2000) Rule-consequentialism. In H. LaFollette (Ed.), *Ethical theory* (pp. 183–204). Oxford: Blackwell.

House, R. (2003) *Therapy beyond modernity: deconstructing and transcending profession-centred therapy.* London: Karnac.

Houser, R. & Thoma, S. (2013) *Ethics in counseling and therapy: developing an ethical identity.* Thousand Oaks, CA: Sage.

Jaggar, A. (2000) *Feminist ethics.* In H. LaFollette (Ed.), *Ethical theory* (pp. 348–374). Oxford: Blackwell.

Jaspers, K. (1932/1970) *Philosophy vol 2.* (E.B. Ashton, Trans.). Chicago: University of Chicago Press.

Jenkins, P. (2007) *Counselling, psychotherapy and the law* (2nd ed.). London: Sage.

Jenkins, P. (2009) Therapy as evidence: legal perspectives on the relationship between therapist and client. In L. Gabriel & R. Casemore (Eds.), *Relational ethics in practice: narratives from counselling and psychotherapy* (pp. 105–118). London: Routledge.

Jenkins, P. (2010) Having confidence in therapeutic work with young people: constraints and challenges to confidentiality. *British Journal of Guidance and Counselling, 38*(3), 263–274.

Jones, C. (2000) Question 2: What should counsellors consider when contacted by persons such as solicitors or the police ... In C. Jones (Ed.), *Questions of ethics in counselling and therapy* (pp. 21–26). Buckingham: Open University Press.

Kaiser, T.L. (1992) The supervisory relationship: an identification of the primary elements in the relationship and an application of two theories of ethical responsibility. *Journal of Marital and Family Therapy, 18*(3), 283–296.

Kant, I. (1785/1994) *Ethical philosophy: grounding for the metaphysics of morals & metaphysical principles of virtue Book I* (J.W. Ellington, Trans.). Indianapolis: Hackett.

Kaufman, W. (1970) *I and you: a prologue.* New York: Touchstone.

Khele, S., Symons, C. & Wheeler, S. (2008) An analysis of complaints to the British Association of Counselling and Psychotherapy 1996–2006. *Counselling and Psychotherapy Research, 8*(2), 124–132.

Kierkegaard, S. (1847/2009) *Works of love* (H. &. E. Hong, Trans.). New York: HarperCollins.

Kitchener, K.S. (1984) Intuition, critical evaluation, and ethical principles: the foundation for ethical decisions in counseling psychology. *The Counseling Psychologist, 12*(1), 43–55.

Kitchener, K.S. (1996) There is more to ethics than principles. *The Counseling Psychologist, 24*(1), 92–97.

Kitchener, K.S. & Anderson, S.K. (2011) *Foundations of ethical practice, research, and teaching in psychology and counseling.* New York: Routledge.

Knapp, S. & VandeCreek, L. (2008) The ethics of advertising, billing and finances in psychotherapy. *Journal of Clinical Psychology, 64*(5), 613–625.

Koocher, G.P. (2008) Ethical challenges in mental health services to children and families. *Journal of Clinical Psychology, 64*(5), 601–612.

Kunz, G. (2007) An analysis of the psyche inspired by Emmanuel Levinas. *The Psychoanalytic Review, 94*(4), 617–638.

Lago, C. & Smith, B. (2010) *Anti-discriminatory practice in counselling and psychotherapy.* London: Sage.

Lago, C. & Thompson, J. (1996) *Race, culture and counselling.* Buckingham: Open University Press.

Langs, R.J. (2004) *The fundamentals of adaptive psychotherapy in psychotherapy*. Basingstoke: Palgrave.

Lazarus, A.A. (1994) How certain boundaries and ethics diminish therapeutic effectiveness. *Ethics and Behavior, 4*(3), 255–261.

Lazarus, A.A. & Zur, O. (Eds.) (2002) *Dual relationships and psychotherapy*. New York: Springer.

Levinas, E. (1969) *Totality and infinity: an essay on exteriority.* Pittsburgh: Duquesne University Press.

Levinas, E. (1981/1995) Ethics of the infinite. In R. Kearney (Ed.), *States of mind: dialogues with contemporary thinkers on the European mind* (pp. 177–199). Manchester: Manchester University Press.

Levinas, E. (1985) *Ethics and infinity: conversations with Phillipe Nemo* (R. Cohen, Trans.). Pittsburgh: Duquesne University Press.

Levinas, E. (1989) *The Levinas Reader* (S. Hand, Ed.). Oxford: Blackwell.

Loewenthal, D. & Snell, R. (2001) Psychotherapy as the practice of ethics. In F. Palmer Barnes & L. Murdin (Eds.), *Values and ethics in the practice of psychotherapy and counselling* (pp. 23–31). Buckingham: Open University Press.

Lomas, P. (1999) *Doing good? Psychotherapy out of its depth.* Oxford: Oxford University Press.

Lott, D. (1999) Drawing boundaries – recognising structure and boundaries in patient–therapist interaction, *Psychology Today*. Available from www.psychologytoday.com/articles/199905/drawing-boundaries

Luepker, E.T. & Schoener, G.R. (1989) Sexual involvement and the abuse of power in psychotherapeutic relationships. In G.R. Schoener, J.H. Miligrom, J.C. Gonsiorek, E.T. Luepker & R. Conroe (Eds.), *Psychotherapists' sexual involvement with clients: intervention and prevention* (pp. 65–72). Minneapolis: Walk-In Counseling Center.

McFarland Solomon, H. (2010) The ethical attitude in analytic practice. In *Jungian psychoanalysis: working in the spirit of C.G. Jung* (pp. 325–333). Chicago: Open Court.

McMahan, J. (2000) Moral intuition. In H. LaFollette (Ed.), *Ethical theory* (pp. 92–110). Oxford: Blackwell.

McMillan, J. & Gillett, G. (2002) Consent as empowerment: the roles of postmodern and narrative ethics. In K.W.M. Fulford, D.L. Dickenson & T.H. Murray (Eds.), *Healthcare ethics and human values* (pp. 225–228). Oxford: Blackwell.

McNaughton, D. (2000) Intuitionism. In H. LaFollette (Ed.), *Ethical theory* (pp. 268–287). Oxford: Blackwell.

MacIntyre, A. (1966) *A short history of ethics.* London: Routledge and Kegan Paul.

MacIntyre, A. (1984) *After virtue* (2nd ed.). Notre Dame, IN: University of Notre Dame Press.

Maroda, K. (2007) Ethical considerations of the home office. *Psychoanalytic Psychology, 24*(1), 173–179.

Martin, E. (2001) The private face and the public face of psychotherapy. In F. Palmer Barnes & L. Murdin (Eds.), *Values and ethics in the practice of psychotherapy and counselling* (pp. 163–176). Buckingham: Open University Press.

Maslow, A.H. (1943) A theory of human motivation. *Psychological Review, 50*(4), 370–396.

Mearns, D. (1997) *Person-centred counselling training.* London: Sage.

Merleau-Ponty, M. (1945/2002) *Phenomenology of perception.* London: Routledge.

Mill (1871/1998) *Utilitarianism.* Oxford: Oxford University Press.

Mills, J. (2007) The immorality of the home office. *Psychoanalytic Psychology, 24*(4), 720–723.

Moodley, R., Lago, C. & Talahite, A. (Eds.) (2004) *Carl Rogers counsels a black client: race and culture in person-centred counselling.* Ross-on-Wye: PCCS Books.

Mordini, E. (2002) Confidentiality in child psychiatry. In K.W.M. Fulford, D.L. Dickenson & T.H. Murray (Eds.), *Healthcare ethics and human values* (pp. 167–170). Oxford: Blackwell.

Moreira, V. (2012) From person-centered to humanistic-phenomenological psychotherapy: the contribution of Merleau-Ponty to Carl Rogers's thought. *Person-centered and Experiential Psychotherapies, 11*(1), 48–63.

Murdin, L. (2001) Success and failure. In F. Palmer Barnes & L. Murdin (Eds.), *Values and ethics in the practice of psychotherapy and counselling* (pp. 100–111). Buckingham: Open University Press.

Murdoch, I. (1970/1985) *The sovereignty of good.* London: Ark Paperbacks/London: Routledge & Kegan Paul.

Neukrug, E., Milliken, T. & Walden, S. (2001) Ethical complaints made against credentialed counselors: an updated survey of state licensing boards. *Counselor Education and Supervision, 41*(1), 57–71.

Nietzsche, F. (1896) *Thus spake Zarathustra* (Alexander Tille, Trans.). New York and London: Macmillan.

Olatunji, B.O., Deacon, B.J. & Abramowitz, J.S. (2009) The cruelest cure? Ethical issues in the implementation of exposure-based treatments. *Cognitive and Behavioural Practice, 16*(2), 172–180.

Owens, P., Springwood, B. & Wilson, M. (2012) *Creative ethical practice in counselling and psychotherapy.* London: Sage.

Palmer Barnes, F. (2001) Ethics and values in our practice: impasse in psychotherapy and organizations. In F. Palmer Barnes & L. Murdin (Eds.), *Values and ethics in the practice of psychotherapy and counselling* (pp. 82–99). Buckingham: Open University Press.

Palmer Barnes, F. & Murdin, L. (2001) Introduction. In F. Palmer Barnes & L. Murdin (Eds.), *Values and ethics in the practice of psychotherapy and counselling* (pp. 1–5). Buckingham: Open University Press.

Parker, M. (2007) Deliberative bioethics. In R.E. Ashcroft, A. Dawson, H. Draper & J.R. McMillan (Eds.), *Principles of healthcare ethics* (pp. 185–192). Chichester: John Wiley.

Patterson, T. & Gottlieb, M.C. (2002) Ethical issues. In F.W. Kaslow & T. Patterson (Eds.), *Comprehensive handbook of psychotherapy volume 2: cognitive-behavioural approaches* (pp. 587–610). New York: John Wiley.

Peperzak, A.T. (1993) *To the other: an introduction to the philosophy of Emmanuel Levinas.* West Lafayette, IN: Purdue University Press.

Phelan, J.E. (2007) Membership expulsions for ethical violations from major counseling, psychology and social work organisations in the United States: a 10-year analysis. *Psychological Reports, 101*(1), 145–152.

Phillips, M. & Poulton, M. (2013) *HIV transmission, the law and the work of the clinical team.* Available from www.bhiva.org/.../Reckless-HIV-transmission-FINAL-January-2013.pdf

Plato (1993) *The Republic* (R. Waterfield, Trans.). Oxford: Oxford University Press.

Poe, E.A. (1840) The daguerreotype [parts I & II]. *Alexander's Weekly Messenger*, 15 January and 6 May.

Pomerantz, A. (2005) Increasingly informed consent: discussing distinct aspects of psychotherapy at different points in time. *Ethics and Behavior, 15*(4), 351–360.

Poole, R. (1972) *Towards deep subjectivity.* London: Allen Lane.

Pope, K.S. & Brown, L. (1996) *Recovered memories of abuse: assessment, therapy, forensics.* Washington, DC: American Psychological Association.

Pope, K.S. & Keith-Spiegel, P. (2008) A practical approach to boundaries in psychotherapy: making decisions, bypassing blunders and mending fences. *Journal of Clinical Psychology, 64*(5), 638–652.

Pope, K.S. & Vasquez, M.J.T. (2007) *Ethics in psychotherapy and counseling: a practical guide* (3rd ed.). San Francisco: Wiley.

Pope, K.S., Tabachnick, B.G. & Keith-Spiegel, P. (1987) Ethics of practice: the beliefs and behaviours of psychologists as therapists. *American Psychologist, 42*, 993–1006. Available from http://kspope.com

Posner, R.A. (1995) Emotion versus emotionalism in law: economics of law: an interview with Judge Posner (Jeffrey Cole interviewer), *Litigation,* Fall, p. 23.

Proctor, G. (2002) *The dynamics of power in counselling and psychotherapy: ethics, politics and practice.* Ross-on-Wye: PCCS Books.

Proctor, G. (2004) What can person-centred therapy learn from feminism? In G. Proctor & M.B. Napier (Eds.), *Encountering feminism: intersections of feminism and the person-centred approach* (pp. 129–140). Ross-on-Wye: PCCS Books.

Proctor, G. (2005) Working in forensic services in a person-centered way. *Person-centered and Experiential Psychotherapies, 4*(1), 20–30.

Proctor, G. (2006) Therapy: opium for the masses or help for those who least need it? In G. Proctor, M. Cooper, P. Sanders & B. Malcolm (Eds.), *Politicising the person-centred approach: an agenda for social change* (pp. 66–79). Ross-on-Wye: PCCS Books.

Proctor, G. (2010a) Boundaries or mutuality in therapy: is mutuality really possible or is therapy doomed from the start? *Politics and Psychology, 8*(1), 44–58.

Proctor, G. (2010b) Working with women. In C. Lago & B. Smith (Eds.), *Anti-discriminatory practice in counselling and psychotherapy* (pp. 53–62). London: Sage.

Proctor, G. & Keys, S. (2013) Ethics in practice in person-centred therapy. In M. Cooper, M. O'Hara, P. Schmid & A. Bohart (Eds.), *The handbook of person-centred psychotherapy and counselling* (2nd ed., pp. 422–435). London: Palgrave Macmillan.

Proctor, G. & Napier, M.B. (Eds.) (2004) *Encountering feminism: intersections of feminism and the person-centred approach.* Ross-on-Wye: PCCS Books.

Proctor, G., Cooper, M., Sanders P. & Malcolm B. (2006) *Politicising the person-centred approach: an agenda for social change.* Ross-on-Wye: PCCS Books.

Rachels, J. (2000) Naturalism. In H. LaFollette (Ed.), *Ethical theory* (pp. 74–91). Oxford: Blackwell.

Rawls, J. (1971/1999) *A theory of justice.* Cambridge, MA: Harvard University Press.

Rest, J.R. (1994) Background: theory and research. In J.R. Rest & D. Narvaez (Eds.), *Moral development in the professions: psychology and applied ethics.* Hillsdale, NJ: Lawrence Erlbaum Associates.

Ringen, J. (1996) The behavior therapist's dilemma: reflections on autonomy, informed consent, and scientific psychology. In W. O'Donohue & R.F. Kitchener (Eds.), *The philosophy of psychology* (pp. 352–360). London: Sage.

Rogers, C.R. (1959) A theory of therapy, personality, and interpersonal relationships as developed in the client-centered framework. In S. Koch (Ed.), *Psychology: a study of science: vol 3. Formulation of the person and the social context* (pp. 184–256). New York: McGraw Hill.

Rogers, C.R. (1977) *On personal power: inner strength and its revolutionary impact.* New York: Delacorte.

Ross, W.D. (1930/2002) *The right and the good.* Oxford: Oxford University Press.

Rowson, R. (2001) Ethical principles. In F. Palmer Barnes & L. Murdin (Eds.), *Values and ethics in the practice of psychotherapy and counselling* (pp. 6–22). Buckingham: Open University Press.

Royal College of Psychiatrists (2002) *Vulnerable patients, vulnerable doctors: good practice in our clinical relationships* (Council Report CR101). London: Royal College of Psychiatrists.

Salamun, K. (1998) Jaspers. In S. Critchley & W. Schroeder (Eds.), *A companion to continental philosophy* (pp. 216–222). Oxford: Blackwell.

Sarkar, S. (2004) Boundary violation and sexual exploitation in psychiatry and psychotherapy: a review. *Advances in Psychiatric Treatment, 10*(Jan), 312–320.

Sartre, J.-P. (1943/2003) *Being and nothingness.* London: Routledge.

Schank, J., Slater, R., Banerjee-Stevens, D. & Skovholt, T.M. (2003) Ethics of multiple and overlapping relationships. In W.T. O'Donohue & K.E. Ferguson (Eds.), *Handbook of professional ethics for psychologists: issues, questions and controversies* (pp. 181–194). Thousand Oaks, CA: Sage.

Schmid, P.F. (1998) 'On becoming a person-centered approach': a person-centred understanding of the person. / 'Face to face: the art of encounter'. In B. Thorne & E. Lambers (Eds.), *Person-centred therapy: a European perspective* (pp. 38–52, 74–90). London: Sage.

Schmid, P. (2007) The anthropological and ethical foundations of person-centred therapy. In M. Cooper, M. O'Hara, P. Schmid & G. Wyatt (Eds.), *The handbook of person-centred psychotherapy and counselling* (pp. 30–46). London: Palgrave Macmillan.

Schmid, P. (2012) Psychotherapy is political or it is not psychotherapy: the person-centered approach as an essentially political venture. *Person-centred and Experiential Psychotherapies, 11*(2), 95–108.

Schoener, G.R. (1989a) A look at the literature. In G.R. Schoener, J.H. Miligrom, J.C. Gonsiorek, E.T. Luepker & R. Conroe (Eds.), *Psychotherapists' sexual involvement with clients: intervention and prevention* (pp. 11–50). Minneapolis: Walk-in Counseling Center.

Schoener, G.R. (1989b) Sexual involvement of therapists with clients after therapy ends: some observations. In G.R. Schoener, J.H. Miligrom, J.C. Gonsiorek, E.T. Luepker & R. Conroe (Eds.), *Psychotherapists' sexual involvement with clients: intervention and prevention* (pp. 265–287). Minneapolis: Walk-in Counseling Center.

Schroeder, W.R. (2000) Continental ethics. In H. LaFollette (Ed.), *Ethical theory* (pp. 375–399). Oxford: Blackwell.

Sembi, R. (2006) The cultural situatedness of language use in person-centred training. In G. Proctor, M. Cooper, P. Sanders & B. Malcolm (Eds.), *Politicising the person-centred approach: an agenda for social change* (pp. 55–59). Ross-on-Wye: PCCS Books.

Sherwin, S. (2002) Toward a feminist ethics of health care. In K.W.M. Fulford, D.L. Dickenson & T.H. Murray (Eds.), *Healthcare ethics and human values* (pp. 25–28). Oxford: Blackwell.

Sherwin, S. (2007) Feminist approaches to health care ethics. In R.E. Ashcroft, A. Dawson, H. Draper & J.R. McMillan (Eds.), *Principles of healthcare ethics* (pp. 79–86). Chichester: John Wiley.

Shillito-Clarke, C. (2000a) Question 26: ... Am I responsible for the mistakes of my supervisee or his future development or work with clients...? In C. Jones (Ed.), *Questions of ethics in counselling and therapy* (pp. 119–123). Buckingham: Open University Press.

Shillito-Clarke, C. (2000b) Question 30: What are the arguments for and against avoidable dual or multiple relationships...? In C. Jones (Ed.), *Questions of ethics in counselling and therapy* (pp. 137–140). Buckingham: Open University Press.

Slote, M. (2000) Virtue ethics. In H. LaFollette (Ed.), *Ethical theory* (pp. 325–347). Oxford: Blackwell.

Smith, K. (2009) Psychotherapy as applied science or moral praxis: the limitations of empirically supported treatment. *Journal of Theoretical and Philosophical Psychology, 29*(1), 34–46.

Smith, L. (2012) Conversations about ethics. Personal communication.

Sperry, L. (2007) *Dictionary of ethical and legal terms and issues*. London: Routledge.

Spinelli, E.D. (1994) *Demystifying therapy.* London: Constable.

Spinelli, E.D. (2003) Embracing the world: extending the boundaries of the therapeutic relationship. *Psychotherapy Section Newsletter (BPS), 34*, 3–14.

Spinoza, B. (1677/1959) *Ethics.* Letchworth, Herts: Aldine Press.

Stoljar, N. (2007) Theories of autonomy. In R.E. Ashcroft, A. Dawson, H. Draper & J.R. McMillan (Eds.), *Principles of healthcare ethics* (pp. 11–18). Chichester: John Wiley.

Syme, G. (2000) Question 25: What is the rationale for having ongoing counselling supervision? In C. Jones (Ed.), *Questions of ethics in counselling and therapy* (pp. 116–119). Buckingham: Open University Press.

Syme, G. (2003) *Dual relationships in counselling and psychotherapy: exploring the limits.* London: Sage.

Szasz, T. (1965/1988) *The ethics of psychoanalysis: the theory and method of autonomous psychotherapy.* Syracuse, NY: Syracuse University Press.

Thompson, F.E. (2002) Moving from codes of ethics to ethical relationships for midwifery practice. *Nursing Ethics, 9*(5), 522–536.

Tjelveit, A.C. (1999) *Ethics and values in psychotherapy.* London: Routledge.

Tjelveit, A.C. & Gottlieb, M.C. (2010) Avoiding the road to ethical disaster: overcoming vulnerabilities and developing resilience. *Psychotherapy Theory, Research, Practice, Training, 47*(1), 98–110.

Toulmin, S. (1981) The tyranny of principles. *The Hastings Centre Report, 11*(6), 31–39.

Tudor, K. (1999) I'm OK, you're OK – and they're OK: the therapeutic relationship in TA. In C. Feltham (Ed.), *Understanding the counselling relationship* (pp. 90–119). London: Sage.

Tudor, K. (2007) Responsibilities in supervision. In K. Tudor & M. Worrall (Eds.), *Freedom to practise vol II: Developing person-centred approaches to supervision* (pp. 26–36). Ross-on-Wye: PCCS Books.

Tudor, K. & Worrall, M. (2006) *Person-centred therapy: a clinical philosophy.* London: Routledge.

Tudor, K. & Worrall, M. (Eds.) (2007) *Freedom to practise vol II: Developing person-centred approaches to supervision* (pp. 1–10). Ross-on-Wye: PCCS Books.

Tyler, J.M. & Tyler, C.L. (1997) Ethics in supervision: managing supervisee rights and supervisor responsibilities. In Hatherleigh Editorial Board (Ed.), *The Hatherleigh guide to ethics in therapy* (pp. 75–95). New York: Hatherleigh Press.

UKCP (2009) *Ethical principles and code of professional conduct.* London: UKCP. Available from www.psychotherapy.org.uk

Urofsky, R.I., Engels, D.W. & Engebretson, K. (2008) Kitchener's principle ethics: implications for counseling practice and research. *Counseling and Values, 53*(1), 67–78.

Van Deurzen-Smith, E. (1997) *Everyday mysteries: existential dimensions of psychotherapy.* London: Routledge.

Wampold, B.E. (2001) *The great psychotherapy debate: models, methods, and findings* (Counseling and psychotherapy: investigating practice from scientific, historical, and cultural perspectives). London: Routledge.

West, W. (2003) The culture of psychotherapy supervision. *Counselling and Psychotherapy Research, 3*(2), 123–127.

Widdershoven, G.A.M. (2002) Alternatives to principlism: phenomenology, deconstruction, hermeneutics. In K.W.M. Fulford, D.L. Dickenson & T.H. Murray (Eds.), *Healthcare ethics and human values* (pp. 41–48). Oxford: Blackwell.

Widdershoven, G.A.M. & Weijts, W. (2002) Diagnostic styles in clinical relationships. In K.W.M. Fulford, D.L. Dickenson & T.H. Murray (Eds.), *Healthcare ethics and human values* (pp. 171–176). Oxford: Blackwell.

Williams, B. (1985) *Ethics and the limits of philosophy.* London: Fontana.

Wosket, V. (2009) Relational ethics in supervision. In L. Gabriel & R. Casemore (Eds.), *Relational ethics in practice: narratives from counselling and psychotherapy* (pp. 44–57). London: Routledge.

Yalom, I. (2001) *The gift of therapy: reflections on being a therapist.* London: Piatkus Books.

Younggren, J.N. (2002) Ethical decision-making and dual relationships. Available from http://kspope.com/dual/younggren.php; http://kspope.com/site/multiple-relationships.php

Younggren, J.N. & Gottlieb, M.C. (2004) Managing risk when contemplating multiple relationships. *Professional Psychology: Research and Practice, 35*(3), 255–260.

Younggren, J.N. & Harris, E.A. (2008) Can you keep a secret? Confidentiality in psychotherapy. *Journal of Clinical Psychology, 64*(5), 589–600.

Youngson, S. & Green, D. (2009) Evaluating personal development in clinical psychology. In J. Hughes & S. Youngson (Eds.), *Personal development and clinical psychology* (pp. 147–167). Chichester: Blackwell.

Zur, O. (2007) *Boundaries in psychotherapy: ethical and clinical explorations.* Washington, DC: American Psychological Association.

Index